Light

AND THE

DARKNESS

HECTOR L. ESPINOSA

www.heaven2earth.info

Order this book online at www.trafford.com
or email orders@trafford.com

Most Trafford titles are also available at major online book retailers.

Printed in the United States of America.

ISBN: 978-1-4669-9080-7 (sc)
ISBN: 978-1-4669-9082-1 (hc)
ISBN: 978-1-4669-9081-4 (e)

Library of Congress Control Number: 2013909229

Trafford rev. 07/22/2013

 www.trafford.com

North America & international
toll-free: 1 888 232 4444 (USA & Canada)
fax: 812 355 4082

Contents

Chapter 1

In the Beginning There Was an Idea

I am delighted to introduce to you my second book, *Light and the Darkness*. Before we start this journey, I want to remind you of the beginning. If we are to believe in a higher power, this power should be described as a tall building with many, many floors. The higher one goes in the building, the added ability to see into the future. We as humans are close to the bottom; as we continue up, there are spirits, angels, archangels, and many other things that are not all good. However, all fall under the reign of the divine plan.

I want to share a very impactful story, one that has marked me. No matter how many years go by, there is always room to be amazed and surprised. I would get together with a friend at least once a month to cleanse each other's spiritual energy. Throughout this book, I will give you many useful remedies for cleaning your energy for different reasons. Most people are unaware of this thing called energy and how important it is in everyday living. Remember if you do not take showers, probably not many could stand to be around you. Well, energy can be an asset or a liability in much the same way. Through proper application like before a job interview, it can be the difference between getting the job or not. It can also help in healing and alleviating health concerns, not to mention sending out the right vibrations and connecting with that special someone.

Okay, back to my story. As usual I arrived at his home, and we started our prayers to set the spiritual mood. I sensed as soon as I arrived that there was energy around him that just did not belong, an attachment I thought. So I immediately lit up one of the cigars I had brought. I clean with many different modalities. Cigars are like a thermometer to me, meaning as I smoke and blow, the smoke around the person talks to me. As it burns, each ember paints a story about the person I'm consulting. I use the smoke and also fresh plants to clear energy around the person until it feels like it flows smoothly and the aura is clear of stray energies and begins to smooth out. The way we use cigars is as we blow the smoke around the person sitting in front of us, it will start to burn in specific ways, kind of telling us a story of what is going on with that person. I like to cover the cigar with different elements. For example, I might cover it with oil on the exterior then add either cinnamon powder or honey or even sugar. I guess what I use depends on what I want to accomplish with the person. How I know, you ask? The spirit will usually show me what I need to use.

The cigar might show holes all around or burn opening like what looks like a mouth at the front or burn unevenly. It would take a chapter to truly explain how much of a story the cigar can give. Suffice it to say that it speaks to me. So as I started to clean my friend, it was getting very hot probably because I like to smoke the cigars that are five inches or more. Remember if you want a story told, it needs to be long enough to create one, so a small cigar will not suffice. The cigar was burning my fingers. I placed the side I was grasping it with on his forearm so he could feel how hot and this was only about a minute into my working with it. At first I thought he was sick because this was one of the possible signs of a cigar burning in this fashion. As I continued, I told him there was energy around him, but I was unable to determine if it was male or female, only that it was very strong.

Remember with cleanings, the ultimate goal is to clear the person's energies, so only what is supposed to be there stays and any stray energy or unwanted spirit will detach and the person may continue their life with as little obstacles as possible. As you can imagine, we live in a world of energy, so it's easy for stray energy to attach. Do you recall a time when you arrived at a place and felt uncomfortable or even developed a headache? Ever remember feeling emotionally wiped out or sleepy after speaking to a friend? These are some basic examples of how energy can affect us negatively in everyday life. Imagine if instead of this, it is a spirit with low energies or someone envious or jealous of you causing a short circuit to your own energy flow. These energy cleansings go a long way and help you move forward on a positive path.

So back to the story, he jumped because of how hot the cigar was. He exclaimed, "Wow! Please focus and take that stuff from my aura!" I continued to clean and asked him about his brother and if he had any medical issues. Since his brother had never come up before, he was curious, so he asked, "Why? What do you see?" I explained that it seemed he had high blood pressure and also an issue in the colon or prostate area. He said his brother was diagnosed with high blood pressure the year prior, and they had done a colonoscopy and had several polyps removed—one of which was a problem. I continued to cleanse him, and I told him about some strange dreams he had been having, and he confirmed they were some very weird messages. Remember we both do the same type of things; only he gets more information from his dream realm.

No medium is exactly like another. We all have gifts, and some are stronger than others. I, for example, have the capabilities to see speak and hear spirits. He can feel and receive messages through dreams. I told him whatever was there was coming out. I sat down in a chair, and it possessed me, definitely not the typical possession as I felt completely taken. What this means is that I could feel my entire body taken over. I usually feel it more in one area or another, but this was heavy duty I thought. My friend began to speak to the spirit and explained to it that it was a soul and should move on to heaven and not waste its time here on planet earth. He told the spirit that all it was meant to do on this plane was completed once the physical death of the body occurred, and as a spirit its job was to go and receive the light of heaven where all things would become clear. The spirit lifted off, and I was left wiped out.

This was no ordinary spirit, I told him. I can usually feel at least a little of who it was: male, female, and type of death along with age. I explained that all I felt was energy and nothing else. I then started to stand up and I was unable to. I told him this spirit had totally zapped my energies, and I was unable to get up from the chair. This was not normal; I usually pass all types of spirits and continue with the cleaning. Remember I was not even halfway done with the cigar. My friend then said he would clean me to detach anything the spirit may have left behind. I agreed, and he cleaned me with the cigar then with plants and it had no effect—I was truly wiped out. After thirty minutes or so, he was scared because I was as pale as my white T-shirt. He suggested calling 911. I told him no since I really did not feel bad; I just had no energy.

He helped me out the front door as I had asked. I thought some fresh air would help with healing, so we sat outside for a bit and I began to recuperate. It was incredible how this one spirit could have done this since I am used to doing these types of cleansings. It should have taken but a minute and back to business as usual. We reentered the home and went into his spirit room where we decided to pray and ask for support from above. After a few minutes, I felt another entity. I said, "Great, this is not something I need right now," and before I knew it, I was back in a chair and a spirit had taken over me. He told the soul to find the light—it was then that the spirit started to speak. My friend told me he could feel his hairs rising. That whatever it was, it had enormous energy. The spirit gave many thanks and many blessings and said we had no idea what we had done today. The spirit explained that the earlier spirit was not a spirit at all but an angel sent down to earth for a specific task and somehow had gotten dislodged and they lost the connection to it. For years they could not find it or know if it was okay, so my friend asked why or how this could happen. The other angel explained that often they are sent down to this planet to fix something or help inspire, but in the history of this, it was rare that something like this would happen, and they were concerned and had been unable to locate the dislodged angel. So again it thanked us. Later my friend said that tears were coming from my eyes like a river because of the super spiritual energy from this angel I was housing temporarily. The angel departed, and I told him I did not need to continue the cleaning since I felt like a million bucks. Usually when one of my spirits channel through me, they clean me, but this was like a super charge.

We began to dissect all that had transpired, and it was amazing how many things are unknown and not understood by us. We both believed the divine plan was perfect, but I guess even up there mishaps happen. My friend stated that things must really be messed up down here, for an angel who is obviously prepared for these types of missions to be so damaged by these lower energies to lose contact with the spirits above. I then recapped what happened from my perspective. I was unable to see the soul because it was not a soul at all. It was never born, so I could not feel how it had died or could I decipher its sex since angels have none. You have to realize that these types of energies are pure and noncorporeal. In other words, they have never had to live life as a human or anything else. As I write this, I can still feel goose bumps. It was truly a once in a lifetime experience. I had never heard of such a thing and neither had my friend. I called several others to share this experience, and they all said they never had encountered such an experience. There must have been a great need in order for them to choose me as their vessel. I thought it was a great honor to have been chosen to channel such an entity and help it go back to where it belonged.

This event was incredible. *I'm starting to see the ramifications or at least some of them.* First of all, having been chosen as the vessel; second, that these things could even happen. I've always thought that when I need help, they have all the answers, but even in heaven, they are having trouble with all the negativity down here. As you can imagine, it's a constant battle just to keep us in the frying pan and out of the fire. We are without a doubt passing through a period in time where both sides are surging to guide or misguide our evolution as free spirits. God's will or the others, who like to complicate things by making a mess, are all around. Since God has soldiers like us, fighting and cleaning the mess bad spirits cause at that spiritual level, the battles rage into no more or less than a stalemate. I know for a fact there are many more people doing harm with their spiritual gifts instead of doing good with them like I do.

People pay more to get what they want other than to get what they need spiritually. For example, I was approached the other day by a lady client of mine. She told me candidly she wanted this particular man in her life. After I focused on him, it turns out that he was married, and she told me she did not care and would pay me whatever I asked to grant her time with him. I asked her that if she could not charm him with her natural attributes, then why she would want it through magic. She replied that she did not care. I told her I do not do those types of spells, so she paid someone else a large sum of money to get him. I know this because she called me to let me know she was doing it.

Last year, another client who I cleanse and cleanse his business asked me to do a spell to get the competition out of the shopping mall where they had their business. I told him I did not do that type of work. The next time I saw him was a few months later, and he advised that the competition had folded. I asked him if he had done a bad spell against them, and he said yes, and the person who did it charged them a large sum of money to make it happen. I charge a flat fee for my readings of $100 and $221 for any good spell or cleansing. As you can imagine the dark side costs more and many spiritually gifted people have been corrupted into making easy money as they call it. I believe once you start on that path, it just becomes easier to do just one more, and before you know it, that is all you are doing. About 75 percent of all the cleanings, I do have something to do with cleaning up messes those people cause. Throughout this book, you will be given examples of heavy-duty warfare waged between the light and the dark sides. Our job as employees of God is to do our part to keep the dark side from running wild and overrunning God's plan for us. We are but simple servants in constant vigil ready to help any soul in need.

We have been taught that there is a plan for each of us. Actually, we choose the life we are to live, and there are always deviations to the plan; so often our plan is changed to fit what is believed to be for the greater good. I don't happen to agree with every part of the plan being the correct one or the only one. Sometimes we see such horrible things happen to innocent people, and we can get angry with the universe. We are narrowed in our view and see this existence as all important, but I must ask you to keep in mind that this is but one life in many we will have and each life allows us to grow. Often this growth is painful, and while we are here, we fail to grasp the bigger picture of our existence.

Remember we are spirits with a temporary body and as such are bound to this earthly existence, at least until this life is finished. Don't get me wrong, living is part of the process for all souls. The only way for a soul to no longer need reincarnation is through growing spiritually each lifetime. Many things can divine our path of life, only one of which is our selected path of life. Remember we choose to come back and what lessons to learn. However we do not live in a vacuum and thus many other pictures develop around us that can cause at certain key points to deviate from our plan.

The plan that shifts more than one soul, the plan that can often shift the greater good toward a more stable or enlightened path is often times blocked by other entities. Mostly by those that work for the darkness. We will in later chapters go into great detail as to who or what they are and what the plan is for them. For now, I want us to discover the why of our existence and how we fit into the divine plan.

Let's speak of religion, its belief. It's a good thing, only corrupted by some hungry for power. Unfortunately through the ages anything created for faith and hope is difficult to keep out of the hands of those that will corrupt it for their own gain. Many, if not all, religions started to unite mankind in a more enlightened direction. We as humans are born pure. That is to say that at the moment of birth and for some years, we are still connected to the divine universal energy we came from. Mankind toils with religion, write about it, fight for it, and die for it. How about just live with it in your heart! It's a personal thing, not to argue over, live and let live I say, if you're happy smile and enjoy it.

There are many religions that create stigma with anyone who do what I do spirituality wise. They believe in spirit but only as so far as their own dogma allows. How many witches have been burned at the stake? How many people have been persecuted because their view or belief is not the established belief? I do consider myself a spiritual person and am part of the only group if I can categorize us as a group, which has no organized religion. If we look at each religion individually, they all have one thing in common: spirit. However, most fear what they cannot control.

Remember, spirit cannot be controlled, so any clairvoyant can channel spirits of wisdom and give messages that might not go with the party line of that particular religion, so they are chastised for being different, even crucified for their beliefs. As I've stated before, I believe that any belief that is for the betterment of humanity is a good thing. Any belief that narrows or eliminates growth because it conflicts with the party line is like any communist or totalitarian regime, a chokehold on growth. Most sound good on paper but very narrow in their acceptance of a different view. In practicality, most are very easy to perverse because anytime the few are given too much power, there is a chance for abuse by any one in power with personal agendas.

It is with time and unfortunately others with less than noble ideas that we lose our connection. I believe this connection can be opened at any time; it's a doorway that can be reopened by all with faith and love in their hearts. We are taught early on to understand the veil does not exist, and we should shut our spiritual view to the universal energy. Remember as children we still retain some more than others an open channel to the spiritual world we came from. So keep an open mind. There is more than one way to heaven, and although your neighbor might be on a different path, this does not mean they have necessarily gotten lost!

Most well-known saints or even God can gain an extra something from us. Our prayers just as our praise can elevate energy of the being and thus giving them a little more to work with. For example, have you not heard of a prayer being answered? That's right, same thing when you put energy out there. Focused energy has to go somewhere. If you pray to an archangel, they will feel the prayer. The stronger the prayer, the more energy is felt by that which you pray to. It is still a choice if they answer your prayer or not. For example, it is my belief that when we pray to God, it is more often than not, others who actually answer the prayers. Remember the levels; God is at the top of the building, and there are many floors with different entities—just like divisions of a corporation that deal with different issues. This is not to say don't pray. Your prayer, when emotionally sent to the universe, does have power.

Let's look at it from the negative stand point. Have you not noticed how people in positions of authority often age to the nth power? For example, take our presidents, Obama for example. Many are not pleased by his presidency. We are not here to discuss politics, but the fact is the bloom is of the rose, and if you look at pictures of him when he was a candidate and much later, the years have been heavy on him. Same as the other prayers we are most familiar with, the ones most of us have sung in church; unfortunately those negative ones also have power, so they impact the person at some level. That's right; you don't have to be a being of energy to get the reward or punishment of prayer. To say prayer, it can just mean in a conversation. Many can say negative things of the president. Most do it with emotion, some of that, if it's strong enough, can have an adverse effect on the life force of the person being spoken of.

This to a much lesser degree is how magic works. When we do a spell, it is just a cane to help us focus. Like the Bible, we have given it power; without our prayers, it is simply paper. As we read it over and over, it becomes more and takes on a life of its own. How true or not is secondary to the energy given to it by us humans. When a witch or the Wicca religion makes a cauldron or any other religion has a talisman such as the cross, it takes on a life of its own. The soul it represents becomes more by sheer will of so many prayers.

This is why in my first book I made such an effort to speak and teach of the power of meditation and visualization. If we were to use just a fraction of our energy in the proper way, we could change destiny. Whose destiny? That would depend on your prayers. Sick people could be healed; those who did wrong would be caught and so on. The uses are endless. Sometimes I fear we humans are not ready for such powers. The truth of the matter is we possess them. It is just our scattered focus that prevents us from uniting in one common thought.

I'll give you a brief synopsis: Last week, I headed out to Boca Raton where I cleansed the energy of a dentist and his friend, the chiropractor. After we were done, they invited me to eat dinner, and I chose sushi. At dinner, the chiropractor had expressed his frustration at the fact that he wanted a new location, and after months of negotiations, the location he wanted had become available, and he put in a contract as requested. It had been over two weeks, and after several calls still no reply. He wanted to know if he should continue looking for another location. I asked him the name of the person who needed to answer. I closed my eyes and said, "Okay, he should be calling soon." The dentist who was there was like, "Come on, that's it?" I explained it is that simple, all the smoke and mirrors that people pull is for the benefit of the person but not necessary. I told them either you have it or you don't. I reminded them of how sometimes I go to the movies with my friends, and I'm asked to move a person for fun. I let them pick a person sitting ahead of us, and I wait till the lights go out then I concentrate and make them switch chairs. They laughed and asked how. I send a simple message, my back hurts, and after a while, they will associate the feeling with the chair and move.

Anyway, we finished dinner they thanked me for the company and I left. I live in Miami, so the trip back was an hour, especially on a Friday evening. Yes, I travel all over! I now travel to about twenty-five states and have clients in fifteen countries, the farthest being Australia. I often feel so blessed because I can do the reading over the phone; otherwise I would be feeling limited as to how many people I can help. The following Saturday afternoon, I got a text from the chiropractor at how blessed he was for having me as a friend. He was surprised that the person had called him over the weekend like I told him. The deal had closed, and soon he would need me to go to the new location to clean the energies there before he moved in.

This is why monks that pray together have had so much mysticism attributed to them. It is not that they are any better than any other person, but their unity makes them strong. Same goes for covens. Witches have that understanding: with unity comes strength. If you take one simple string and grab it at each end, you can pull it apart. If you just double it, it becomes more difficult; and after each time you continue to double it, it becomes consistently more and more difficult to pull it apart until it becomes impossible to break. Such is the power of unity.

Although we as individuals can accomplish much, in unison, we are invincible to all except a larger group, and then only if they are in unity of thought. Two hundred does nothing if not together in thought, and a small group with focus can break right through.

I get recurring questions about my communications with the spirit world. No matter how I put it, the middle man is what I am. So with this, I will give you an example of a recent telephone reading I had with an old client. She had been read by me many times, and about a year ago, her husband died. They were a relatively young couple with two kids, and it was hard for her since losing a loved one often is. With this in mind, I will walk you through her reading, and in doing so, answer what I'm sure are many common questions about communications with a loved one. Overall life is pleasant, death is usually peaceful, most just fear the transition. Don't waste a minute worrying; after all, it's over in a flash then you have eternity to rejoice.

During the call, she told me she needed to know how her husband was on the other side. I had done a reading for her a few months before, and he never showed up, so I reminded her and we continued. Without too much wait that her husband showed up with tons of proof that it was him. He began speaking about her brother and how his health was not well. He detailed some of his problems and told her about the name of a woman she confirmed to be his previous wife. He told her she was the one who had damaged him, and she agreed the whole family believes it to be true. I sent her some stuff for him to do since he lives in Spain. I also told her about her brother's current woman and advised that I did not see him getting married to her. She confirmed and stated that they lived together. I explained how the spirit showed that they were not a good pair. It had to do something with age, and she again confirmed he was about twenty years older and she definitely was not the best for him. She did say she was so nice he did not know how to get rid of her. I explained that for his well-being, he needed a relationship where they had some things in common.

The spirit jumped in and told her how sorry he was about her daughter, and I inquired why. She told me about a week before, the little girl was talking and the mom asked her who she was talking to and she said, "Dad." The father said he did not realize the little girl could see him, so he briefly spoke with her and left. Again apologizing because it was not his intent and he would be more careful in the future. He also told her that he had recently visited a man with an *a* as his first initial, and I was not able to understand the full name. She jumped right in and clarified that a cousin had called her. His name was Alex, and he told her that recently he had seen her husband. Further confirming his presence, he told her she would be getting married again and not to forget he would make his presence known to her by the tug. She laughed as she told me one of the last things before his passing was to tell her that upon her next marriage, he would come to tug on her toes at night.

He conveyed to her that his only concern and why he was still around was that he needed to know she and the kids would be fine. He could not go until she let him go and moved on in her life. She cried and agreed she would do it. She confirmed that even his demeanor of expression was his; with this, the spirit spoke a bit more and left. I want you to understand that I cannot summon a spirit or can anyone else. W are just translators for the other side.

Never believe anyone that can guarantee anything with relation to that other side. We merely can communicate and affect some minor things, but they are in charge. In this example, you should realize that only when a spirit sees the folks that are left behind moving on can they truly find peace; so while we might feel anguish, there is nothing more important than that soul, and we must do all that is necessary to help with this transition.

Another important thing is that the more light a spirit has or more evolved the spirit, the clearer the message. If the soul was in a dark place, the messages would have been very scrambled much like a person that was drunk just as an example. Although it is not common for a recently departed to make an appearance, they can and clearly if they are souls are with light. Again, and I cannot stress this point enough, it's about them. Once a soul reaches the other side then they can choose to come and visit. This enlightened soul is the one who can see beyond and can truly give valuable input into the lives of the living. This is the type of souls I work with and with them by my side is how I am able to help so many that call me for advice for something as simple as a job or health concerns or even future relationships. The type of advice has no limits since they have pierced the veil to the unknown. Spirits also have rules and there are penalties; so what they can speak of is to benefit the living and not beyond as they have told me, everything they do is to help in our spiritual evolution. No one should know everything, since coming to learn is our very purpose, it's why we come to temporarily inhabit a body.

Before I forget, I want to tell you about some preparations I take before I do any cleansings or any heavy spiritual work. This would definitely be covered by any haunted places and exorcisms. So in a nutshell, I always let my spirits know what I'm getting ready to do and why. I try to speak to them as much as possible so they can be on the same wavelength and on board with what I'm doing. If by chance there is something I'm missing or doing incorrectly, they have an opportunity to tell me what to do to fix it. Once we are in tune for the activity, I usually ask some to go to the location ahead of me, often days before to get the location ready for my arrival. Let's face it, walking into a big problem is not the same as if they get there before and soften up the ambiance prior to my arrival. There have been times when I've gotten feedback from the location regarding something unforeseen they ran into and they give me ideas on what to bring.

Where spirits are concerned, you can always walk into a trap. Don't think any of the entities causing problems are happy that I'm there. I'm an intruder in their mess, and they do not need me in the mix. Remember causing problems is why they are there and my intervention just makes me their enemy more than the folks being spiritually attacked. Over the years I've made friends and enemies. The souls that I've helped have become grateful, and the ones I've prevented from doing harm have become enemies. Here is a secret with every person I help. Their guardian angels, unable to help their charge, often tap me with a small gift of positive energy for helping their charge get back on track.

I work with the light. Unfortunately, for every one of me, there are literary hundreds that work the darkness. It is a lot more work to fix a mess than to cause it. It takes a second to crash a car, to fix it; it often takes weeks, that is, if it can be fixed. Sometimes if the damage is bad enough, the vehicle is trashed. Unfortunately to heal physical and emotional damage takes longer, and it is sometimes impossible to completely repair. It is, however, just as easy to cause the harm to the life path of a person or situation as it is to crash a car.

This is why in a later chapter I will discuss energy maintenance that can help keep our energy healthy. At the very least, make it more difficult for damage to be caused. Remember negative energy must have something to grab. If our aura is clean, that makes it more difficult for attachments to attach to us. I said more difficult, not impossible, so learning some of the signs of a spiritual assault is very important, just like there are signs before people get migraines. There are signs of a problem building in our energy space. Okay, we are here to learn lessons which vary with every time we come back to earth.

Energy is eternal. Sometimes it's used for good and sometimes used for negative purposes. Just as humans are good and bad, so are beings beyond our scope of existence. Here on earth, we speak of spirits, but this is just one small realm compared to the many that exist. Yes, spirits can and often disrupt the natural order of our earthly existence, but in the scheme of energy, they are very low on the scale. Why do I say this? As free spirits when we pass, we are still in our early realm and don't remember anything other than this existence.

Disoriented, often the newly freed soul does not even realize that the death of the body has occurred, so in its disoriented state, it can lose focus of the next steps to freedom from this early confine. Most souls find their way to the afterlife, heaven or the astral plane, whatever you call it—it's a place where the soul will remember all the reasons it came to earth in the first place. Why they associated with certain people and the experiences it endured. I say endured because this is a learning place, so all the lessons are not perfect. I guess this is why it's called a lesson. Be assured when the soul does arrive at its destination, all memories are restored.

Unfortunately, sometimes the soul comes to earth and not all memories are wiped out as it should be. This is why some people have difficulty adjusting to life here. There are no absolutes and sometimes there is a clear-cut reason why a baby is born with some difficulties, making life here a handicap. When on the other hand there is no reason why, then it's a good time to start looking into other options to find out. I've seen on many occasions regression therapy having a profound effect on an individual. Remember there are alternative therapies. Hypnosis is another I feel can be of help in cases like this.

Look, I'm not saying it's always successful, but if there is a glimmer of a chance a loved one can benefit from these therapies, then why not? What do you have to lose? I feel there are more things to help us than are currently available. I believe all that is, was, and will be is already out there for our minds to find it. This book is just like my first one offering teaching tools for self-discovery. If you are willing to go through the techniques I've outlined, better is what you will become in the understanding and use of this spiritual realm.

For the longest time, I would travel to other places with my mind. On occasion I was guided to certain places to show me or teach me something. These souls are very enlightened as their job is to help humanity, one person at a time or in groups. On one occasion, one of my spirits was talking to me about the constant engagement between good and evil.

In this case, I was taken to an area I had not been before. To me it looked like a vast emptiness on one side was the light and on the other was a deep empty darkness. He explained that in this place it is decided what will happen in the future. He explained that the darkness always wants to rule while all the light wants is balance. The light understands that there needs to be darkness for light to exist, the balance must be maintained, he said.

As we wandered this vast emptiness what seemed like hours, I heard a noise, and all of a sudden there were things I could see on the emptiness side where the darkness was before. I cannot explain what it was exactly as it seemed to be far away. Another wind or something came past us from the other direction. As I turned to look at the light side, what seemed to be entities of some kind were popping up. At this point, the spirit that had brought me said perhaps it was time for us to go back from where we came.

It's funny, well, now it's funny; I've always been told that we are specks of light in a large universe. I never imagined how accurate that statement was. I soon realized we were in a place where we were specks of dust amongst giants. So my earlier analogy of emptiness was accurate, like an empty football field would be to an ant. Back to the story, I want you to get into the scene so you can appreciate the enormity of where we were. I looked at the spirit and asked if we could stay a bit longer.

I got the message, without the spoken words the spirit agreed but only for a short time. I agreed and we continued exploring. You must understand we were noncorporeal in this place, kind of just floating around is the best way to describe the scene. Every once in a while, I would feel a brush of energy, but nothing seemed to be there. As we started to float toward the light side, the dots became bigger and bigger until I could determine with some accuracy what I had been looking at.

This incredible scene was beginning to build before my eyes. It was all kinds of energies with different sizes and shapes. I could even see nature or animal shapes as well as what looked like trees and birds as well. I mean this was like a menagerie of everything that existed in our world and other places. I was shown how we are but one place in an infinitival number of places in this and other universes. As we got closer, I could discern that not only were they far away but gigantic in perspective to us.

As we got even closer, I could tell there were groups, the animals, or at least that is what it looked like to me and trees or nature area, angels, and other different groups. I could not see what they were but could tell warriors or at least ready for some event that was to come. As I glanced to the darkness, I no longer saw emptiness, but it was filled with what seemed to be millions of little eyes—at least, that is what it looked like from far away.

One of the angels approached, and as it did, it began to shrink to our size. I guess that is how they visit our planet to make it easier for us to comprehend. It approached the spirit that was with me and told it you know this is not a place for us and definitely not at this time. The spirit agreed and began our journey back to the portal where we arrived through. I continued to go where I was being taken but not taking my eyes off the big picture developing.

As we were halfway to the place where we originally arrived from, it felt as if the place was trembling and lots of things came from the darkness toward the light. Instantly the light opened up, and all those we had seen earlier had lined up to what seemed infinity and approached to meet the darkness. If I had a body, I could tell you shivers were up and down my spine, metaphorically speaking. The energy of the place had changed, and it seemed stuffy like too many people in one place.

As they got closer, I could see the anger in the faces of both sides. All these energies were just glowing everywhere, and at the moment of clashing, it seemed like a million atomic bombs exploded at once. It was vicious, and the devastation was mind blowing. I'm a fighter, so observing this was getting me in the mode. Let's get it on, and as I started toward what I now understood to be a battlefield, the spirit grabbed me and took me back. When I arrived back which seemed to be hours, the person who was sitting next to me said, "Wow, where were you?" I asked why; she said it seemed like you were dreaming or talking with someone in your sleep. I asked how long I was in the trance. She replied only a few minutes; I was sobbing, and she asked if I was okay I just smiled and said yes; it was just intense.

To date, every time I tell this story, I relive that time, and my eyes get watery. It was an incredible experience. Since I've been on many other journeys but none showed me the big picture more than that moment in that place. I guess time passes different there because I could swear I was there for more than half a day. I guess this is partly why we don't see much of what happens here from that side. They come do their thing, and before we blink our eyes, they are gone. The spirit that took me to that place explained to me that the balance must be kept.

To a lesser degree, every inch counts, so here on earth we are constantly attempting to maintain this balance. He said it's all important. He said imagine if all the worlds lose ground to the darkness. He said this in itself would weaken the lights position and strengthen the darkness. I understood that we are all important, and we each make a difference. So I will stay vigilant and keep my little part in balance. He told me that seduction is great, but we must stay faithful to the ideal of free will for all. When we give in to another's ill will, this weakens the whole of one side or strengthens the other side. With enough weakening, the other side might gain a foothold and plow through a stalemate that has existed since the beginning of time. That outcome over there would trickle down to us and it would be hell on earth.

In my first book, I was not ready to speak of this universal truth of good and evil, at the very least not at this level. I believe that if fewer people are sheltered from the truth, the snake of illusion cannot corrupt the good in everyone. The taste of the proverbial fruit is only eaten because of ignorance to the facts. So enlightenment to what is out there, I mean good and evil and what it's doing to us and countless other young civilizations should be looked at and understood. It is how we grow to eventually reach the stars and beyond, to become the new protectors and take our place in keeping the balance for everything.

Our perception of reality is very limited. Take a cube for instance; place a strong light at a wall, step between the lamp and the wall, hold the cube, and place it directly in between the light and the wall. We are creating a shadow. If you move it, there are many angles that the cube just looks like a two dimensional square. So if we were to look at the shadow of the square without the knowledge that it is truly the shadow of the cube, we would be totally unaware that behind this shadow there are other dimensions out of our perception. Have you seen the vehicles with the tricked-out tires? The rim has spinning parts. If you look carefully as the car goes faster, the spinning piece seems to stop spinning all together. It is, however, moving or spinning at just the right speed so as to make it seem to be still. You know the law of gravity, all things that go up, must come down. So how is it that you take a metal object securely on the ground and take a simple magnet and it can move it away from the grounding forces of gravity? Could it be that there are other forces working on gravity, other dimensions that vibrate so close that we cannot perceive it but it exists all around us?

I'm often asked what makes one person evil and another one good. I don't think it's that simple. Let's break it down to the fundamentals. If you do something wrong and you know it's wrong, are you weak, or is it peer pressure? Don't know? Neither do I. It could be a variety of reasons. Only studying each case individually can truly and justly answer that question. Going back to the good and evil thing; I've met many practitioners over the years, and what I've found, and this is just my opinion—if you do something and you think you are justified, then how can in your eyes this be wrong or evil? The arrogance of some astounds me. If you truly believe it's your divine right to do such a thing, then how can that thing be wrong? In other words, it's justified. I like to tell people there is no right or wrong but only what you can live with.

If you in your heart truly believe that, in the case of magic, let's say a client or you yourself want a position at work and you have the tools to get the person in that position fired, why not then? You are doing it with the belief that it is in some twisted way a good thing. People can justify just about anything. The practitioners that live from the misery of others justify it by stating they have the power and it's for hire. It's not their responsibility if another is willing to pay for any act; and it will benefit him, her, or their family. They do not lose sleep over it. They have completely bypassed the judgment portion that most people have in place.

These people are dangerous since they truly believe it is their divine right to take any action paid for by another. They believe if it were any different, they would not have been given these powers. You know the old saying, power corrupts and absolute power corrupts absolutely. This is why before I take on cases where magic spells have to be done, I have to be clear about what is being asked and that the request is just and for the right reason.

Before I forget, I want to tell you about another question that kept coming up from the folks that read my first book. The question was straightforward, and I think that it needs to be answered. Why are there more women getting readings and cleansings than men? I told them, and I will tell you as I'm sure in the stories and testimonial section of this book, you will again see more female testimonials and stories than male.

The answer is really quite simple. Women quite literally take better care of themselves than men in almost every sense you can think of. They go to the doctor with more frequency. They cater to their looks more than men, etc. So why should this be any different? Women are more curious and so on. I must have had thousands of e-mails and wonderful feedback about my first book, and this one question came along with about a quarter of the e-mails.

There are many types of people that can channel from birth and just as many that grow into it as they grow older. We are all able to perceive energies from other planes of existence as primal man found it useful to fine-tune all the senses. The fight or flight instincts were necessary during that early time when we were roaming the wilderness with the animals. Since heightened instincts were at a maximum, they were able to know when danger was around the next rock. So in a sense, this extrasensory perception much like modern psychics today helped our predecessors in the wild.

It is very important to us as humans to stay in touch with the other side. No matter what country we are from, there are rituals for family members who die. Know that part of keeping in touch with us is the soul of the departed visiting this plane from the afterlife. So if you woke up and had a clear moment when you just knew a relative who had passed came to you in a dream, it's true. They are able to visit us and even give us advice from the other side. Keep in mind that they are always with us, and when we have need, they will always try and give us faith.

You ask how we can believe in another area we cannot identify with just because it is outside of the sphere of our vision even outside the sphere of our technology. At least for now, as we grow and advance technologically, I have no doubt that we will touch on these spheres all around us. If we were to look at existence scientifically, we could answer at the very least state questions that make us question *what if*. So let's look at some examples, some in the big realm, and some in the microscopic or even smaller. For example, if we blow something up, the explosion expands, but eventually it slows down and stops. Like if we throw a rock in the middle of a lake, with time even the ripples dissipate, right? So why is it that the idea of the expanding universe has already collapsed? If you did not know the universe, it is not only expanding, but it's picking up speed. Contrary to all the laws of nature and science, we have described till today.

Could it be that it is within our realm of reality, amongst other things we have yet to identify there are still unknowns? Could it be that some energies or conscience travel within these realms, in and out without our understanding? All curious questions, these questions will eventually be answered. Will they show that God or the divine does not exist? I do not think so. I think spirituality is just another science in its infancy. I do this for a living, and with every reading and cleansing, I discover yet other things. My life has become an adventure. I'm so glad I was chosen to work this realm, the realm of the spirit. Let's talk about the small science, atoms, and smaller particles, science keeps on looking deeper and deeper into that which cannot be seen in hopes of answering the big world we live in. Some supposed proven and accepted theories have been disproven. For example, the theory of atomic decay was proven flawed, if you are interested perhaps a look into it on the Internet.

It was discovered that it can be predicted when solar flares would come by this variation in the decay. I'm not a scientist but do follow technology in the news, so I've seen the articles and believe that in the long run, this discovery can save our planet from catastrophe. For example, if a giant flare were to engulf the earth, it could knock out all satellites and other sensitive machinery. Not much would work for years to come until it was rebuilt or at the very least fixed. This discovery about the variant in decay happens in days if not longer before a flare, so now scientists must use this information to predict and protect our satellites and other possibly affected machines so we are not thrown into a temporary dark age again.

Now to the more regular things some mediums do, like how to cleanse energy, might as well ask how doctors heal. It's not entirely about the doctors and their abilities to a great extent; it's about the individual person and what works best for them. So with this in mind, imagine every medium or healer like every doctor comes with some things they do better, but perhaps it's not that ability that the patient needs—it's something different. So it is with cleanings. Perhaps one medium is better at energy passes, but the individual needs more of a healing with plants. So we must adjust, by the same token even the person that gets better results being cleaned by plants often needs a different form of cleansing. Not everyone works well with penicillin; even those that do if you continue to give them the same medicine, the body and those viruses or infections can become immune. So like in medicine we must also try different frequencies and different tools to keep the people that come to us clean. So yes, maybe energy passes for a while then switch it up to a cleansing with incense or a cigar. Maybe use different plants or make it into a bath to pour over yourself; whatever the change, it should be effective in keeping things fresh so the negativity around them does not acclimate to the tools being used.

There are many types of cleansings: some are superficial, others go deep into the person's psyche, yet with others, I reach the astral plane. This is why some cleansings are not successful and people might feel let down. If you do the superficial, one you are working on the aura, and this is where most need help. Deep cleanses often deal with the person's past. They usually have been stuck or held back because of an emotional and/ or spiritual anchor. In these types we have to reach deep inside and often travel along the life line to break that anchor or chord that is preventing the soul from truly moving forward. The last is when something has been done to the person, but it's not necessarily an attachment; it's sitting in the astral plane much like the sun radiates warmth, but it's not near us. These energies are often the most difficult to find and eliminate because they could be well hidden. Along with these, there is another where, if necessary, I can also cleanse for healing purposes. I feel that most of the folks with sickness have at least one of these components causing or enhancing the infirmity.

I never believed in any of this. Growing up there, I had no examples. I lived a very normal life. I have a younger brother who was also ignorant of this spiritual world. Upon reflection, I believe my spirits saved me many times and my meditation sessions saved me as well. I also was at some level using magic even if on a conscientious level. There was one incident in particular when I was a marine recruiter that I worked for this master sergeant. He was a guy who thought people under him should look up to him at all times. Out of seventy-three recruiters, I was number 3 in performance, so I did my job and did not feel I needed to look up to anyone all the time. On several occasions we had run-ins. He point-blank told me he would make the remainder of my three-year posting a living hell. I began to meditate on this issue and would visualize sending large red fire flames at him. It was within a month that he got transferred to Puerto Rico. He had only been at the posting for less than a year, and he and the wife had just purchased a new home, so there was no reason for him to be transferred. Now I realize that I caused this through my meditations.

There was one time while I was a network administration that a friend advised me that someone was selling memory chips very cheap, probably stolen he said. I agreed to go with him to check it out. Turns out it was a trap, and about thirteen other people were caught purchasing stolen chips. Fortunately I did not buy anything. My friend and several others were arrested. Coincidence maybe, but I can tell you the deal was so good to this date I have no idea why I did not buy them. One time while I was doing bounty hunting—yes I've done many different things in my life—I was about to break into this house to catch a guy who was running from the law. This overwhelming impending fear entered me, and I did not crash into the front door as I would have done and did on many occasions. Instead, I decided to go around and look. The front door was a trap with a shotgun placed facing the front so that anyone who opened the door would get shot. All these and many other moments that had no importance then have now become clear. They were always there protecting and guiding me toward what was my destiny.

I was working with computers and teaching at a local college. I was the teacher for the network + class and the A+ certification courses when I began to feel and see things. I was told by my spirits to leave my job, that they would not abandon me as I embarked on this spiritual path. After some soul-searching, I decided to go for it. That first year I made $5,000 and was devastated financially. They kept telling me to have faith. During the second year, I guess about $15,000, another financially catastrophic year for me. My faith was wavering, but they continued to push me to stay on course. The third year, my income jumped to $50,000, and I started to see the light. I will not betray my beliefs or will I ever tell anyone that did not need one to get a cleansing. Don't need to, there are so many in true need that need it. I don't advertise; I've grown by word of mouth, a slow process, but the truest way to grow is from someone else that was satisfied by my work. Those of you who want to embark on this path, it tells you it is not an easy one, but the rewards come by seeing how many people you can help. So if you can weather the difficulties, I say follow your calling. We need your help.

Chapter 2

The Subconscious

A paralyzed teen regaining ability to walk, I've done this exercise. I have shown that one sentence to a client, and he has read it at first glance as paralyzed teen raging ability to war! Think of this and analyze something I was told by the spirits, at times people are misdiagnosed. They are told they are dyslexic or labeled otherwise. All the while, it is their psyche that needs to be looked at. The example above was of a new client, but after I did this simple test and discussed it with him, we realized there were some latent anger issues with regard to his job and how he was being treated.

Before we can find our place in the universe or just our path of life, we must have peace. Internal peace is very important in all aspects of energy. How can we wish well on others if we are at war inside? War in a loose sentence can just be turmoil. It is this turbulence or unsettled energy that more often than not keeps us out of balance. We are ruled by our emotions. We need them, and we must have them. This is a large part of who we are as humans. Managing these waves of emotion is what I'm talking about. Do not let it get the best of you; make them make you the best. You know the saying if life gives you lemons make lemonade; as for the companionship, find the one who got vodka and have yourself a party!

It's iffy, life does not bring us what we want, but it should. All we need to do is actually believe, not play at it, but truly feel the emotion. We are given a canvas and a scene. The canvas is where you are born, and the scene is the key people in your life. You know, mother, father, and the family circle you are born into. Then you are given looks that is physical and emotional. By this I mean, are you funny or are you sarcastic. Good health or not, long life or short, some predispositions, talents like painting, or good talker, or a numbers person. Most things are, like I said earlier, canvas and scene; what we do with it all is life.

Now, let's get to how to work on our life path. Let's not talk about problems, and let's talk about solutions. There is nothing that cannot be fixed. There is nothing that cannot be turned around, and we as human beings can overcome most complications. Most of us in our youth develop certain abilities that stay through adulthood. We can reinvent ourselves, over and over, with every turn we change our life. Some changes are great; some are minor in the scheme of a lifetime. All changes can potentially be life altering. One needs to keep an open mind on these potentially pivotal events and when they started.

You thought, yes, my life would turn out X, and it turned out Y. I'm sorry to say it can still turn out Z, so don't give up on yourself. Just when we think it's over, some new possibilities are afoot! Yes, a new turn to give us a new perspective on our future, that is right. Learning to let go of old habits and really start anew is the secret. Not to bring any echoes of old relationships or old hurts into new scenarios, we are all given constant restarts for our lives; all we need to do is choose to. With this basic idea, there are variations. For example, parent with kids or very young and without recourses or very old or sickly. I don't care the variables; each will be given parameters for new beginnings that fit into the essentials of the particular life.

Some say teach to control impulses. I say release them from who you are. Reeducate your desires, expunge the ones you no longer wish to satisfy or that no longer satisfy your needs or desires. For a long time I desired a popular brand of cola until I realized how it made me gain weight. I decided to get rid of the vice that no longer met my desire. I began to think of it as not good. Every time I took a sip, I thought of a negative. Did not matter what. Think of the most disgusting or just something that tasted horrible to you. With time, the cola or whatever you want to get rid of will taste like you want it to until your desire for it is gone. You have just rewired yourself to dislike something that at one time was indispensable as cola was for me.

Another example, I've never been a big coffee drinker. My wife, on the other hand, is, so guess what? We have coffee for breakfast. Initially it was not very palatable. With time again, I thought of my wife as I drank it, and coffee began to remind me of my wife and how I felt about her. I'm sure that technique might make some think of this. What if I did not like that person anymore? Yes, it could backfire, and I won't like coffee again. I know, nothing is perfect, and with every possibility, there is a possibility for change. Is this not what we are talking about? Not all change is favorable; however, it is change. The flow of life does not stop just as a river flows and meanders around rocks and other fixtures. We must try and stay on a good path. What is a good path, and how do we know the changes coming won't lead to a better one? Trust your instincts, don't run on fear and insecurities, and allow the flow of life to guide you. If you do, you will know what is right and what does not feel right.

The mind is all important. We have therapists, psychologists, psychiatrists, many ways to help our minds. Throughout our recorded past, humans have realized a large percentage of their issues have come from some sort of psychological issue. What are the odds that things just happen? There is a pattern to everything. Most people that fall into certain patterns, and we can play back to a point when things just got off on the wrong foot. Today we have crime scene investigators and many other experts to decipher the how and why of things. I remember a case where a young man got into marijuana. He got into trouble. The police pulled him over, and he was given an opportunity in court to repair his mistake. The officer in charge of his case told him that if he did his course and stayed free of any problems for three months, his record would be wiped out.

Unfortunately for him, within two months of his having completed his course, he once again got pulled over. He told me that the stuff was not his, but it was his car, so guess what he was found guilty of possession again. Unfortunately for him the law of the land was that second offenses with marijuana would carry a sentence of suspended license for no less than two years. Imagine two years without a license to drive for a young man of twenty-one going to college and working to pay for his bills. This was disastrous.

Often we are careless in our selection process or decision making, so we need to get on focus and live our lives as if it were the only life we are going to have on this earth. If we choose that it's worth our time to learn spirituality and all that comes from it, I feel all can benefit from this awakening, awaken to a more interesting life. Awaken the sleeper inside each of us. We must awaken and grow into our maximum selves. Not for the sake of self-benefit but for the benefit of mankind. I know, a lofty goal but a worthwhile one, I think. An attitude of gratitude unlocks the fullness in your life, try it, I guarantee it will be enough!

For transformation to occur, desire must be part of the equation. I'm often asked, why them and not us? I believe the answer is within the question. If the talent is equivalent, the missing part of this equation is desire. How far or long will you be willing to go to achieve what you want? If all other areas are equal, then he who wants it most is who gets it. I can help level the playing field. If you can maximize how others perceive you, this might also give you the edge you are looking for. In this book and my first, I give many recipes that can put you over the edge in the running, perhaps even winning.

We are born perfect. It is with experience that we are sometimes hit hard. What is belief except an opinion? There is not one opinion that cannot be reeducated or fine-tuned like a car. We can take a car and make it different, not necessarily better. Take any car and change the computer chip and modify it for better performance, better gas mileage, or for higher speed. With each modification something gives in another. For higher performance, gas mileage will suffer for example. So check our beliefs. Are they true, or are they true for you? Is it absolutely true, or only the part that is important?

Each of our thoughts has the power to shape or reshape our lives in powerful ways. What we send out comes back. If we send out anger, it can come back in the form of some body defect. Try and always send out joy, hopefulness. Remember a thought can become reality. Choose words and emotions to enhance our calm, to live productive and loving lives. You will with time form new thought and experience. Both will become a realization of your truth, make it a truth you will be proud to share with the world—a life you will want to share with someone just like you. Remember if you but cut a weed, it will come back, often stronger than before so go to the source, the root, and pull it out. Educate or reeducate your thought patterns. There is nothing that is beyond your reach if you believe and invest the time to change it. Remember this, to forgive someone is your gift to them; to move on is your gift to yourself. Dwelling is the beginning of the end of freedom. Happiness cannot be traveled to, earned, owned, worn, or consumed; it's rather a spiritual experience when we live a life filled every minute with grace and an attitude filled with gratitude.

Let's talk about testing. An ugly word you may say but oftentimes a gauge. A meter of sorts is needed to see where we are as a whole with the rest of society. After all, we do not live in a vacuum or do we just compete against ourselves. A reality check of sorts is often needed to reevaluate where we are and where we should be based on the society we live in and our personal goals. As people, we grow and develop at different pace, so it's important to gauge our general intelligence and unique gifts that may be overlooked or unappreciated. Find your talents, or at the very least, you're standing within your particular group or society. It's never enough. Perhaps the type of education you receive is not the most propitious to your learning style and growing the right goals for your future.

There are common methods psychologists use to assess certain cognitive processes. They involve evaluating not only the psychological aspect but educational abilities. Most tests should be a reference and can be a good gauge for you or your children, never to substitute professional help but as a basic guide into your subconscious. There are tons of standard tests and educational ones out there like the FCAT, SAT, MCAT, and many others. When you are out of touch with yourself and your emotions, it's difficult to connect with others. Realizing this is the first step to getting back to the basics and then move forward and get back in touch with the rest of the world. There is nothing wrong with looking for help. I believe we do whatever it takes to be right with ourselves and the world around us so get to it!

I don't like to get very metaphysical, but in this instant, I think food for thought is in order—to think and analyze this thing called life. First and foremost, some say we are living a dream and life is but a dream. If this is so, and the only reason you know, meet, and greet and live with the folks in your life is because they are dreamers in your dream as well. So this is why those who are not living your dream can, like ships at sea, cross and continue without any major interaction. If we mix this with karma, then we can look at all the people living our dream as past, present, and future dreamers of this dream called life. Some intersect and then leave our lives. Remember we are not alone, so even as dreamers in separate dreams, our karma often calls for experiences not in our dream then the universe allows much like circles that intersect at the edges the capability for separate dreams and dreamers to intersect.

Let's look at this from another angle. If we are in our individual dream and we sleep, when our brains are off, or dreaming within our dream, so technically our dream is off as it were temporarily. Then does our dream continue or does everything cease to be; does the dreamer stop to exist while the brain is slumbering? As they say, if a tree falls in the forest, did it really fall? Did anyone hear it? Does it even exist? Again, food for thought! If you get my e-mails, this is why I call them food for thought! I want to briefly talk about emotions. We have them. Why is it that so many of us often cry with no reason? I know it happens more often to many people that will never admit it; they, however, believe there is something wrong with them. They are mistaken, just as the pressure cookers of the world vent so as to not explode, so does our subconscious mind. It vents through these events and lets out our pent-up emotions. Many have bottled-up issues and would otherwise have breakdowns, so the mind releases slowly, and often unexpectedly, these feelings often turn to tears. Feeling gratitude and not expressing it is like wrapping a present and not giving it. Show it, give it, welcome it into your life and be more tomorrow than you have been today.

If what I have been discussing above is in any way or shape true, even to a lesser degree than totality, then what does this mean to us the dreamers in our own dreams? If as we suppose, it is as suspected, then each of our destinies is in our own hands or in the hands of the dreamers. Interesting concept, what does that tell you? Most if not all misfortune we bring to our own life so the most important concept to understand is we create our future. If for some reason throughout our lives we have lost our way and become so discontent as to dream our own obstacles, we can through rewiring of the subconscious place our lives back on track. In a similar way, by looking into our subconscious mind, we can truly release some of these pent-up emotions that cause us to break into tears without rhyme or reason, at least at a conscious level.

Let's talk about the body and mind. Oh, don't forget emotions; our bodies are new or renewed regularly. I guarantee you that the muscles, skin, and even the bones in our bodies are replaced regularly; so if our bodies are a do-over, then we need to identify if our bodies are built to be renewed. Why does cancer exist and many other abnormalities in our bodies? Let's forget about genetic predispositions. We know there is a percentage of things our bodies are predisposed to suffer. Let's talk about in the grocer sense why is what's naturally occurring going wrong more and more within our modern society now that we have more technology and advancement in medicine than ever?

Obese people are growing themselves into disease; they decay because they grow beyond the norm. They can control one-third of all disease by just keeping fit for life; we can all grow younger by keeping our bodies fit. All fine and dandy, but what about all the diseases that we cannot justify occurring in normally healthy bodies. Through negative thinking, we are killing ourselves. If we could only learn how we are damaging our lives, we can heal and prevent disease. It's never too late, we can get healthier, and our life or quality of life can improve with positive thinking. Our bodies are programmed from the beginning to grow and continue to regrow until we die, so why is disease getting into this cycle of regrowth that the body goes through regularly?

Remember that every month the body rejuvenates from the cellular level to organs to limbs, etc. The legs you are walking on today are literary not the same once you were walking on last year. So if this recycling occurs regularly in our bodies, and it has since our birth, then what changes, barring accidents or other external occurrences? Why are our own cells not being duplicated as our genome has programmed? Could it be that our emotions, mind, and spirit is sickened and causing these otherwise perfect machines we call the bodies to malfunction more and more? Some modern diseases—I say modern because they were not commonplace in our history—are here today.

I would say that we need to reevaluate how we are dealing with our spirit. The closer body and spirit become, the healthier the body becomes. One of the tools at our disposal is meditation. The more we learn to control our bodies with our minds, the more we learn to better manage our emotions, the closer we become to health and the balance that is our birthright. Always remember we are but parts in this planet, so even as we sicken, our part in this echo system becomes weakened. We must learn to become one with nature, not regress from our technology but incorporate our nature as human's right along with our technological advances.

I believe it's true, our future is in our hands. Set your ship back on track, write your future with every thought much like a writer does with a pen. He can change parts and place them, replace them, and pretty much do what he wants. Create your future with but a thought, rewrite your script. Remember we can crisscross other circles or dreamers, so use caution not to damage or interfere with other dreams or dreamers more than necessary to change the course of yours. After all there are consequences with every action. There are reactions and ramifications, so stay on course and pick your path of least resistance. When the universe shuts one door, it always opens at the very least a window or two. It is a funny thing about life. If you refuse to accept anything but the best, you very often get it. Be one of those, and you will be rewarded, and why not you deserve it!

As explained before, with every action there are some unforeseen turns of events, so before you act rashly, make sure you know what you want and try and achieve it with the least of obstacles to the rest of the world. There are circumstances in life where you may exhaust all other options and the only solution is war. As it is with countries, unfortunately with magic you can be caught in a cross fire or even worse in the cross hair of another person with less than honorable intentions. When this occurs, the options are few. Run and hope like the bully in the playground. They don't continue the harassment. You can fight and if equally matched hope you win. If overmatched, hit-and-run tactics are in order. In other words, clean self and fire back quietly in hopes you hit with a bull's-eye shot. If you are stronger, send a magical message. They won't soon forget or ever mess with you again. You need to make them understand niceness is not weakness.

Is this psychic stuff for real? Are mediums real, or are they another manifestation of our subconscious mind asserting itself and giving us something to rationalize the things we cannot logically deal with? Remember that part of our minds that is not reasoning always attempts to give us an answer we can live with. That same part of the mind is the one that when tragedy strikes a person, and it's so awful that part of the mind wipes it out so we do not even remember. It's that part of the mind that fills in the gaps and why standard therapy does not often acknowledge hypnosis.

When a good hypnotist works on a person, this does not happen, but when amateurs tinker with the psyche of a person without knowing how to do it the information that comes through is often skewed by the subconscious mind. If the mind cannot retrieve the real information or it was never there, it often will fill in the gaps with make believe it generates loosely from other memories or imagination. So if you were witness to an accident and saw the tag but did not remember, hypnosis will retrieve the correct information. However, if you were a witness to a crime but really did not see the tag or a detail needed, that part of the mind might make it up if pressed for an answer.

Now back to the question, is all this spirit stuff real or just another joke our own mind plays on us to perpetuate the idea that there is something else out there besides us? Is it our mind reaching out and perceiving what is already out there in the ether? Both good questions, I can only give you my answer. With faith, all things are possible, cop-out maybe, but the science of spirituality (and it is a science) all questions need to be answered. I have never been a "take it on faith" type, so I ask the hard questions. Why, when, where, how, sound like a detective—that's right, you need to investigate. Why, because there are some unscrupulous people out there that takes advantage of people in need.

Over the years I've proven to myself and many others through readings and cleansings that I perform and the results that occur because of them. I have found missing items for people. I've been told where to dig and have found items that have been underground a long time with no living person knowing where it was. I've divined things that no living person knew but only the dead and passed on the messages. People at death's door have been given a new lease on life, and they said they were not believers until then. How can it be? Perhaps there is something else out there? I've always been a practical person, so when I told my family that I discovered this world, I did it with proof. Giving messages and I continue to astonish them by telling them things there is no way in this world I could have known.

I've given clients the name of who they are going to marry and even before they meet; I've done this by describing in detail the person's occupation, height, and in some occasions even their eye color. I've told clients about jobs they would get and details of the boss before they even started working. Could this mean there is something more, maybe, still needs more, then given the clarity of some messages? I predicted two years before on the radio that the president of Venezuela will become sick and have a need of an operation and that operation would not be a complete success. I predicted on that same radio show about Jennifer Lopez's breakup with Mark Anthony and the reasons for her leaving him.

My mother reminded me of a prediction I made when the pope took his place. I told them that it would be a short reign but not for death but rather to give entry to another who would bring a renewed strength to the church.

These are just a few of the hundreds of predictions that are mind-blowing truths before they happen: what do you make of it, no matter if they are fact, and there are always people that come with the idea of just creating doubt. I don't read people unless they come to me in need. Although I charge for my readings, I want to help people, so if someone comes to me just for the challenge, they are barking up the wrong tree. Come to me with genuine problems, and I will do my best to help you.

I have specialized in doing general readings. I can go into special areas such as animals. By this, I mean if you have a pet, I can often feel their energies or give a message—sometimes finding things someone had lost. Remember it's rare to find a medium that can do everything, so most will specialize in one area. This does not mean they cannot do other things; for example, I'm not a great dreamer, but I do on occasion get glimpses into things through dreams. I remember when I told people about a dream about an island with volcanic activity and subsequent floods because of it. Then about a year later the incident in Japan occurred, very similar to what I had predicted.

I do all kinds of things with spirits, but I feel the strongest tool to us is the mind; he who learns to develop it will be king in this or any world. We are limited by our imagination, and fortunately the human race has an incredible ability to dream and then make it reality. I feel that we can accomplish anything as long as we can stay on task. Our minds are not even running at a quarter speed. As we unleash our potentials, we begin to explore more of our minds and thus more of the world around us and to the farthest reaches of the unknown. We can touch any plane of existence and beyond to understand everything. It comes naturally to learn and want to know more. Our lives are made up of time. Regret is the one truth we must overcome, so as our lives flow through time, enjoy and live every moment. Upon reflection you will realize it was all worth it.

There are many ways to find our center; the one that most helped me was through meditation. In the first book, I covered many ways to learn how to meditate and many ways to use these techniques for our betterment. These different ways to use our minds to manage our spiritual lives can enhance our calmness and without limits rewire our destinies to reach an end of blissful balance in our everyday lives. Let's say with but a breath, we can enhance our calm. That's right, one deep breath and exhaling, opening our jaw to relax the tension in the mouth, closing our eyes, and inhaling again, this time a strong exhale giving our bodies permission to release, to let go of any tension still within us. By doing so, we allow our inner light to cover our mortal bodies and allow the one true spirit within each of us access to that universal energy available but limited because of our erratic mundane way of life on this planet. While taking several deep breaths, ask yourself if there is any tension, if there is focus on it, and once your mind is at the spot, could be the neck or back just ask yourself what animal it represents? Don't analyze just the first thought that comes to mind and look at it with your spiritual eyes. Ask the animal what it wants. You will get an answer in the form of a reply or simply the animal with disappear. In either case, when you focus back on the spot, it should feel much better. Blessed are the flexible, for they shall not be bent out of shape, so let's go with the flow and bend with the changes. Time is a blessing for those willing to change with it.

Once we connect to the divine universal truth with our aura and our body is fully elevated to that realm, we can see and sense things that were out of reach to us before. So once we find that center—that calm we can easily access our reality and without all the jumbled-up information from our subconscious to interfere—we can truly see our lives as they are and will be or at least should be. It is at this moment of clarity that we can rewire ourselves and get on the right track. Unfortunately, with time our subconscious can rear its ugly head and interfere, so every once in a while, it's a good idea to tap in and allow this beautiful calm to cover us and envelop our being to once again gain a view of where we are truly meant to be, continuing on the right path to enlightenment. Change and growth are part of the natural order of living. It's never too late, or else you would not be reading this. Make it a choice to be alive. Grow with these new concepts, and the evolution that is life all around you will nourish instead of blocking your inevitable growth.

I have an idea or a thought on how to best help others see it my way. Here it is in a nutshell: if you want to get people on board with your idea. For example, if you want to build a ship, don't get people to cut down trees. Don't get them to do their part. Teach them to yearn for the ocean and to yearn for a sea voyage. As they become passionate, they will willingly do all that is necessary to get there. Too good of an idea to be true? Try it. When you work with emotions, you can succeed where logic alone fails. Get your passion mojo flowing and get others on board with your ideas. True time is lived, impossible to hold on to, so stop looking at the clock as it will only seem slower, get in the game.

I've had situations wherein a group many people are looking at the same situation yet see different things. Our perception is warped to a certain extent by our experience; for example, green represents money to many, but to someone who likes the outdoors, it might represent nature. This is a very raw example of how we can feel, see, and hear, even smell differently according to what we know to be true. So if we appear to be something, we are not depending on how good we get at sending out our vibrations. We can actually get people on board with that idea. Never say never. I've walked into an office, and before walking in, I've visualized myself as invisible, as part of the tapestry in the office; and more than half of the people I walked by never realized it was me or never realized anyone passed by them.

There are many exercises that can be done. My first book worked briefly on this subject. Now let's go into greater detail. In my experience, first and foremost, we must learn to relax. Meditation is part of that process. Once you have achieved a level of proficiency in this, you can continue your development into this very difficult art. I myself have scratched the surface, never truly having a reason to perfect it, I chose just to experience its range. Once you started working on this like anything else, you must devote regular time each and every day just to get with the program.

I don't believe there is anyone that can become good at something without practice, so practice as much as you need; the level of perfection depends on your natural abilities and how much effort you put into the subject. I can imagine several reasons to perceive this talent; for example, I have a friend who is a police officer. For him being able to overcome the significant signals the uniform sends out takes extra effort, so he must also send out energy of control. Wherever he walks, he must also send out the vibrations that he knows what is going on and people should listen to him. In situations where violence occurs, he wants to send out a calming energy so that the situation does not escalate out of control.

I know a lady who is very good at handling a room. She can go around and where needed; she is friendly, and where she wants to be attractive, she sends out some vibrations that, well, it's almost like she has some pheromones. I have also seen her with her back to a person, and they turn to see what they are sensing. It is incredible how we can extend our reach even beyond the visual range of others, to a lesser degree all of you have at one time or another walked into a room or building and a headache occurs soon after. Sometimes I've been privy to a person walking into a room, and a sense of fear has taken over. This is not someone who is claustrophobic and enters an elevator. This was someone who had no phobias and fear struck for no reason. He told me the hairs on the back of his neck stood, and a weakening of his legs took over to the point he said, "Let's get out of this place."

Likewise, I've walked into a room and have been pulled into a particular direction to find there was a hidden skeleton in the closet. Believe it, all these are different energies we are capable of harnessing and using for our own benefit. Remember there is always a cause and effect. Changing or manipulating someone's will for self-gratification can, in the long run, cause repercussions in our own lives, so make sure you have an agenda and there is more to it than just your benefit at the cost of others. Back to the exercises, as I've told you before to target specific people, it is imperative you send a thought or feeling directed at that person. You have to generate a tip or way to identify when that person got the message.

I like to send messages from my third eye and have the person receive the message through the base at the back of their neck. I'm sure with time you will develop your own tools. I like to close my eyes once I have the person's image in my mind. I visualize sending the message. Simple is best at the beginning then I've worked out a technique that if they get it, they are looking away and they turn around and look at me. What we are speaking of here is broad, so you will be like an antenna sending out a signal everywhere and to everyone. You must practice working on your aura, but more than that, you must strengthen your mind and focus; your concentration must be absolute.

Here is a good one: sit in a chair in a busy place, make believe you are not there. Your energies are shut down, to the point that you feel like part of the chair, part of the scenery. The nothingness of thought sounds easy, but for someone who cannot quit their mind from working, it is a very difficult proposition. After a while, you will take in visual information, but your surroundings get nothing from you. Believe it or not, even your coworkers will just pass by and not even realize your presence. This is what we are looking to accomplish, so try it until you get it right. Stand next to a wall, become the wall, become part of the color or features. With time people will walk by and might even bump into you as if you did not exist. These are great little exercises that with time you will perfect. This is but the beginning, get in a pool, and become part of the water. Some might swim over you as if you did not even exist, cool stuff. Don't get frustrated if you need to work on this for a long time.

After you have mastered the nothingness, try and become whatever you need to in order to blend into moving scenes. If you are in a bus, be careful someone might even try and sit on your lap. Don't believe it, try it. On more than one occasion more than a large portion of the readers are standing in thought and someone will step or bump into you. They will apologize as they truly did not see you were you so gone in thought that they could not measure your existence at that moment. Curious topics, it all begins and ends with the mind. The more you control your thoughts, the better you will become. The good poker player will also be good at these exercises. They have mastered the art of the tell. They can give nothing for another player to decipher what they are holding.

Once all these exercises are completed, you can take it to the next level. I've only been able to accomplish this twice. I've stood in a place, and a friend walked by. Later I told him if he saw another friend. He said yes he had seen another friend standing where I was. I attempted to project his image and clothing, and it was properly perceived by him. I thought this is very cool stuff. Keep it simple is the key. Live the scene just like an actor gets into his or her role; so must you but deeper. You must think and become that person, or it will not be believable. Time ends, just not today, so to truly know what we are capable of accomplishing; you must give it time. Time rules. It holds all the cards in its hand, know when to hold on and when to fold; also know, you must only play the winning hand, the one time deals you!

Sleep

There are many things that the body needs in order to function at its maximum. We must never overlook sleep. I feel that as you get older, most of us need less sleep. Let's look at this logically: as we are born, the body is being built into adulthood. We need more sleep. As we get older, our bodies start to deteriorate more and more until it can no longer run and therefore falls apart and we die. So while we are growing, our bodies need more sleep. It is during this time that the body is being built. The chemicals in the body need sleep to balance out and expand not only our physical growth but our psychological stamina. I feel that for our spirit to truly evolve in this lifetime as well as to maintain good health, our bodies need a certain amount of daily sleep. What is this amount you say. From my experience with thousands of readings and cleanings, I feel this differs from person to person by many variables. Age is the most crucial. As children we need more. As we grow to adulthood, this will decrease, but as a baseline, I would say most adults need seven to nine hours of sleep to maintain good health, not only physical but spiritual health.

Many of the body's autonomic systems need to be regulated. This is not done while awake, so as we sleep, our body repairs and replaces what needs to be. For example I've found that most people that are not getting regular sleep in the amounts I've spoken of above might develop hypertension or a blood sugar imbalance or other physical problems. Even more important in determining if you will live longer or not than family history of high blood pressure or other determining factors that science has outlined today is regular sleep. I feel a good night sleep is very important for our health. The hormones that the body needs to regulate are done at night not during our waking hours. I've really found many of the problems that people call me with to be related to lack of sleep.

I want to give some specific examples. I believe you are not alone in this. Many people with intimacy issues have found with better sleep they have repaired the lack of sex drive or even improved their communications. The messages are of long-term solutions. If you are sleeping less than six hours a day, you may be experiencing some debilitating emotional issues like depression or irritability. Let's clear something up if you are living long term with little sleep and are not feeling tired or sleepy then probably you are getting the sleep you need. There are always exceptions to any rule, but as a baseline, I would continue to emphasize seven to nine hours' sleep a day. Not everything has to do with a spiritual problem, never forget this.

I recommend to the people I read not to obsess. Look for any and every other possible solution and then and only then if there is nothing else that can be causing the particular situation, then we look into negative energy. As unlikely as it can be, it does happen, but always look for the mundane answer first. Let's get back to the big picture of sleep or lack of it. Let's start by telling you that a good night sleep is one of the key things needed if you do not want to gain weight. Yes, if you don't sleep well or long enough, your own body might have a problem fighting off weight gain.

I found several instances of women who were having problems getting pregnant. After I place them on a regular sleep treatment, they all ended up pregnant. This showed me that lack of sleep also affects hormone levels. So many issues are related to lack of sleep; this is not a magic pill or is it a cure-all, but if it is something so important for so many reasons not to mention living longer, then perhaps we need to take an active approach and get that good night's sleep. I want to cover some of the things I've been told has worked to get regular sleep.

I don't want to scare anyone, but the less stress in your lives, the better your chances of avoiding a stroke or heart attack. Guess what, the better night's sleep, the better your body can manage that stress that can cause these problems. For those who snore or suffer from sleep apnea, I suggest sleeping on your side and place a pillow between your legs. This will or should decrease these problems. Gaining weight and not sleeping enough, then a longer night's sleep may help your body to fight off that weight gain. A power nap as some call it during the day may be a quick fix so keep it between ten to thirty minutes, not longer. If you take a longer nap, you might feel sluggish and sleepy instead of it giving you that quick fix. Consider this option, sleep apnea, a greater and more common threat than we can imagine. How many of us snore? There is a good chance you also may have it. Go to your doctor and talk about it. Remember sleep is essential for life as is the quality of sleep. Imagine if we are in bed for eight hours but only sleeping four, not good enough for the body to replenish. I'm sure if most people slept the right amount of hours, life would be better. So don't forget if you're having or think you might be having this problem, go see your doctor.

I've had several clients over the years with sleep apnea or other sleeping disorders, and the one thing they all found in common was weight loss when the problem was attended to. My clients will tell you I have simple rules: eat big meals in the morning or at lunch and then later in the day, the smaller your meal should be. Never eat late at night or consume any alcohol or coffee at least four hours before you go to bed. Sometimes I will give this advice and not go into the details of hormones or weight issues; I try to help my clients without becoming an alarmist.

The bottom line is giving the help each needs, and I'm content without having to get the credit. I like to exercise early. You want your body to be wound down before you go to sleep, and while on this subject, keep computers and other electronics like television to a minimum as you come close to bed time. Yes, keep the bedroom for sleep and intimacy, no fooling around with television or computers or those smart phones.

I've found that we need sun, constantly harping that people need to get it regularly. This will, believe it or not, regulate hormone levels. Our bodies produce melatonin before we go to bed; if we get enough sun during the day at least one solid hour upon our bodies, then the body will be more likely to release this melatonin in the evening hours. I'm definitely antipills, so unless all else fails, try and stay away from most of the habit-forming pills to help you go to sleep. I've had several students that were not doing well in school. After suggesting changing the sleeping habits, their grades slowly increased dramatically. Remember natural changes don't happen overnight, but if you are consistent with the changes, so will your results.

I've even recommended to people to change their sleeping habits. For example, eating more fish can help with your sleeping. Look into the foods that might bring chemicals that help you sleep naturally. A nice warm tea before sleep might help. Don't drink teas with caffeine. Use logic and find the ones that will help you fall asleep. I'm big on meditation, so simple breathing techniques are a must for anyone having sleeping issues. Keep it simple. If it makes sense, try it, if not, do I need to say it. If we use common sense, then our solutions will be right in front of our very noses. I've spent quite a long time on sleep because I've seen what it can do when we sleep enough.

One last thought, no matter what the problem to sleep, even if you are a drug user such as marijuana, after a while, it will have a negative effect. You will need more and more, and eventually your body will not respond positively, no longer keeping you asleep. So here it is down and dirty: For those who are desperate, you must go to sleep consistently at the same time and awake at the same time. So for thirty days, you will pick a time to go to bed, let's say 11:00 p.m. and awake at 7:00 a.m. No matter what happens, you will not go back to sleep once you are up at 7:00 a.m., even if you only fell asleep at four in the morning. You must reeducate the body and give it guidelines. So no naps, keep in mind the things I've told you not to do video games before you go to bed. Bed is for sleep or intimacy, so in bed by 11:00 p.m. and up by 7:00 a.m. You must not lie down or sleep at any other time. Be consistent, and you will find your body will cave in and you will regain control over your life. Remember when you oversleep, you disturb your body's natural sleep rhythms. Don't quit this technique before the thirty days I've outlined. It needs consistency for the change to occur.

Let's talk about dreams. Most of us have the capacity to dream a good dream. I mean receive messages during our sleep time. Does this mean we are getting messages from departed beings? Maybe, but as a general rule, most dreams are our own subconscious mind unscrambling problems we cannot cope with or find a solution for. For example, many people have dreams that inspire them to create. You've heard the saying, thinking outside the box. This is what I believe happens when we dream. We can navigate outside our structured world and construct often in abstract ways our way out of whatever situation or problems we might be encountering or will soon encounter. One of the key and interesting elements to dreams is our ability to predict what will be. Over the years I've encountered many people who are vivid dreamers and many who sporadically get a message. We need time to dream. It's Important to our well-being. We dream in spurts, and if we do not sleep enough, we are shutting down this very essential part of who we are. Over the years many have told me their success was sparked by a dream.

I like to tell my clients to write down their dreams in a diary. For those who have an issue remembering them, I suggest giving a simple posthypnotic suggestion just before sleep, like I will sleep soundly; and when I dream, I will awaken, write down my dream, and go back to my sound sleep. So keep a notepad next to the bed along with a pen or pencil and start your diary. If you do it when awake, try and do it immediately after waking up because as you get input from the day, you might forget your dreams. Find a friend or a nonbiased observer that you can discuss your dreams with. Someone you can talk these dreams through with, someone who is not judgmental and can share their dreams as well. There is no one answer and dreams can be very subjective, so analyze them. After several weeks or sometimes even months of dreaming, you can make a better assessment of the meanings. I've been told in dreams when you dream with calm waters it's a good sign, and when it's dark or turbulent, this means difficulties.

I would take a back seat to these statements and find your own way to interpret dreams. We do not all speak the same sleep language; your own subconscious mind will develop its own ways to speak to you in a way best understood by you.

Chapter 3

Stories

Ashes

I want to tell you about a constant I've found in almost every situation where people have kept the ashes of the deceased. Over the years I've done home and business cleansings where I've found the ashes of deceased people. In every single case the area felt as if a dense fog, spiritually speaking was covering the place. From the beginning, the business or the homeowners have called me because something was wrong with where they lived or worked. If you can understand life, you can understand death. What I mean is how folks go through the stages of grieving. Some who are not ready to pass often suffer the same stages upon passing so they might feel remorse or sorrow, but somewhere along the way, they will or might feel the anger of leaving. These are the souls that can potentially become dangerous. They inadvertently pass this rage into our world. Could be as simple as breaking objects or causing you to drop things; sometimes lights turning on in the middle of the night might be their thing.

Let's speak of one or two home scenarios and at least one business. I had done a reading on a lady, and as part of what I saw, it seemed that her life had taken a wrong turn about a year before. She agreed that things did not seem to go her way for the last year or year-and-a-half. She agreed that there must be something going on that was not right or normal in her life. I could not pinpoint the source, so we agreed to meet at her home and do a personal and home cleaning. When I visit a home, I only charge for one cleaning, so I would clean her and her sister who lived with her and her home also for one charge. No matter what, my price is always $221. This was decided by the spirits I work with from the beginning and I don't change that.

So the day arrived, and as I got to her house, I started to feel heaviness even before I entered the home. It was the very first cleansing of a home where there were ashes of family members so as with any situation, we learn. As I walked in, I told the lady I wanted to start cleaning the home and then I would clean her and her sister. I asked permission to walk around the home and use the tools I had brought to clean the energy of the home. She agreed and I started to walk around the house. It had two floors so as usual I started with the top floor and worked my way through the home.

As I started downstairs, I felt this wave hit me as I passed the mantle in the living room. I had to go back and forth a few times until I pinpointed that it was coming from a beautiful looking metal or brass vase. I asked the woman if I could bring it down. She said okay but explained it contained the ashes of her dead husband. I immediately realized that it had become a beacon of energy, not at all her husband's. I explained that once the body dies the soul does not stay attached.

She seemed open and understood what I had explained. I also told her she would have to get rid of the ashes. I took the ashes out and wrapped it in something I had brought with me to clean. I told her this was not a permanent cure but a temporary patch to give her time to get rid of the ashes. She asked what she should do. I said the ashes really have nothing to do with her husband. I like the ocean, but anywhere they could be scattered will diffuse the energies that had gathered around it. She agreed, and I finished the home cleansing. Her life had taken a wrong turn about six months after she brought the ashes to her home. Coincidence maybe, but would you take the chance, understand, nothing of the spirit is ever left in the ashes. So keeping ashes is never a good idea, and if you know someone that has them, let them know to get rid of them before they become a collector of all sorts of negative energy.

On another occasion, I was called to clean an office energy, and while in the middle, I was shown how the woman who ran the place had ashes from her mother and dog in her home. Although the ashes were not physically at the office, it was having a very similar effect because she was bringing those energies from the home to the office. Since she was hired strange things were happening. I informed the owner that it was not that the woman was bad luck. This had become the consensus of the folks who had been working there for years. I explained that she herself was having personal problems and why. The employer offered her a home cleansing if she got rid of the ashes or she would have to be let go from work. She agreed, and within a couple of months, things got back on track and she became the asset she was hired to be.

I was called by a client of mine, she said she started a new job at a big company; she was a client for a long time, so she could tell that there was some sort of problem, spiritually speaking. After I was done with the reading over the phone with her, I told her she could recommend to the owners to do a cleansing of the business in hopes that we can set right what was obviously going wrong in the last couple of years. This organization had several hundred employees. Many strange incidents had been happening—things they could not explain, production had also gone down.

They would try new avenues to drum up business and in other areas things would go wrong, so they were considering among other things to sell. The man agreed and called me for a reading. I gave him many proofs during the reading about not only work but personal stuff, enough so that he agreed to do the work cleansing. Once there, I realized that all familiar fog of ashes in the area. It took me a while to find it. One of the managers had brought the ashes of his dead son into the office and placed it in his cubicle. Once I found it I suggested to management to get the person to get the ashes out of the office.

The man was not comfortable with getting rid of his son's ashes; he became very defensive and ultimately quit his job. Soon after things began to get back on track with the business, it's been several years, and my client still works there and with every subsequent reading things improved until not even a flicker of that problem existed any more. I got several new clients from that business, and all has been well. No one ever heard from the man again. I've asked about him because I know his life will not improve if he keeps those ashes that have nothing to do with his son.

Things Can Change

With destiny we can estimate or guess as to when things will happen. I remember one case where I told a woman who lost the man in her life it was not over, but she would have to wait if she truly loved him. She wanted results right away, so I was able to tell her when the tide would turn and an opportunity for them to get back would begin. I told her she would have a chance encounter with him. It would be indoors she would be making a turn, and he would be in front of her. I told her like idiots neither would say a word and about a minute later he would flinch and walk away. I told her although he walked away she would be able to tell through his facial expression that he misses her and had changed his mind about what had happened. It took about a year of nothing from him before this exact situation occurred. I know this because she continued to call me about other matters throughout the wait and see period. She always asked about him, and I kept telling her the same until it occurred.

I read a woman about five years ago. The client was from Greece, and I had told her she would divorce her husband of eleven years. I told her she would leave her home and move to the United States, and she would have a different career and remarry. Well, I recently heard from her for another reading. It had been about five years since I last heard from her because she was not happy with my predictions. Unfortunately I was right, and all three major events occurred. I told her that things don't always happen within a certain time frame but usually the events come to pass.

Again she was not happy with the reading as I did not give much energy to her current relationship, she thought it would turn into marriage, but since the man hardly had any energy with her I told her to keep looking. I told her to get a cleansing, and as usual, she wanted to hear what she wanted to hear so she just thanked me and said I hope you are wrong. I just told her me too, so good luck to you and God bless. I'm sure with time I will hear from her again. I tell my clients if you are open, I can guide you and help you. Most things can be changed, so with proper energy work we can lessen bad outcomes to situations. Life is worth living is a mantra we should all practice. Remember if you believe hard enough and often enough and it will become your reality.

Anything can be changed; I remember about a year ago, I helped a family whose husband had been unemployed more than two years. Well, not only did he get a job but at a very good salary; it was about a year before the problem arose again. This time, they called for a reading when I was informed the boss had told him he would be getting his walking papers by next Thursday. Guess what, they called me on a Tuesday, so without hesitation, I gave them a spell to use on the boss to change his mind. It was not much time, but I had faith.

They called me on Friday. The man arrived at work and spoke with the boss, and he was told he would no longer be fired, so they were very happy. I was very content. I had faith that their need was great and the firing to have been done was not right. You must remember right and wrong does give a little extra or takes away from any spell. What I mean is, if I do a spell and it has merit, it will work better than if one is done but not for the common good of the one or the many.

I've visited many homes. I've cleaned many energies that needed to move but none to this day ever felt so real as this one I'm about to tell you about.

It was during my time of early learning that I would attempt all sorts of rituals. One in particular was called a spiritual mass. It was during one of these that I discovered how powerful malevolent energies could be. During these sessions there is always a group of people like me that meet to help a particular individual being assaulted by something not of this world. This time was a group of people with a mix of male and female energy. Since we did not know what we were going to find, it's often good to bring the mix. Not all spirits will channel through every medium, so a good variety of hosts offers the best chance to channel whatever is there and vanquish it.

So it begins, we take part in cleaning the energies of the home and the people there to soften any difficulties we might encounter while in the session. As we go through the home, sometimes we find clues as to what is really going on. We each take on one of the people in the home and clean their energies to again further soften the energy or energies we are to encounter during the session. We prepare the area where we are to work and place the chairs in a horseshoe form to have the person in question sit at the head so again we can absorb most if not all that the person in carrying.

Oh yeah, who we came to help was a young boy who had been in the hospital multiple times for no apparent reason. Fortunately, there was someone in the family that could see this was not natural and reached out to one of my friends who in turn called us to assist in this endeavor. As a group, we had worked together in other occasions. I gave an example of another session in the first book, but this was something different. We were all ready and everything had been placed just where it needed to be. One of the ladies in the group started the prayers. Yes, we pray. We invoke in God's name all the spirits in our group to come forth and assist us in our endeavors.

We call upon all our ancestors and the ancestors of the people in the home, their guardian angel or spirit guide. In any case it's the same thing, just different belief system, so as we start to fill the room with positive energies, we focus on the boy in question. We focus all our energies to getting whatever has been bothering him to go away. One of the ladies tapped in first and started to shake as the energy attempted to tap in. I could tell already that whatever it was, causing this child to sicken was not a simple soul. I felt it was feeding on the life force of the child and if not stopped it would eventually drain all the life force and eventually kill the boy.

Another in the group began to pray again, and she told us that we must stay focused in summoning our energies as she felt this thing as she called it was getting angry. We use prayer to diffuse the hold of the entity and allow the person under assault breathing room. Remember this child had been in the hospital at least seven times in the last four months. Each time it was for something different and the outcome was the same, doctors could not figure out why so many different organs were being affected.

We knew and thus arrived I feel just in time to prevent the thing from taking the life of an innocent boy. He was pale and weak although he had been in the hospital with an IV for about a week. I stood up and walked behind the boy. At times when the entity did not want to let go, we would go through motions and prayer pull at it until it angers and jumps to one of us. Yes, take on the thing causing such harm to another person; this is part of what we do. Do not think this is an easy task, and I don't recommend it until you have practiced taking on a possessing spirit multiple times.

I also recommend you learn to channel your own spirits before you take on any other souls. Remember this is like driving a car, only a car with a mind of its own. Yeah, we are the car, so these beings are inside we can hear, feel, and just about all they can manifest. It's often weird when I allow a female spirit to take over. I feel the other sex and it's a bit overwhelming. Some people who channel spirits are conscious during the process; this makes it even more difficult. There is another mind in there with you, one that you willingly temporarily let take over your physical body.

Some of these spirits have a very foul mouth, so you must try to keep it from speaking atrocious words; they had not been in a body for a while so you never know what they will do. This is why we make sure where we are is difficult to get out of or you might find yourself running out of the house and into the middle of the street. Yes, these souls are not always bad or malevolent, but they love life just as you and I, so any opportunity to walk or speak will often make them run amok.

Anyway back to the moment, I called in God's name for this evil to let the child go and come into me. Oh, it did. The rest I'll tell you from the accounts of others of what happened next. That's right I can usually stay there, when a very powerful energy takes over my consciousness, it is sometimes out of the picture. Well, I was told I got on all fours and took a solid tile from the floor and ripped it out, with my bare hands. I could tell because my fingertips and nails were dirty and scratched from whatever I did while on the floor.

As I was possessed, the boy got scared and ran out of the room. It's not the best thing to happen and often can cause the possessing spirit to release and go back to the boy. Fortunately it was by this time fully funded inside me, and it was not about to let go, so the other mediums began to work on it as I in a minimal way prayed to God for help and to take this evil out of me and take it away from here. My friend told me it took over good, and she was glad there were others as it took the power of all of them to get the spirit out and gone. She said at one time she saw my eyes change color and other manifestations that scared her a bit.

I can tell you the kid never got sick again, at least not from any paranormal stuff. It's been years, and I happened to hear from the lady of the house who to date is very grateful to all of us. She remembered how scary it was when the entity possessed me, and she said the energy of the room got dark and she thought I would not be able to handle it. I must admit it was one of the hardest possessions I had to channel.

The Client

Dear Hector:

It's been two years since my last reading. I didn't think I'd have a follow-up testimonial to write so far down the line, but as it turns out, the spirits must have known I wouldn't have a reading for a long time because they managed to cover all the bases when we last spoke. You did a cleansing for me once before at your center and read me then, too, but the call we had was so detailed, I wrote everything down to be sure I'd remember everything. Truthfully, the specificity of the experience was so astonishing, I've never had to refer to the notes I jotted down. Everything made an impression and has stayed with me since.

To give you an update, at the time, many of these things didn't really make sense to me but I knew they must be grounded in truth because you were able to provide names and dates you couldn't have possibly known. Looking back on our conversation, I can now see you were pinpointing events before I even knew what they were. You read me in May of 2010, when I was worried about getting a job, I had interviewed for and been back to for follow-ups several times. You told me it would happen in August and, sure enough, that was my start date—August 2. (I stayed there for a period of eight months, so the number 8 must have been important for whatever reason.)

You also told me to go to the doctor to get checked out for something in my ovaries. At the time, I was too scared to go get tested but I finally decided to go (I kept getting the feeling like I really needed to, so I stopped putting it off). When I saw my doctor, he scheduled some tests and found out I had a cyst in my ovary and three small fibroids. I'm glad you had told me it would be ok, because that really gave me reassurance as I was waiting on results. After two weeks of testing (and *lots* of prayer), my biopsy came back negative and the doctor told me I was more than fine.

The doctor also mentioned that I should start trying to get pregnant to see if it could happen. This was also related to our reading. You asked me about a miscarriage. I hadn't had one yet; in fact, I'd never been pregnant to my knowledge. Well, this is the reason I decided to send you the testimony. On Sunday, I found out I was pregnant. I went to the doctor on Monday and got the blood test done, and they calculated I was at five weeks. For whatever reason, though, I had a feeling it wasn't the time and by Tuesday, I had lost the pregnancy. I do feel at peace, though. I recall you said it wasn't the right time, and I knew that deep down inside. My husband and I are trying to buy a house now and are under a lot of stress with the process because there will be an intense amount of work to do on this house, so I know that wouldn't have been good for a healthy pregnancy.

I'll be going to see my doctor again on Tuesday, but I still remember something very reassuring that you said during our reading—you told me to stop worrying and that I would be a great mom when the right time came. That has stayed with me until this day and I hope it will come to pass. There's definitely hope for the future, and I have you to thank for it.

After reading your book (I'm about 50 percent into and I can't put it down!), I felt the need to write and tell you how much you've helped me with just that one reading. I'm looking forward to chatting again and scheduling another cleansing as I venture into this other phase of my life. If it's one thing I've learned from this experience, it's that the spirits have given you a gift, and I'm grateful you're there to communicate the important messages our spiritual guardians offer us in hopes of providing a fulfilling and abundant life.

Thanks for all you do.

I hope to be in touch soon.

Warmest regards,

Alicia

In this testimonial you can see how sometimes the time line can be a bit skewed, but remember time is flexible and the events cannot only come out of sequence; but also past, present, and future can come in the wrong order. So when you get a reading, always take it with a grain of salt, take it all in however, and keep an open mind as most of the time a large portion of what is revealed does become reality. With that said, the reason we peak into what can be is in hopes of changing what we do not like. So if in a reading I tell you within the next two years or so you will go on a trip to Europe and it will have negative repercussions, then you can change this by not going. If I tell you that you can get pregnant within the next twelve months but it will not be the right time, make sure you use contraception or your companion does as well. All things being equal knowing makes it easier to change the outcome.

I am more than happy to write this testimonial for Mr. Espinosa as his help in one of the darkest hours of my life has no words. I was in the middle of a chaotic and at times unstable marriage with recurring thoughts of leaving yet never having the courage or signs to guide me and tell me whether staying or leaving was the right thing to do. A papaya-smothered bath, dip in sea water, and personal reading later, I felt refreshed, rejuvenated and empowered enough to finally let go of something that was clearly not going where I truly wanted it to go and was causing my more harm than good. The aftermath has obviously not been the smoothest ride in my life, with constant ups and downs and moments of anger, depression and doubt. But without Mr. Espinosa´s words of enlightenment and of courage, I would probably still be stuck in the relationship limbo, asking myself, "Is she too good to leave or too bad to stay?'" His direct and always kind words will allow you to see the light after the tunnel. He doesn´t walk you through the door but merely shows you the door and provides the tools to make it through with self-confidence and courage.

Changes in life are unnerving and always makes us uneasy, but sometimes all we need is the right nudge in the right direction.

I hope this helps, Mr. Espinosa, and thank you again.

Best,

Richard Tampa, Florida

Lady Looks

I want to affirm how good your cure for dark eyes was. You told me to grind fresh washed mint leaves. Your suggestion to place on the dark areas under eyes for fifteen to twenty-five minutes and wash clean was fantastic. I've told all my friends with similar problems, and I've become the popular friend with my girlfriends. You gave me lots of good health type tips in my reading that I've incorporated into my regular routine. If you remember you told me to get my husband to drink one lemon a day for breakfast, wait fifteen minutes, and then have his regular breakfast. Well, his cholesterol has lowered, and he's lost a few pounds, don't know if because of it but it's all good. You also recommended I eat at least two bananas a day; if not more and I'm on it, oh yeah, your suggestion to take the inside of the banana peel and rub on to my teeth has actually caused them to whiten enough for my friends at work to ask if I've done a bleach on my teeth. Last but not least my drinking three tablespoons of pure apple cider vinegar twice a day with a half cup of water, once in the morning and the other before bed, has really made my overall feeling better, not to mention I'm digesting better and not as hungry. I know you told me three times a day, so I plan to step up this routine. Again, God bless you and all you do for so many people.

Alejandra

The Message

I've had many readings where the first thing that comes out is the spirit of a recently departed, and then I will get a flood of readings from friends and family looking for messages. Folks, I am only the person in the middle. There needs to be someone on the other side willing to come through and give a message for me to convey it. Although I do not disappoint, I can only tell you what is being shown to me and not always what you want, especially concerning the other side. We as mediums can foretell the future and see into the past as well as the present, but when it comes to spirits, we can only interact if the spirit in question wants to come through. You will always get what you need and not what you want.

It was during one of these that a spirit came through, and the first questions out of my mouth was did someone in the family or close to you die within the last few months. She immediately said yes, and this was the reason for the call. I continued to express what I was being shown; I believe the reason for the spirit's appearance was that her son was in trouble. Moving out of the country was it seemed to the father a good thing. He wanted in no uncertain terms for her to know that he was behind her idea to leave the country and take the son completely out of the environment he was in. She asked about the daughter and all kinds of stuff, but he kept going back to the same thing. I explained that when a spirit is so stuck it must be for a serious reason, and she should wrap things up and complete her plans to move.

Once she affirmed she would soon move. The spirit of her deceased husband moved farther away, and we continued the reading without his help. She was concerned about money and what he had left and how disorganized the death and his paperwork was. I told her that it was his time and that there was not in my opinion anything weird about the death or how he died. I told her that she would not be alone or should she worry as the spirit had shown me repeatedly that if she moved the situation with the son would get better and his path to destruction would be avoided. She seemed pleased and thanked me for the reading.

The Aura

I got a call from a new client. I usually would schedule for another day, but my spirit said make room. I know that what she wanted must be important for this to happen, so I gave her my lunch hour. As soon as she called, I connected with her and her aura seemed to scream, clean me. So I asked her if she felt tormented and if she could not sleep well. She told me this was an understatement as she had not been sleeping at all for a couple of weeks except for an hour here and there. I began to look deeper into her and found so much energy in her aura that I was amazed how well balanced she still seemed. As I've stated before the aura to me is the extension of the soul. In other words like a shield or protection for not only the body but the internal soul itself. So no matter if you hold on, let go, go up or down, side to side, forward, backward. These are but a few movements in the art of living. Remember years wrinkle the skin, quitting wrinkles the soul. No matter time passes, so take an active role and smooth out the edges of your life.

I gave her some remedies and told her she needed to change how she was living. Her stress level was out of this world, and although she was still fine within a year or so, she could become a basket case if she did not change gears. She agreed but explained that she was going through a tough divorce and the ex-husband was really messing with her. I asked her about the person that was speaking to her and had to make a report to the court. She explained that there was a court appointed person who was investigating the husband's allegations against her. I told her that nothing he said was true, but she would be found guilty. She was freaking out at this point. I explained she needed to calm down and listen. I believed that he had a new girlfriend, and although she had not caught on to her yet that was the person who was orchestrating everything that was happening to her.

After asking her a few question, I realized that she knew nothing about this woman who in my opinion was the true enemy. I asked her what the woman did for a living, and she did not know other than that she held some sort of government job. I asked her to make a call and find out what she did if she had the means; she explained that some old friends of both of them had been going out with the ex-husband and the new woman. She hung up the phone and called me right back. She was truly panicking now as she had found that the woman worked for the Department of Children and Families a government agency that handles these types of allegations.

I explained that that husband did not have a clue, but as soon as he started to date her, she decided to help by corrupting the system or using her knowledge to mess with her life and try and take the kids away. I told her to speak with the attorney and explain what she had found out perhaps there was something that could be done now. I was certain this woman knew the man sent to do the investigation and was manipulating the system for her benefit.

Here's my question to you with this story. Did I help her? Yes. Did I change the outcome? Maybe, but I believe knowledge is power, and packing this new information would most certainly help her with the attorney and the court. If they properly showed the connections, I'm sure it would mitigate many issues currently being brought up. So with this newfound information, she was able to go to the court and a new person was put in and the woman who worked for that government agency was disciplined and the playing field was level; now she was able to fight and win these unfounded allegations.

The Bookstore

I remember one time I walked into a bookstore. I was looking for something specific when I approached the lady at the counter. I asked her for what I came for; she looked it up and told me where in the store the book was located. I found it and started to look for another. Again I approached the lady, and this time I told her uncharacteristically that she was correct in her thinking, but she should not doubt as the person who did it was, and I gave her the name given me. I explained how this person had been doing damage and how he had left some black magic to cause the place to have problems. She was astonished as I spoke and could not believe it. When I was done, she admitted she was conflicted as to who could be doing damage to her and why.

She told me she had thought it was between the men whose name I mentioned and another woman. She continued to explain to me how much peace of mind I had given her. She found what I had told her, and she threw it out and soon after everything in the store started to flow again. She happened to be a very good astrologer, and over the years, she has done my natal chart and predicted my astrological future.

I believe nature will choose for itself from itself what is to be discarded; nature has a way to create a balance even when a balance has changed. A new balance is always attempted, so the universe will always find a medium to any situation. Things can be thrown out of whack, but eventually after the turmoil a balance is achieved. Turbulence is not a natural state, so eventually a new state of balance is achieved in all things. In most if not all of my stories, I try and show that you are not alone and what you are going through is not just yours to own.

Vice

With this in mind I want to tell you a story, one in which the natural state was not respected and the change was drastic, swift, and permanent. It's the story of a family that because of the father primarily that balance that natural state of stability was not achieved. They had been married for six years. The first time the wife called me for a reading. He worked a government job. She worked for a bank in a senior position and they had three kids, three girls. I want to give a synopsis of their lives together as I lived many of their ups and downs unable to help straighten them into balance.

With my first reading, I was able to identify that the husband was a cheater, but as I continued the reading, so was my client I discovered. She immediately told me not to go into that but instead to concentrate on the husband and what he was up to. So I did and gave her some remedies to help her get her husband back on track in their marriage. I could see the three little girls and the need for a stable home. I also gave her some remedies to create a better and positive home life for the girls. I did suggest to her if I was to help her she should consider stopping her own activities outside the marriage and put her energies back into the family. There is no recipe for living: a shoe fits one, pinches another, a suit fits, itches another, how to do this thing called living, walk out, and do it. If you are in it, do it as trouble free as possible life should be lived and not struggled against.

It was six months or so since that first reading, and she again called for a second reading. I started with a question. I asked her if she did the baths that I had recommended for her and her family. She said some of it and some was just too difficult. I know what I give people is simple. I have a practical approach to any cleansing, or clearing of energy, if what you have to do to fix the problem becomes stressful to find the ingredients or in any part of the process then it's not worth doing. If I could recommend nothing or a magic pill, I would. Unfortunately I don't have one yet. I'll keep working on it in the mean time while most of what I prescribe is easy and pain free.

So as I continued with the reading, I realized she was yet on another affair. Again she brushed it off and told me to concentrate on other areas. As we progressed on these areas, I saw the eldest daughter would get married early and the second would get pregnant out of wedlock. She asked about the little girl, and I said her future was uncertain, I continued to talk to her about where the family was going and I told her how an opportunity to move would manifest and it would be a positive thing if they did leave.

Again I gave her some remedies to help things along; I told her this time to e-mail me once she completed it or if she had any questions. I truly felt the life they were living was in constant flux, and the children were not in a very loving or stable environment. You know children can feel things even if they don't know what they know something is not right and their little girl was one of those types of children so she suffered silently.

Yet another seven months or so later, the woman would call me for another appointment, so I gave her one a few days later. Once she called me, I told her I really feel a huge change in their lives. She told me that in the last reading, I had predicted a big move and indeed that opportunity had arrived. Her husband was offered a post in another state, and they were considering it. I told her not to give it a second thought and suggested they take it. As the reading progressed, it had come to pass that the little girl was showing the signs of a maladjusted young person as I had told her in previous readings.

Again I asked her if she had done the remedies I had instructed. She said no, but after all that was happening, if I were to give her any remedies, she would surely do it. I smiled to myself and said, good, better late than never. We continued, and I told her that it would be good for the family to have a fresh start without those distractions. I was kind. I was really talking about those extra people in both their lives, and she of course once again told me to continue but to leave her and her friend alone.

I gave her a hell of a reading, even some dead relatives chimed in; I don't know how to get through to these people, primarily my client who I don't understand. It's almost as if she has these two distinct personalities and they can coexist in this weird life they are all living. I can see the disasters that might befall them if I cannot help get them into some sort of balance their derailing is certain just as a train will derail and crash if it does not stay firmly on the tracks. I gave her this analogy in attempts to get through. Together takes work, like a beautiful vase its worth is whole, but if broken, it becomes worthless. Even so it can be picked up, so it is with relationships, you can always pick up the pieces and become whole again!

I'm usually good at dealing with the different temperaments and types of client, but this family was getting to me. I can see the movie of their disaster and so far have been unable to change anything. I feel hopeless when it comes to truly giving the family a chance at survival. These people are so strange both the husband as much as the wife. My hope is that if they make this move to another part of the country, they will leave behind so much baggage and give the marriage a true chance to work.

It had been about a year before I actually heard from her again. When she called I was shocked. I thought she had given up on the readings. Once we got to the reading, she told me that the move happened, and she had been at a branch with the same company but in another state. Her husband she said seemed to be doing well at his new position and the kids were seemingly happy in the new home. As the reading continued, I asked how she felt. She said restless. She asked me about the husband, and I told her that at the moment he seemed to be content. *I did not tell her what I was seeing. The spirit warned me not to; for some reason, the realignment did not take and soon both would revert to the course that would eventually take them to disaster and the end of their family life.*

I asked her to take some baths and asked her husband to do them as well so they could settle easier and things could run smoothly in their new environment. Over the last few years I've tried as best I could to guide her and help her, but she is far and there is so much I can do without actually cleaning her directly. She seems to believe but only as far as it suits her and her own desires. So with this new reading I again could see a very cloudy future. No matter what they keep in flux, this huge change by moving states should have grounded them. Unfortunately life is not one thing or another; we must of our own free will want to find balance.

As I told you, a life without balance is doomed to crash and burn. At one time or another, being out of balance is part of the human experience but continually so is not correct and eventually disaster strikes. So I will continue to give my all in hopes to change this destiny that continues to get closer every time I read this woman. I was really frustrated at my inability to help these people; I have come to terms with the fact that I cannot help everyone. I refuse to let this be the epitaph of this family, and I hope by the time she calls again. If she does, I've come up with a plan to help them.

Like clockwork it was about seven months later when I got a call and request to get a reading. I gave her my next appointment three days later. I had been busy but took time to think about her and her family and what I would say to help her. The day of the reading arrived, and I told her what I saw and how the future looked very bleak unless she took action and stopped her extra marital habits. Oh yeah, she had taking up with one of her new coworkers. I told her before she asked me to stop that I knew the second or middle daughter was not from her husband and she would hear me this time.

She said nothing and just listened; I guess I rattled her with that eye-opening statement about the middle child. She was so silent. For a second I thought she might have just hung up on me, so I asked if she understood. She said yes, and I continued. I told her that unless she stopped and she got her husband to try and be a husband, she and he would get divorced. She said, no way he is also at it again. I said yes, and this time it's someone from his job.

I continued to give her a full account of what I saw and how it could be prevented if she but tried to make it work. I asked her if she felt anything for her husband, and she said yes. She asked me the same question about her husband, and I said yes, he still feels for you as a man feels for a woman or I would not make a case for keeping the marriage alive. So she agreed to try and I was so happy, although I had my hesitations if she would really keep her word to give it a try.

I got a call about thirty days later. She had gotten caught with the lover, and the husband asked for a divorce. This was one situation I was unable to make work. After several years, it was finally over for this family. I always saw a strong window of possibility that this could happen, but destiny had something else in mind for this family's future. I meditated on this outcome and came to the conclusion that no matter what your future, it still takes work on the part of the person to make it happen. What I mean is no matter what is written, free will always overrides destiny. If the destiny is good and you are on a destruction path, you can override your good destiny. Take the other side of that coin. If your destiny is less than good by sheer will, that destiny may be diverted and you can create a new future. I believe we can all write our destiny, with the scenario I just told you about, I saw how things can be changed and it gave me that understanding.

The Clash

I have been fortunate, blessed you could say, to have avoided many energy classes with dark energy practitioners. Dark magic is just as powerful, and like any fight, both get bruised no matter the victor. I will tell you of one incident where one of my clients was being assaulted by a black magic practitioner. I'll give you a brief of how it all started for him; he and his wife were upper middle-class people, a tight knit family with many cousins, aunts, and uncles. In other words this was a large if not huge and tight family with regular get-together. No matter if alike or different, you just know without the spoken word that together you are better than apart. Don't let life, external to you and him, don't let past traumas damage this beautiful thing called together. You know it, you feel it. Say cancel whenever you begin to bring in destructive and needless emotions from a place not of love but of panic, anger, depression, confusion, misguided loyalties, stay true, stay together. So it is with this story they knew they belonged and reached out to me in this case. You will be astounded how many obstacles, and they stayed the course.

This dark power practitioner was paid to break this family apart since the person who hired him wanted the wife for himself. She was quite beautiful, successful, and full of fire for life. Only one problem, she had given her heart to her husband, my client. The world can have very strange friends as the man who wished to possess the woman in question had been a good friend of the husband. As it were they all knew each other since high school; they all went to the same college and had kept friendships for many years. The one she chose was the man she married, and they had two children together. They had lost touch with the other friend, so after several years, they hear he was doing great and had amassed a small fortune.

He, one day, came to visit the wife at home, and she greeted him as she had always, as a friend. He came clean with her about his feelings about her and now that he was where he always wanted to be his only need was to have her by his side. She told him that she was happily married, and after all those years as friends, how was it that at this moment he decided to say and proclaim all these things to her. He explained to her that before he had other priorities, but he always had a desire and love for her, even since they were going to high school together. She told him news to me, and she never saw him in that light. She confessed that even back then she had a crush on her husband. She told him she always held out for him to step up, and when he did, she accepted without hesitation.

This guy was a very driven person and point-blank told her he would change her mind and he would not stop until she became his. Later that evening, she told all this to her husband who was flabbergasted at the story she told him. He could not believe it as he was friends with this man all this years, and he never had an inkling that those were his feelings. As a matter of fact, he attended the wedding and then returned to his life and endeavors for success. Playing the fool sometimes is part of learning the ropes of life, so it is important for your growth to admit imperfection is built into the system.

I had them explain all this as I had to make sure that what I was getting into was a righteous situation. As I got all the details from both husband and wife, I felt more comfortable in what I was about to embark on. By the time I got on the case, it had already been a year since the issue began. The man was apparently obsessed with the occult and with unlimited funds was bearing down on this family with all cannons.

He did spells to get her to fall in love with him. He did spells to break them up, and he did spells to make him loose his business. He felt as if he were living with them. They were at a point where it could fall apart for them; the stress they were under was not an easy thing to bear. I feel when the husband called me that they were close to a breaking point, so right away, I started to clean them, the home, and his business. Then I began doing some protection spells on the home and on the business. I made some custom talisman they could carry, so if more was done, it would at least soften the blow.

Pretty much I gave them a crash course on magic, explaining some spells and also included cleansings for them to do as needed. With an assault like this, the more you do, the better it is for protection. I knew that as long as this person was fixated and had the backing of whoever was doing all this negative magic for him, he would not give up. I'd been so busy cleaning them up that I had not really had a chance to focus on the guy or who he hired to work all this dark stuff against the family. By the time I learned of the mess, a year had gone by and there had been plenty of other problems, like brothers and sisters distancing themselves from the couple.

I still did not have all the spirits I have today on my side, but it was an experience that if it had happened today would still be a large undertaking. Back to the situation, after I did what I needed to do for them to stabilize, I knew it would take a while for the person doing all this to realize that his spells had been broken and the people being assaulted were on their way to recovery. I was counting on this, the longer I would have uninterrupted to clean them up, the easier my position will be in keeping them safe.

I know things are getting stable since the family members that had distanced themselves from the family started to call and some even set up lunch dates with the couple. I spoke with the client who was ecstatic of the results I was able to get after only working on the big mess for a month. He asked me what next; I told him point-blank, this is just the quiet before the storm. I explained that so far their friend thought it was freewheeling by him; I told him that soon when it was discovered that the magic had been undone, I was sure who he hired was going to recommend to him to escalate the level of assault.

My client now was a believer. He told me okay, whatever you need to do, please do it; he told me this as he looked into my eyes, "I don't care what happens anymore. All the gloves off, this guy is after the destruction of my family and I won't have it." I smiled and agreed. I told him this type of problem can get expensive as the magic becomes darker. He smiled and said, "I've lost close to a quarter of a million dollars because of this, so I doubt it's going to be any more expensive than that. I told him no not at all, but it will be expensive. He said no problem, and he gave me a retainer amount to start the work.

Up to this point, most of the stuff I had done was simple cleansings, even a couple of haunted houses but it was stagnant. What I mean by this was there was no one creating new magic against a client. It was just the situation and done. If it was like that, then after all I had done for this family it was over and off to a happy ending. Unfortunately I would soon find that the trouble was just beginning for them and for me. Yeah, the person getting paid to do the damage took it personal. My interfering was not part of his plan. Apparently he had made guarantees as to how long it would take to accomplish what he was paid to do.

I started to do some magic to neutralize the fixation the man had on this family and along the way figure out what to do if anything about the black magic practitioner. I did a few binding spells on the man, and it seemed to start to work. He would from what they told me try and reach out to her on a regular basis. Since I started to work my stuff, they had not heard from him. I assumed it was working. I believe wisdom begins by stating God keep me humble before my peers, keep me away from perceived wisdom or philosophy or the greatness that does not keep me grounded to this world and allows my success to ground me in the thought that we are but one world together. I do this simple prayer because I never want to let my successes get the better of me. Remember stay humble. It will keep you grounded in reality and not let you be thrown into a world of self-grandiose belief.

It was a couple of weeks after I started to work against the dark magic that I realized they knew of me. I almost had three accidents within a two-day period. I decided to clean my own energies and look into this guy in detail. Sure enough, no more accidents or negative energies. I called my clients and told them we needed to do a follow-up cleansing. I did not mention what I had felt because I did not want to worry them; after all they had me to protect them. I asked them how they liked my recipes; they loved them and all the energy work I included. He even recommended me to some people, this is my source for clients, and from every client I get I always get a few new ones.

Back to the situation: I'd been having some nightmares; I'm not a serious dreamer, so for me, these dark dreams are just messages of negative energy flowing in my direction. I got some feedback from one of my spirits; he said that the person who was working for the guy definitely had plenty of experience. I was given some insight as to who the person was and the type of magic he could wield.

I'm sure since he realized that the couple sought help and he probably cleaned his client of the spells, I sent his way. I was correct. A few days after, he called the lady on her new cell phone. Yeah, they changed their cell numbers to avoid the calls from this guy. They even called the police on him but could not prove any malice or intent. They gave him a hard time, but the calls continued. I told them no matter what sort of difficulties we encounter or how painful the experience is, if we lose our hope that would be the real disaster.

As it escalated my clients found blood at the perimeter of their property. I had instructed them that if they found something strange in or around their house, they should not touch but just call me so I could see what it was. After arriving, I told them to each pee in a cup and go around and sprinkle a little pee onto the areas with the blood. I explained to them that one of the best spell or energy breakers is simple pee, so if you happen to run into some uninvited magic, sprinkle some pee around the area.

After some inquires, I finally discovered who the dark-side practitioner was. I spoke with a mutual acquaintance we had; I sent a message with him to meet with me so that we could maybe come to an accord. We met at a coffee shop, and from the moment I walked in, I felt all the vibes were wrong. Our mutual friend was already with him waiting for me; he introduced us and asked me to sit down. We will call the other guy Harold since I don't want to start another fight if he reads this book.

Harold started by telling me that he has a job to do, and I was interfering with his job. I told him that my job was to clean any energy that did not belong. I told him unfortunately that covered all the negative things he had been throwing at my clients for over a year. He told me if we could come to some accord that money was no object and his client would not have a problem to pay me whatever I wanted just to step aside. I told him I was well paid for my work by my client and would not fold for money. He asked me how much. I was confused and asked what he means; he told me how much the clients had paid me. I told him they retained me with $5,000. He smiled and just told me his client was prepared right then and there to pay me four times that amount and all I had to do was step aside. For a split second I entertained the thought, avoid what could be a long dragged out battle, and I would not have to harm anyone just stop protecting them. This thought was but a few seconds, and quickly I told him I was sorry but that was unacceptable to me.

Harold stood and told me then I guess we will see who wins, I told him it does not have to be this way. He knew that what he was doing was wrong on many levels. I don't think he cares; the pay was good and that was all he cared about. I saw it in his eyes. All he cared about was being paid. For money, some people have a flexible moral code. Unfortunately these types of people do not scare easy, and once they are paid, they do not like to lose.

My reality is the light and not the darkness, and sometimes you just have to fight for what you believe in and I did sign up for all of it. That sometimes means you have to get dirty along the way, so be it. I just made sure I was on the side of the light. I have been in situations where the client just to get me to work for them will only tell me half-truths. No matter how difficult a situation, right does equal to might, so if you are outmatched but in the right, the scale might still tip in your favor.

Many things I could do from home but others I had to go and clear the air as this guy was relentless. I decided to escalate and sent as many things as was pitched to my clients back to its originators with a little extra something of my own. It's easier to send back to where the spell originated since it is easy enough to trace back. I even did some spells to separate both men from their own protections. To really hit someone with wining shots, we must study the person and ask before you send the spell if they are with good energy that particular day.

I don't care what you do if you do it or send the spell on a day where the universe is watching over the person it will have no or very little effect. So you need to see if it's a bad energy day for the subject, and when you find the opening, then you shoot. I was doing stuff weekly as they were as well; I knew when I had a homerun because my clients would tell me the guy had not called that week or even two. This was a relentless bastard; I was in awe how arrogant he was. From my client's experience with him, that was how he had been throughout his life. Remember they knew him since they were young.

He took a drastic turn to some very strange magic, almost like he shifted the type of magic being used, and within a couple of days, both the husband and wife crashed their cars individually, and she had been getting some weird headaches over the last few weeks. I decided to go see them and clean them again. Remember cleansings work great to take out negative energy or even spiritual assaults, but like any infection, if your antibiotics cleared a throat infection and you walk into another biological minefield like a hospital, then you can pick up another infection and need another cycle of antibiotics.

It was a back and forth. At the time I was dating, and I decided to stop as when this type of magic is in constant flux, it can hit a loved one, so better safe than sorry. I still went out and had fun but nothing steady. It was, I must admit, beginning to upset me. I decided to call up on my witchdoctor, the guy who initially came to me when I was getting started. I try to only use him to clean black magic, but he had to do it all as his job was to defend the tribe in Africa.

He showed me some dark stuff; I started by getting the ingredients he suggested, then cleaning myself as much as possible. Most people think getting cleaned once you do something negative or to get rid of it. I learned that like any disease, if you have a strong base, it's harder to attach to that person. So it is with energy. If you are clean and your aura is in good condition, many things won't be able to attach. Remember most energies need something to anchor to, so if it's smooth sailing, then perhaps it's more difficult for any unwanted energy to attach.

So after taking every precaution, I looked for my opening. Every morning I would ask by name if either of the two subjects was wielding bad universal energy that day. Like everything, there are good days and bad days: days the star alignments are showering us with good fortune and days the stars are not favorable to us. So I was looking for unfavorable days. I don't care if you throw the kitchen sink at someone if it's on one of those cycles that you are on a roll it will just bounce off with very negligible effect on the person. That is a secret most energy practitioners won't tell you. We also have to rely on a larger power, the universe, so in its infinite wisdom it gave us good and bad days.

I constantly counsel business people. They call for the best days to have important meetings or do important deals. I do not guarantee that you will win or make the sale or convince someone else, but it does increase your chances from a one to three on a bad day to an eight to ten on a good day. I use the one to ten rule; as there are just average days and if you must use a day, make it a day that is influenced in your favor by the universe.

If the day cannot be changed, then we can always try some magic to soften any negative effects or even better an already positive day. I have a philosophy; if it's not broke, don't fix it. What I mean is that I have clients that want more and more. I simply tell them if it's a good day already leave it alone. We might be able to tweak it. Unfortunately it might not come out as expected. I hope you understand we only go to magic if we must and only to fix a problem not to create one.

Okay, don't want to keep on rambling, back to the story. I finally got a bad day. I was not looking for an average day. I was looking for a day I could knock the heads off these people with no scruples. At this point, I was mad. That is a very hard thing to do, get me to that point, but I was there. I wanted to help these poor people but also stop the nonsense. I'm sure you can read between the lines. I wanted blood. I'm now sorry to say, but I was at my limit with these people.

I fired first at the money man, and a few days later at the other person, the one actually doing the harm; if done right there is no defense from an assault such as I was doing. To this date, I've never invoked such powers again, even less to do harm to another. I wanted to stop the entire movement with one swift blow. As time would tell and not too far from those dates, I found out that the money man got sick, and I believe my clients heard he was diagnosed with cancer of the pancreas. Who knows what was the outcome of the other person? Suffice it to say that within a couple of months, things began to get back to normal for my clients and their lives got back to a point where their day to day lives was once again on track. I heard from them once a few months later, the man asked if he owed me any more than what I had received from him. I told him to be honest there was still money leftover. He told me not to give it another thought. It was mine and well deserved. Today I might have done it differently. Well, today I have many more options available as I now work with six different spirits each with their own gifts and an abundance of knowledge which means more wisdom.

I've never heard from those clients again. Over the years the folks who gave them my information and told them to contact me initially have kept in touch and they tell me the family is together and doing well. I think like me the way we took care of the problem was acceptable but left a sour taste in all of our mouths. As it should be, no one should have to resort to these extreme measures on the other side of the coin; we all have the right to defend ourselves from brutal attacks like the one they endured for almost two years. In our last conversation, my client said, if it were not for me, he did not know what would have happened to their family.

Family Matters

Let's bring it down a notch from that last story. I happened to be here in the book when I did the reading over the phone I am going to talk about. Life has a way of giving people just what they need at the precise time and date they need it. I got a call from a young woman who when we started the reading was curious but was not sold on the idea. She had been told by another client months before about me and had just gotten the courage to call me but with apprehension. I started the reading about someone around her who might be cooking for a business or starting a restaurant, whatever this was I told her it might be happening soon.

She confirmed that her mother-in-law wanted her husband to start running one of those little trucks that feed the people from a location or drive by businesses during lunch times. I told her that she had a spirit of a teacher. She said, "I am a teacher." At this point I had her undivided attention. As the reading progressed, I gave a name of someone thinking of her. She said the only one with that name was the principal of her school; however, she explained that until school started again she had no dealings with him. If I had not mentioned it, at the time of the reading it was midsummer and all the kids were out of school and so were the teachers. I jumped to her husband and told her he needed to go to the dentist. She laughed and agreed.

I continued and told her I believed she might be changing her job to some sort of management position. She did not think so since she was not looking for any change. She liked the classroom. I told her with insistence that to me she would be offered some kind of raise but not in the classroom. She just could not see that happening. There were many other things discussed, intimate things I feel would not be prudent to discuss here. Suffice it to say some time later that day, she called me back and apologized for the call but told me she had to confirm some things. She told me in a much excited manner, she reminded me of the name I had given her and she told me the principal called her and offered her a management position as I had told her. She was so in awe that it could be this accurate and that it happened this soon that she had to call me. I'm always happy when clients tell me that something I told them happens, so please do.

Hard Messages

I remember one instance when I used to take clients to this spot off the beaten path; it is a place where the river meets the ocean. Although the place had great energy, it did have its drawbacks. On several occasions, I or my client saw alligators or, on the other side, sharks. After several sightings, I decided prudence was the best way and started taking them to a different location. After all it would not look good if one of my clients got eaten while on my watch. Can you imagine it in the local paper, psychic gets client killed by alligator or shark? I still consider it a powerful place and on very specific circumstances I still do take a client or two there.

I would like to talk about information I gather while working with clients. This one incident was a bit mind-blowing for me. The person who called was as are most of my clients referred by other clients. The reading started about the creative energies in her hands. She confirmed with her painting abilities. Next a spirit manifested with metal in his hands. I was not clear as to why he manifested in this manner, and the person said another of her creative vehicles was making designs out of metal.

As we continued I mentioned the name of her partner and his son. Continuing with the reading I spoke to her about the partner of her lover and also the person who betrayed him. We discussed another partner, and then we arrived at several health issues including some family health issues. Once done with the mundane we went to the topic of her call, the death of her previous lover. She was still overcome with grief of his untimely death. I told her to tell me a little about the person. She explained the death was violent, and she told me that they had separated months before the death and it had been a while since the death and she was already with another man. She confided how she still thinks of him; I switched gears and told her about the man she was with and how he felt trapped in his personal life. I asked her if she was with him why he did feel trapped or boxed in. She confirmed by stating that he was in a bad marriage, and although he was still married, he spends more time with her than with his wife.

At this point I tried a different approach since no one can summon the dead. They have free will, and they come only if they want. I asked where he was at that moment to at least answer some of my client's questions with reference to him. My spirits told me he was with her. Let's call her Maria, just to have a name and not divulge intimate information. She recognized the name as his mother, still alive and in another state. She did not really know what the dead son was into, my client explained. He was into dirty businesses, and it was that business that got him killed and she continued by stating that is also why I distanced myself from him.

He showed me the name of the person who killed him and the person who put him up to the killing. In all these years this was the first time that I got such a direct answer without even asking the question. What is even scarier is the lady knew the two names as coworkers of her dead ex fiancé. I explained to her that this soul was not at rest, and she and her mother had to let him go. The longer a spirit attempts to stay in this planet after they leave the body, the worse it becomes and with time they can become permanently stuck here on earth.

I did some prayers and spoke to him, and he was not listening. He felt like he was where he belonged. I told her that she and her mother and any other relatives had to let him go. She tells me that she feels him, and sometimes she feels she gets answers from him. I explained that with time and without malice, he will start to harm those he is around. I explained that his energy is dirty; all spirits that are earthbound generate dirty energy. I spoke to him and asked him to reach for the astral plane and he will remember the reason he took on this life and why it ended so badly for him.

As I tried my therapy, I told him to go to God's right side, to his good graces, and he would be healed from all this dirty energy he had gathered since staying behind to accomplish nothing. As a free spirit, he has but one mission, to regain memories of past lives and replenish his spirit with those souls that are urging him to move on. He was just not in the mood to listen. He was as if he still had a physical body and did not want to hear of heaven. He told me he belonged to a drug cartel and that it was one of his rivals who got rid of him. Lucky for me that all this stuff just evaporates in my brain soon after I get it. Can you imagine if I kept all this useless information? This is what happens to some mediums a brain overload; all these emotions can literally drive a person crazy.

Out there in the west coast of the United States, this whole thing played out with all these people and their drug business. Thank goodness I'm all the way east in Florida. I know bad exists everywhere, but I don't have to mingle with it unless my clients are in danger; then I will do what it takes to help them spiritually. We spoke some more about the wife of her boyfriend and the previous one. Oh yeah, I forgot an important part of the puzzle—the guy who got killed had a girlfriend in another state. He told her the nickname of the girlfriend, which was only something he knew. She told me that he could be mean-spirited. She continued to explain that his reason to tell her such hurtful information was for her to know without a doubt it was he at the other end of the conversation. He was very chatty. Remember at the beginning there was nothing. Fortunately or unfortunately he was very earthbound and made his rounds to all the folks that mattered and my client was one of these people.

I recently read a woman whose daughter is my client; when we started the reading it flowed from the beginning. I asked her what she really wanted to concentrate on; she said on her guy, it was not her husband but a lover. She wanted to know why things cooled off; she did not feel she had done anything wrong. I explained to her that it was stress and financial problems; she confirmed that he was having money problems. I continued the reading with her sister and brother who she wanted to know how they were. I told her what she needed and then asked her about her mother; what was going on that was not resolved. She told me that she and her mother were not speaking because of her sister-in-law. I gave her the wife's name and that is I believe when she really began to believe, I told her that the sister-in-law was a bad person, confirming what she had believed.

I told her of a strong thought related to the boyfriend and the name was of his ex-wife, I also told her of a strong thought from a man, I described his name where he had lived and what he did. I confirmed to her what I got about him in detail; I told her to call the boyfriend and explain she got a reading and all the information about him including this one she knew nothing about. I told her it would give her some topic of conversation that might stimulate their getting back together. I hope to hear from her and the confirmation on the guy I gave her such a detail account of.

Remote Viewing

I remember one occasion I was talking with a girlfriend I had at the time. She was calling me after she had left the doctor's office. She called and told me she was on her way to my house and had stopped to pick up some snacks. After a few minutes, she told me she had to hang up so she could not hold on to what she had in her hands and pay. I, at the moment, did my first remote view. I could see she did not have anything in her other hand, and no one had asked her to pay, at least not at that moment. A moment of enlightenment when one realizes I'm happy without what you thought was needed to achieve it. Happiness is not perfection but looking past those imperfections. Some say it isn't what you have or who you are or where you are or what you are doing that makes you happy or unhappy. It is what's on your mind, so I pose this same question to you: what's on your mind? I challenge you to make it a happy thought!

So I called her right back and told her what I had just seen. She asked how I could possibly know that, I told her I saw it. She thought I was kidding and asked me to tell her. I told her with clarity that she was facing the counter and to her left was a cup with coffee next to her left hand and she was straitening her hair after a gust of wind had blown it in her face. I continued to tell her if she turned around she could see to her then right side two kids going around a pole and one was wearing cowboy boots that looked like cow boots.

She said, no way. I continued to tell her to turn to her left and she would see a fat man sitting on the table there with the bottom of his shirt unbuttoned. I told her if she turned around, there would now be a bill being held down with what seemed to be a glass jar filled with sugar or some white substance. She was astonished and confirmed everything I had told her was fact. To this date I remember as it was so unexpected and clear to me. It was as if I was standing right behind her and could see everything; since I have been able to do it several times but it is still beyond my control to do it at will. I imagine if it were a regular part of what I did I would become proficient at it as I have become at many other abilities.

Voodoo

I'm currently involved in a case where this old client of mine had hired this famous voodoo priestess to give her some classes and develop her abilities. She told me what had sold her on the woman was that she had been on national television several times and sounded like she knew her stuff. She studied with her over the computer and through the mail as the woman lived in another state. During this time she had not called me except to say hello and just to see how I was doing. I believe we all have a destiny and how we get to it is up to us; I never asked her anything about the woman or did I care to give her advice. This simple background just to set the stage for what is now going on. About a month ago my client called back for a reading. During the reading I told her she needed to come and get cleanse as the stuff she was dealing with was not easy and required more than a simple bath.

The lady agreed and made the appointment. Upon her arrival, she began to ask for forgiveness; I'm very easy that way and told her it was just a lesson she had to learn. She gave me in great details from the beginning, but I'll start at the important stuff. She was told that forgiveness could be given to her by the priestess in the form of a donation of $5,000 or else the Voodoo woman would have to help her find forgiveness by calling the husband and telling him how she was spending their money and many other secrets she had discovered as their friendship grew. My client is a smart businesswoman, so she knew she was being blackmailed but she still feared the woman so she came back to me and caught me up on all the stuff that was happening. I cleaned her and told her not to pay and to stop communicating with this person. She wanted it all to go away and was willing to pay to make it go away. I looked at the supposed voodoo priestess and told my client that yes, at one time, she might have had some powers; but today she was weak as many spirits turned her back on her and her materialistic endeavors.

I asked for the letters and pictures and full name and a signature of the woman; this woman was fairly confident that my client was scared and would do nothing other than what she was told to do. I directed her to buy time for me to do my stuff. I told her to answer the woman's calls and stretch it out as long as she could. This person was arrogant and had already broken a deal the husband was negotiating. The deal on the table was an $800,000 dollar loan that just needed a signature to be approved. My client knows enough to realize she was being attached; the woman sent her a message and told her that from now on things would get difficult unless she asked for forgiveness. She was pushing that forgiveness stuff down her throat with no wiggle room.

I started doing my routine of cleansings and baths; after a few days, she felt powerful again, the fear had subsided. I gave her some instruction on cleaning her home and herself over the next thirty days. She was diligent and she noticed the difference. I started to do my own stuff against the woman with no scruples. It's incredible how someone with these powers can use them or misused them so flagrantly. So be it, I will have to intervene as what this woman is doing gives all the people that do what I do a bad name. As of the writing of this book, we are in the process of straightening out the mess. Hopefully by the time the next book comes out, this story can be told to its final outcome.

The Realtor

I have been a realtor for eleven years, and I can say that during all this I have met all kind of customers, but without a doubt Hector was the most unusual of them. Four years ago, Hector started looking for a house to buy and contacted me over an ad I had placed in a magazine.

The first time we met to see some properties it was kind of surreal for me. I did not know anything about him and started asking him questions regarding his family in order to have an idea how big of a house he needed. He told me that he had a daughter, but that he was engaged to marry a lady and she had three kids. Then, he turned to me and asked, "How about you?" I told him that I had a boy and a girl. After that, he started describing my daughter just as if she was right in front of him. My jaw dropped to the floor. "How do you know all that?" I asked him with a shocked look on my face to which he answered, "That's my profession, I'm a psychic," and he proceeded to ask me: "Who's a person with the name starting with an F?" I thought and thought and could not remember anyone. We continued our journey looking at houses and chatting. I am a very spiritual person, and I started telling him some of my experiences, especially with a spirit named Frederick, who had been a doctor and was always on my side helping me whenever I needed him. Hector looked at me and said, "That's the F person I sensed was close to you!"

Our next encounter was on the next weekend and this changed my work a lot. We went to see a big house and the owner was there showing it and we got the sensation that he was very eager to get rid of the property. When I entered the house, I started having a very weird feeling. It was like something was pushing me out of the house; it was like a voice was saying in my head, "Leave now, leave now." We did tour of the house, and when we got to the back of it, we found a little room. The owner explained that he had built that addition for his in-laws. The feeling of uneasiness in that place was almost unbearable. Finally we left the house, and I told Hector about my experience inside the house and, most of it, in the back room. So calmly Hector explained to me that, when moving from a house, people leave some of their energy behind. So when they are bad people, they leave behind bad energy. That's why sometimes the house is beautiful, but we do not feel comfortable inside it. He pointed out to me that, that house in particular was used to perform black magic rituals, so that's why it had a very dense and bad energy. The addition was used to sacrifice animals. It would be very difficult to sell that place.

From that day on, with Hector's help, I learned to sense the energy of the houses and every time I enter them with my customers, I always tell them, "This is a happy house or this is not a happy house." They get used to asking me how I feel about the house.

Since that first day, I met Hector on several occasions, we became friends, and he has been helping me a lot in my personal as well as in my professional life.

I've done many cleansings for this family. One occasion I brought my stuff, but after a few minutes, I asked one to come over and placed my hand on her stomach. I immediately told her not for you as you are pregnant. They were in awe as no one had told me and she was so new that nothing showed. It's often that when I do cleansings only the lightest portions are done for the pregnant. Just as certain medicines are good but not for pregnancies, so it is with clearings of energy. You want to do the best and sometimes that means keep it simple for women while pregnant.

I would add many things to this client's statement since I've continued to work with her over the years, she worked for a company, and I told her she would do great on her own although it was not a good time for this country and definitely not in her industry. I continued to urge her until she took that chance; I try not to tell people what to do, but when asked, I will let them know when the window of opportunity is open. She took the chance and started her own business; well, let's just say that she is doing better than ever as her own boss.

I'm happy for her and her family. Over the years I've done some cleansings for properties she wanted sold and they did. I recently visited her and her family and within a week of my cleansing. She told me that ten new people had made offers on some of the properties. Remember the heavier the energies the quicker the results; if you have a headache and take an aspirin, you feel the difference. If you don't have a problem and take an aspirin what can you possibly feel, you get the idea. This is a person that deals with strange people every day, not strange in a bad way, just different with different issues, and as a realtor, she has to create a bond to better understand their needs. Automatically you will tend to pick up on some of their energies, so it's almost a certainty that she will need some sort of cleansing regularly to keep her energies at their best.

Most people that I work with will feel a difference right away. Imagine if you are not 100 percent and I work on your energies and you go from 40 percent to 80 percent. Oh yeah, you will definitely feel better but more than that; usually things that had become difficult will start to clear up and things just flow better in your life. So it is with her. Every time she gets a cleansing of energies within a short period of time, she sees a positive change. So the moral to this story is simple. If you clean your body to smell and feel clean, energy is no different. The more you clean naturally, you will fall on the positive side of your life. So how do you measure life, not by its duration. It's how much you've given to others, your donation in time and emotion. The return on the investment will be written in the book of your life!

Back to the story, another good one with her and the family. Her son was already in his early thirties and was single. He wanted to find a girl to have a family. I suggested he go and do a specific type of cleansing. On this last visit I was surprised to know after his cleansing he met a good woman and they just got married. During this cleansing I had an opportunity to meet his new wife and cleansed her as part of my visit. Often we want our lives to move in a more favorable direction, it's kind of like a TV set with the rabbit ears, and you can move the antenna a little to the left or the right and you get a clear channel. Life is the same, if things are not quite right; we look for ways to get it going in what we call the right direction. To think like a winner we must not fear failure but embrace it as part of the path to success.

Guess what, energy has a lot to do with this, so call me or find a person that works with energy and can manipulate it. Remember, you don't want to change your life you want to put it back on track, so as I've said, we live life within ninety degrees. If you are all the way on the left of that ninety-degree mark, do some energy work, some cleansings and move toward the right side of that ninety-degree mark. I guarantee as you move your energies your life will move in a more positive direction, no matter what, it does not change your life it just makes it the best it can be. To some it might feel like a miracle because the changes can be so impressive but be sure it's still within the ninety degrees of your life.

So it is with life. Little movements can often cause major changes, so what do you have to loose, a good reading and subsequent advice. After all who better to ask than the person that needs that change. I do some difficult cleansings when it's needed or when the person wants to make sure it's done right. I believe more often than not when you do things with faith, they manifest in the solutions you were asking for.

I'm sure she will continue to call and I will continue to give her advice, often I can recommend what to do, remember I do all my readings over the phone. I do this in fifteen countries and about twenty-five states currently. I like consulting over the phone, there are no visual distractions, only what the spirit needs to express to the client comes across.

The Grandmother

I had a reading today that was interesting, I do many readings and often a spirit will pass through giving messages. Well, today was one of days, a very funny spirit, not ha-ha funny, but a character; she gave her name and the client thought it was her grandmother. She continued to speak and gave advice for relatives. She spoke about four different relatives and she spoke in a way that without a doubt my client knew it was her grandmother. A little pushy for my taste but entertaining, never the less; she reminded my client of her sweet tooth. The client laughed since she knew much her grandmother liked sweets; her demeanor was funny; she asked about her grandfather and the grandmother said he hit the road running and never looked back.

She was very opinionated, she told me a little about her grandfather and she could understand as when he lived he told her that there was nothing after life and when you die it's just dust that remains. The client explained that her grandparents were married for seventy-five years and he died about six months after her grandmother did. Her grandmother told me that was his problem since she did not invite him to that party, I guess she meant death. She was a tough old bird; I know, she even told the granddaughter to move it along because she was talking too much.

Again the granddaughter confirmed it was her grandmother since on more than one occasion the grandmother had told her to shut up. Wow, some spirits are more spirited than others, so the reading continued. One of my spirits told her that she had been a good-looking chick when she was younger. She asked me how I knew this. I explained that she had much better relationships with men than with women and how with experience I had discovered that the more beautiful the woman the more distance women created because of competition. She agreed. I continued and told her many things. She, I think, was very surprised at how clear the grandmother had come through and how I was able to hear her.

I work through examples, so I asked about several people in her life by name. I gave her some examples on how I got the names. On one I told her if she remembered Popeye the sailor man, cartoons. She said yes. I further asked her if she remembers the skinny girlfriend, she said Olive Oyl. I said correct, so who is the lady with the olive name? She was amazed as this was one of her coworkers, and this is not a common name. I gave her several other examples of people thinking about her and their names. In other examples, I told her about a relative with a specific initial in the first name and the sex. Minimizing the possibilities of which it could be, I would even tell her if it was a spirit or a living relative.

The Translator

I have clients in seven countries as of this reading, and this story is about a client in Greece. She was using a translator since I only speak English and Spanish. I prefer the client to let me give my input first as within this time most of what the client wants to know will come out. After, I will always ask what else they wanted me to look at. I'm certain as has been the norm most of what they had to ask would have been visited before; however, I will look at everything they need.

Okay, back to the story. These readings with a translator are fun; the translation is never 100 percent as I say things in a certain way, and only the client will understand the meaning. With this reading, I started to speak about her mother. There were many health issues, and she needed to get on the ball or they would get worse if not tended properly. She acknowledged all of the statements I gave her with regards to her mother. Unfortunately, the root cause of most of her mother's health issues was her emotions. Again, my client agreed and expanded that there had been some issues in the relationship with her father and her mother.

I again stated that this and more were the root causes of her mother's health issues. I itemized the many issues and explained how I would approach fixing some of them. As she was a very TLC type of woman, the mother that is, she felt lack of attention and needed to be better tended to. I explained that I was not speaking of sex but of tender loving care. In other words I told my client that her mother was high maintenance. She laughed and agreed that her mother could be a handful and was not easy if she was not catered to. We briefly spoke about her father and some of his shortcomings and explained how he needed to be more attentive to her mother for her to feel more fulfilled.

We addressed some of her issues including some shortness of breath that was affecting her and explained that in a previous life she had been a soldier and was killed in battle with a shot to the chest. Sometimes that type of death will come in, and she would feel that way. I explained how her life was supposed to be a life of service. She agreed. She is a social worker in this life time. I told her in her next life she would most likely be a teacher or she would work more directly with children. I did discuss with her where she lived (what country) when she was a soldier. She loved the past and future life stuff and how certain issues like the shortness of breath was due to her previous life and why.

The translator was also a client, so she was listening to the reading and was a bit put off by how her friend got so much karma information in her reading. She has been my client for so many years, and I have never spoken to her about her past or future lives. I explained that each person gets what is important to them, and although she was bothered by it, she had never asked or thought of asking about these things. I told her that next time she called for a reading to remind me of this, and I will do my best to look into her previous lives and if there was anything I could see in her next life. She seemed to like that idea, so I'm sure I'll get a call from her soon. I finished my reading with my usual remedies to help her with her everyday life and some for her mother, and oh yeah, her brother also was in need of some help, so I told her some stuff about her brother and some of the things he need to do in order to put his life back on track. I don't do past life readings as such. I touch on all aspects of a person, past, present, and future. Over the years I've developed a good well-rounded reading. You can call and tell me where you want me to concentrate and that will be the area where I will spend the greater part of the reading.

Gym

I want to tell you about a couple of gym experiences. I go regularly to do my elliptical and steam room workout, and three times a week I go to the weight room. On one of those days I saw my friend working out with his partner. I had approached my friend and told him of a message that was to be delivered to his workout partner. I ran into him some time later, and he refreshed my memories of that day I had approached him and told him he should tell his fried to see a cardiologist as I felt one or both of his main arteries looked clogged to me.

Time passed, and about six months later, my friend called his friend, offering him a job where he worked. His friend told him that it was not a good time. He had been feeling a bit dizzy, and when he finally visited his doctor, he was told that his carotid arteries were both clogged and he needed surgery immediately. The man had remembered my message and confirmed that if he had not been told the message before, he would have chucked it to indigestion and maybe would have dropped dead if he did not tend to it as quickly as he had. My friend could not wait to let me know what a difference I had made in that life. Especially since he had told me so many months ago his friend's reaction to my initial message; he told me that although he did not practice, he did believe in spirituality and I had given him insight that had panned out for him.

The Confirmations

At the beginning of this year, I happened to literary bump into an old client. She was at the gym where I go to regularly. I had not seen or heard from her in over three years. She got married and had a baby girl. Anyway, she bumped into me as I was walking down the aisle and she was looking into the aerobics room. When she bumped me, she said I'm sorry and then recognized me and told me all about what was happening in her life. All was great, and many things I had told her in the past were confirmed. She was glowing with happiness.

I was looking at her and realized there was an upcoming event with health with regard to her female organs. So I was unsure if I should to tell her. She seemed so happy and full of herself. The spirit told me that it did not matter, and she would understand with time why I told her the things I would tell her. I agreed and told her how I saw her need to go and see the gynecologist; she told me she had gone the year before and she was fine. I explained that the spirit told me she needed to get a detailed checkup, something not done normally but only if there is a history of problems in the family.

She agreed, and I did not see her for a while. A few months later, she called for a reading. She reminded me of all this stuff and told me after she had a number of checkups. The doctor told her he discovered a small cluster of cells that came back positive for cancer. The doctor said if she had not asked for all these detailed tests, it could have been easily two more years before symptoms would have manifested.

Testimonial

Hi Hector,

Thanks:-)

Hector is truly gifted. I first heard about him from a friend who had seen him on several occasions. I knew my friend was trustworthy, so I decided to call him. He immediately told me things about myself, my children, etc., which were true. He presents the information in a nonthreatening way, and he makes you feel comfortable as though you are his friend. He also gives you specific instructions on what you should do to clear your energy and restore balance. Everyone needs that, right! (EW)

For all you naysayers out there, I wish you could all call me so that I can let you know about my experience with Hector. A friend who had their house cleansed (and totally helped them) referred me to

Hector, and it was one of the best referrals of my life. Throughout the past couple of years, my readings have been so spot on and specific that only someone with a gift like Hector has could know of the personal happenings that occurred or have occurred. My pregnancy, situations with my husband, and other family members have all been topics; and he has just completely enlightened me. There have been way too many things that nobody would know that he knew and it is simply incredible. I highly, highly, highly recommend that you get a reading, it will change your life!" Oh yeah, that other insight you gave me with relation to my father to have him sleep on the right side or on his back only turned out to be great advice. He had a heart problem and the doctor's diagnostics of him showed that after he had been sleeping on his right side and sometimes on his back actually improved his condition.

Michelle

Message

I had a nice reading today with a new client. I must tell this little information about readings. I cannot summon spirits, no one can. They are either there or not. I can, however, talk to the client about the deceased family member. Often this can get a spirit that is not present to appear; anyway this particular reading today, as I started, one of the first things I told her was the presence of her deceased father. He took over the reading, giving her advice about all aspects of her life. How did she know it was him, he started by giving me his name, and how he died. He also spoke of her alcoholic former husband and how he never liked him.

He continued to give her proof. He told me about her son and baseball. He reminded her how he used to go and how he was there during the game the day she day dreamed about telling him how it would be nice if her father had been there for the game. In other words he was confirming he was definitely there with them for the kid's baseball games. He continued to give her all kinds of advice to include the name of her former boss who was calling her and asking her to return to work for her. Her father explained how it would be better if she continued with her present employment and why. She agreed to everything her father was telling me; it was an incredible experience for her. This happens every once in a while. I cannot, however, make this connection unless the spirit is willing and if he is even available to this mortal world.

As usual after I give the information that comes to me, I asked her what she wanted me to look at. She cried and told me the gift I had given her was incredible and how she felt at peace. She had not felt that way in a long time, but if I could look into a couple of people she would appreciate it. I agreed and we started to talk of about her former husband and how he had alcohol abuse problems. I must remind you that all through this reading the spirit of her father continued to give his advice as a matter of fact he was the one who brought up the alcohol abuse. She then continued to ask about several other people including her kids. I described what I saw and even the colors that would vibrate best, and she agreed they liked those colors. I explained how one of her kids was very smart but lazy so she had to stay on top of him. We continued to her sister and a gentleman. Again her father put in his thoughts and she again agreed. She was so impressed how much her father was around. It was a great comfort to her.

The Wicca

Over the years I've had opportunities to meet witches. These are interesting practitioners of nature. Some were solitary but most have been part of a coven. As I've stated before there is always strength in numbers. This is no different and my personal opinion a group is always more powerful than an individual, so it is with a coven. Like me, each according to their spiritual strength can summon and combined with the others pack a wallop so to speak. The solitary witches are much like I am. They believe that not all are here to do right and prefer to go at it alone than to risk being tainted by the negative ideas that others might bring to a group.

There are things that a group can do that an individual no matter how much power or energy amassed is limited by the power of one. So for example, a few years back while at my center, we decided to do a cleansing spell to clean the world. It's a cool thing to do. I wished we would have done it more often. Unfortunately we did it only once. It's like a bath. If a car is very dirty it might need to be cleaned several times to get it right and then a good waxing to keep it from getting dirty again. So it is with this type of cleaning. We all have to view the world as if from above looking down. One person does the cleaning and the others pour their goodwill, concentration, and guidance from the cleaner to help in the job. It was like a temporary super charge. I was feeling great, and I could see better and channel more energy.

Before I get ahead, as always, a good ten-minute meditation and then visualization to get into trance, allowing a clear view of the earth. Once the breathing and visualization was right, I began to channel for divine universal energy. For this energy to flow through us, allowing my body to channel this and direct it toward the earth. With enough time we can affect some measure of change on the whole planet. The more people the more change.

I believe we can pray and create prayer for just about anything, so it was in my first book that most of the prayers I've either modified or created from scratch. Prayer is nothing more than words with emotion behind it. We can read whatever we want or say whatever we want. Without intent to back up our words, they are nothing more than words. If, however, we wish to impact with our words we must have intent, emotion, belief in our resolve, then and only then we might reach our goals. No matter what the reason, no matter what it is, unfortunately so many of us pray for self-gratification and not for the common good.

Back to the story, I met a witch who was having some difficulties in her craft. She had been at this for many years. With limited success I gave her a reading and immediately found that there were several spirits with her that followed the Wicca ways. Interesting enough they felt she had what it took to achieve great things and were frustrated at the poor advancement, even after the many years. As I progressed in the reading,

I found she had done some wrong things in how she began her alter and how she was doing her rituals. I told her and gave her some examples of things she had done and failed; the two spirits that were guiding this reading had lots to say and had very productive advice.

She decided to take me up on the offer and cleanse her energies and her home. I explained that the spirits with her wanted her to start her altar from scratch and to start everything she had been doing again but without certain preconceptions she had picked up from one particular book she was reading. Apparently these spirits thought the book was not what she needed and guided her to an earlier book she had discarded and told her to read and work from that book again. Over the next few months she did as the spirits suggested and after the process of rebuilding from scratch was done she felt much more secure in her spells and rituals.

Soon she called me and told me how her life was back on track. As a matter of fact, she had been working with a coven and they welcomed her in. She told me she was really learning a lot and thanked me for the messages and the cleansings to get rid of negative energies she had acquired by accident. As of today I have not heard from her again, but I'm confident with the two spirits she has guiding her and the backing of the coven she is without a doubt reaching new heights in her evolution.

Gotcha

She was mad when I had told her that one of her friends was having an intimate relationship with her husband. She hung up the phone and that was the end of the reading. Several months passed and I got a call from her to schedule another reading. I remembered her since this was not the typical way my clients work with me, but I said let's not jump the gun and see what she wants. As she started to speak I could tell she was embarrassed to be speaking with me, so I let her sweat it for a minute and then opened up to her. I told her not to worry that whatever it was we would look into it together and together we would find a solution.

I could hear a change in her voice, and she seemed more relaxed. I gave her an appointment that very next day as I was as intrigued to find out what had manifested to cause her to call me. I had never physically met this woman or did I know what she looked like; pleasantly surprised she had a different tone, and as we began the reading, she expressed to me that what I had told her many months ago now seemed to be a possibility, if not a reality.

I asked her to tell me what took her in this new direction, a direction she was so opposed to a few months ago. She explained that over the last thirty days, she had seen a shift in many aspects of her husband's habits that included a lack of sexual appetite. She was very candid with me, and I listened. She wanted to know why and with whom he was with. After looking at her for a few minutes I told her again that her husband was not faithful and that he was with someone they both knew. I suggested it was probably a friend of hers and not his, but time would tell specifically.

She wanted more but that was all I was getting. The spirits gave me a spell, one I had done in the past with success so I told her what she needed to do. I told her to get a pen and paper. She needed to get a branch from a tree on her property, and then she needed to burn one end like charcoal. Then she had to wait until she realized who would be coming by. She had to write toward the entrance of the house the woman's full name, the one that would be coming over that is. Making sure this name would be along the path she would take to enter and thus stepping on her own name before she entered my client's home.

Within the first month, she had checked off about half of her friends or their friends with no positive results. She called for another reading, and I confirmed that she would find out who her husband was with. She agreed to continue to write the names as I had told her the name was not visible and all were oblivious to their stepping on anything. Soon after our last reading, she called distraught. It was her own sister, a person she was hesitant to write the name down for stepped into the home, and as I had described, soon after began to suffer with extreme leg pains. She asked the sister if she had it before. The sister confirmed that she had never had any leg pains. She wanted to know what to do; she was freaked out with the discovery but had no solid proof. I told her just to keep an eye on her sister, and she would lead her to where her husband was meeting her. She agreed and started keeping an eye on her sister. Within a week after working hours, her sister visited the office where my client's husband worked. She waited, entered, and discovered her husband and her sister making love. She called me for one more reading where all this information was given to me. Remember this worked for her, but I'm not sure if it will work the same way for all. I suppose if you have a need, you can give it a try; most spells that work well are living spells. This means for the case and not written on some paper and people just apply it to their situation.

The Free Loader

This client came for one of her regular cleansings; she's a businesswoman so most of her cleansings have to do with work. While I was working on her energy, I asked her if she had been extra hungry lately. She looked at me and said the last month she had been unable to control her hunger. I also asked her if she had been sleeping poorly. She said her sleeping habits had definitely changed over the last month. She was curious as to why I had asked this. I explained that there was a spirit attachment that died of over eating and exhaustion. She said, "I'm not going to die, right?" I explained that I would get rid of the spirit although he told me that she was also going through depression. She told me that he was correct.

I told her the spirit was of a gay man, he liked her because of her creative energies and he would leave when good and ready and not before. She said, "My god, are you kidding—he's going to stay" I laughed and stated, "No, this is what he said, but I had other plans for the extroverted dead guy. I had to negotiate with the spirit and it gave in, not before telling me she, my client, was also going through depression.

Tormented Soul

While on one of my trips, I was doing a cleansing to a family at a beautiful river with a cascade. While in the water, I cut my hand with a glass. My clients were horrified at the blood flow. I was okay and was confident that I would not die of this nor loose the hand. They took me to several hospitals before finding one that could take me in. The doctor on duty looked overworked and my client still stressing asked what the distance to the big hospital was. She called a doctor friend of hers who asked who was the attending on duty. She asked the doctor for her name and her friend seemed to know who she was and told her it would be good if we stayed and let her do the stitching.

They put me on a mobile gurney; it was at this point I met the spirit of this story. He kept insisting I speak with his sister; I was bleeding and my hand was wrapped. His request was not a priority in my mind, so I told him if he had not noticed I was bleeding and no one was attending me. He was very single-minded and continued to insist by telling me that nothing would happen to me. I tried to ignore him, but he was very insistent and in my face. Over the years I've gotten very good at ignoring spirits, so they do not realize I see them. If I go to the mall with my wife after a couple of hours of keeping up the act, I begin to drain of energy. I can handle short term but constant barrage of the mall or other very busy areas can drain me.

Back to the story, the doctor finally got to me and asked what happened. I explained, and my client and the rest of the family were all very concerned since the cut was very deep. The spirit kept on insisting. I did not answer. Can you imagine I'm talking to myself in front of the doctor and nurse? Society as a whole does not acknowledge what I do; rather, we are given drugs and called crazy. Over the years I've met many people whom were misdiagnosed as bipolar or any number of multipersonality disorders that were really undeveloped or obsessed people. These folks over the years become reclusive or just plain weird because they are given pills to fix a spiritual problem. Anyway, I did not want to be given some drug because of any side effects of the cut.

The spirit was really pressing my buttons, and I finally asked the doctor if she knew a dead man by the name I was given. She said no, but then the nurse who I had not paid attention to jumped up and said my brother's name was the same. He got in my face and said now tell her that I was not killed. She said *what*. I said this is what he is telling me. She explained because of how he was found, the family believes that he was murdered. The spirit jumped in and explained in detail what happened. He explained that while driving his motorcycle he died, and as the body and motor bike where splattered on the road, a passerby saw the body and moved both to the side of the road so no one would run them over by accident. He explained it was at night and on a dark road. He again expressed how important it was that she understood it was his fault and no foul play happened. The nurse was in tears and now could put this drama behind her. I looked at the spirit. He looked at peace, and I saw him floating up toward heaven now ready to move on.

The lady told me how happy this made her to close this injury to the family and now they can all move on. I told her that as I spoke with her brother, I could smell alcohol on his person; she smiled and confirmed that he used to drink more than he should have. I told her several more family-revealing information, and the doctor who was listening to everything told me if I had a message for her. I told her not to be embarrassed, what happened to her husband could happen to anyone and she should move on. She was flabbergasted and her jaw dropped. She told me, "Oh yeah, I understand and that was a very kind piece of advice." I told her a couple of other things, and she thanked me very much. Another nurse came in, and the doctor asked if I would give her some advice. I said yes but not in front of anyone. The nurse invited me to one of the rooms where she gave me an antibiotic shot.

I told her one piece of advice to stop having relationships with three people; I asked her if she understood the message. She walked up to the door in the room and made sure it was closed and turned and said crystal clear. I was shown she was having an affair with someone's husband that worked in the hospital with her. This was why I had asked her to speak in private I was not sure if it was one of the ladies in the area where we were. As I was leaving and my clients asked how much for all the service, the doctor said there would be no charge for anything including the pain killers and antibiotics they gave me to take. They were so grateful for my messages they wanted to show their appreciation by allowing me to get all the wonderful treatment at no cost.

The doctor was so impressed with my messages she advised her husband to come and see me where I was staying. When he arrived, I told him all he needed to know and he thanked me profusely. I saw that he had been in trouble before for the same problem he was in trouble now. He was shaken that I could see something that had happened over twenty years prior. He started to take me seriously; he had come because his wife asked him to and not because he believed until this moment. He left as a believer with new insight to his future and told what to be careful with.

Bad Spirit

One of my clients visited me yesterday. He brought his mother to my home for a dual cleanse. As I began with my client, we spoke about his work and girlfriend, just another cleanse, nothing jumps out. He told me he did not expect anything because he had really come to get his mother cleansed. I told him okay let's get to it. I began with a gage. If you remember from the first book, one of the things I do in a cleansing is clean with a cigar. To me how it burns lets me know what is going on with the person, like a thermometer. It looked horrible, so I stepped up my stuff. Somewhere in the middle of the cleansing, I took another cigar and started to clean the back of her neck, I asked her son over to look at something.

I gestured to him not to make a big deal, definitely not to tell the mom. He was freaked out by what he was witnessing. A lump had risen from the back of her neck; it contained what looked like to very small eyes looking out. He looked at me, and I explained that sometimes when something has entered the body and does not want out but is ripped as I was doing it can hold on and fight to stay. This sometimes can cause a physical manifestation. The exit point is not always the same, but it can manifest physically as in this case. You must understand this was a very elderly woman, and I did not want to cause her more trauma than needed. I did want her son to see this event.

I've had situations where a spirit physically holds on to a body part and people witnessing the scene can see fingers pressuring the area, and there is no physical hand attached. Scary stuff. If you can see the entity or spirit, you would understand better. Suffice that the event is so intense that it shows in the physical world for all to see. At best you usually feel a wind a chill, a touch, a sense that there is someone watching you; remember most of these are good souls watching over us. The stories I mention here are the exception. So feel safe. This world does have intrusions from the other realm, but most are good energies. This is a very magical world with energies of all levels sharing our world. Belief is not necessary, and you never know who will experience its reality. Many things we don't want to happen but accept, things we don't want to know but have to learn and people we believe can't live without but let go. The world is not fair it just is. So it is with energy. We don't have to understand its details, but it's there as sure as all these other examples, and we must learn to deal with them as well. Some we let go, others we embrace, but this realm is our constant companion never the less.

Young Man

This is a very interesting case. A good looking, smart, and outgoing twenty-year-old man who everyone liked was alone. He had no girlfriend, and when any of his friends had a girl, the girlfriends all loved him. No one understood why this young man was alone and neither did he. I too was not able to understand why this was happening. I took him to a good friend and medium, a woman who I spoke of in my first book. It happens that in a certain situation is not clear for a medium. The good ones will admit we all have limitations and we seek help; after all it's about helping and finding the answers for the person coming to us for help. I always tell the folks I've helped develop that it's about the people and we should check our own issues at the door and do the work and on the way out pick it back up. Anyone that claims they are perfect, run, no such animal exists in this planet. Perfection is for God only, and we are here to strive to achieve it. Once we get closer, we no longer need to reincarnate into this mortal world.

Back to the story, when my friend got to see this young man, she knew nothing about him. She identified a spirit of a woman who had been with him for years. She described a party he attended years before. He remembered the house and so did his mother. She described the woman as a person who sleeps with him and has intimacy with him in his dreams. She asked me to set up a session so we can get rid of the spirit. We scheduled it right away and brought on board yet another woman who channels. She took on the entity, and it gave her a message and was very reluctant to let go of the young man, but eventually at the end of the session, she was detached. His life soon after started to take a turn for the normal and away from the twilight zone he was living.

The Car

I went to a dealership with my wife. She wanted to turn in her lease and get a new one. I recently did the same thing. After she found the car she wanted, they discussed with me that there was too much wear and tear on the vehicle and therefore I would be charged additionally. The person helping me knew me and knew what I could do, so he brought me the man who decides how much the car we were turning in was worth. He was introduced to me and advised of what I do. He told me he was not sold. I told him intimate things about his wife and some emotional issues his stepson was going through. He was surprised, and I told him some things about a trip to Europe he had placed on hold and also of his dissatisfaction with his job. I advised him that it was not the time to change jobs. I told him about some health issues that no one knew about, not even his own wife. I told him it should be easy to overcome—the issue by drinking more water and drinking less milk. By the time I was done, there was no charge for any excess wear and tear on the car I was trading in. I guess sometimes it comes in handy having insight about situations and being able to give guidance to certain people.

I had just purchased a new car, I did this before selling my old one so I would not be pressed to sell or shortchange myself. After two months I was getting worried that the car would not sell for the price I was asking. I did some research and found it to be a very good price and people were calling but the car would not sell. Yes, it was a truck with a big engine at a time when gas prices were high but still other trucks were selling at the same price and mine was not. My wife was asking the cards question one evening and she told me she wanted to inquire about the truck. I was disappointed to hear that it would not sell for several months to come. She said let's see if it needs a cleansing. Okay, I said, and she asked if indeed the truck would sell sooner if cleansed. To my surprise the cards answered yes, the very next day I did a cleansing to the truck and within three days it was sold close to the price I wanted. People tell me my life should be bullet proof but if you understand how this spiritual world works you would understand that for most people like me the messages are for others not me or my family so unfortunately I'm the last person to get messages. Remember what I say, each of us choose a life to live and we must live it, irrelevant of the jobs we have.

Contrary to what many believe we are not our work or should we be described that way. Things change, life moves on, so appreciate what you have today before tomorrow comes and time forces you to remember and appreciate the things you once had!

Death Coming

It had been a year since my client had been told her ex-husband was sick. I did not see him lasting and the problem was cardiac related. I told her in great detail and in multiple readings that her former husband was not going to last long. She continued to tell me he had high blood pressure but had everything well in hand. I even mentioned it to one of her sisters that year that I felt my client was not taking me seriously.

The day came and unfortunately the two kids were with their dad. I was told it took a while before 911 arrived and their daughter was told how to resuscitate him over the phone while they waited alone with their dying father. He did not survive the heart attack, and his daughter has lived with guilt thinking she may be at fault for not saving him. I knew it was his time and there was nothing she or anyone could have done to save his life.

I believe we can intervene in many situations, but when death comes and it's your time, there is very little that can be done to change that.

Over the years I've seen it coming. Death, that is, for many and in some circumstances due to their own way of being they shortened their lives. In one case I was cleansing the person and death's energy was already upon him and I was able to intervene. He was going to die because he was overweight, and by giving him a harsh warning, he lost sixty pounds in six months and the stench of death left until it was truly his time.

Condolence

Usually what comes in the first few minutes of my cleansings are what is most important. There is no rule to this it just turns out that way. About a month ago, I started a reading by stating how sorry I was about her loss. She told me that there had not been any deaths in her family for at least two years. I apologized and continued what turned out to be a very productive reading. She also was thinking about selling her portion of her business, and I told her how a business separation would be a good thing and why. So after the reading she recommended me to a couple of people who also called and about a month later. Out of the blue she called me and reminded me about her reading. She reminded me what I had said at the beginning of her reading regarding a deceased relative. She reminded me how she told me no one had died for a long time in her family, and then she explained why she called. She had just lost her mom. She said it was about a week after my reading that her mom had a stroke and died. She told me how she thought of me and what I had seen. She called to ask if she had gone a different direction would that outcome been different. I explained that usually premonitions can be changed by just knowing it could happen, but in her mom's case, it was her time, and I doubted it would have had a different outcome because to me it looked like destiny had her leaving us. She felt better since she was beating herself up as she dismissed what I had told her. Now she knows better and she can rest from that self-imposed torment. It's hard to start anew if you continue to revisit old chapters. Things turn their best by making the best of how things turn out so move on and remember.

The Parents

I did a cleaning very recently to an old client that comes for regular cleansings; she works at a very stressful job with a tyrant of a boss. As usual I started my cleansing of her relating to her work, but out of nowhere both her mother and father who are deceased arrived. This woman has been my client for over ten years, and the parents died before I met her. Neither one of them had ever made a visit during my cleansings and to see them both was as surprising to me as it was to her. When I informed her, they were both there she told me that it was funny because when she chose this day for the cleansing she did not realize it that it was or would have been her mother's birthday.

I told her they both had messages and first to confirm who they were. I told her the woman was a teacher and her mother was a teacher. I told her the father always wanted to do something in medicine. She confirmed although he was also a teacher they always discussed how the profession he truly wanted was to be a doctor. He felt a bit off to me and she said in life he was a functioning manic depressive person. She told me he always thought that if he was a therapist she might better understand his problem. She, the mother, walked over in front of her and got on her knees and placed her head on her daughter's lap asking for forgiveness. She said she was very detached and was not a very good mother to her. She continued to express that my client was a much better mother to her own daughter.

My client started to cry, and she said that it was true, but she had long since forgiven her mother. Her father was not the most talkative, so I asked her if her mother had been the boss in the relationship. My client laughed and confirmed that her mother was the one in charge. Her mother went on to give examples of situations where she could have been a better mother and again asked for forgiveness. I asked why they had chosen this time if it was in fact because it would have been her birthday and she said no. She explained that her husband was getting ready to come back and reincarnate soon, and this would have probably been the last time that they could have come together and tell her all these things. Again the client started to sob, and she said she understood and they should go in peace as she had forgiven them.

She talked about an uncle by name and told my client that this had been the person that helped her transition when she passed. She told my client that when it was her time, her father would be the one to help her transition since she would be here on earth again during that time. The daughter asked if she had not told us that the visit was because the father was getting ready to come back down onto another life. She explained that my client was not going anywhere anytime soon and that the lifetime the father had chosen would be a relatively short one so he would return to heaven with plenty of time before my client would move on.

The mother said that in the year 2087 she would come back and live a life with my client as sisters. My client was excited and asked why; then, the spirit stated that this would be the very next life my client would come back to live another earthbound experience. I asked the spirit if she was better and the soul told me yes. I asked my client if there were any questions for her mother or her father. She was still sobbing from the experience; she told me to ask if they felt she was a good mother. Her mother smiled and told her with all the shortcomings she had been left with by them, she was a much better mother than she had ever been to her and asked again to forgive her. I guess it was a very moving experience for her. The cleansing wiped me out emotionally.

The Second Chance

This story was over eight years in the making. A woman came to me after seeing three specialists that had advised her that she had no more than two months to live. She was diagnosed with pancreatic cancer, and modern medicine could not save her. After her reading, it was obvious that her time was not up. I told her that destiny did not have her death marked at that time. I also expressed my belief that even if it's not your time and you step in front of a bus, you will die. So with this I told her that destiny was on her side, but other deciding factors could change that destiny. I explained that if she drank, did drugs, or any participation in other self-destructive ways of life, a person can change their predetermined destiny and this is called free will.

This story is not about that. I was able to help her, and she has become cancer free for all these years. Recently she called on me again. Now she has liver cancer and again inoperable. She had gone to the specialist, and they opened her up to cut the cancer. Unfortunately when they saw how much cancer was covering the liver, they simply closed her up and told her she was done. She questioned them about any programs to kill it through another form and the protocols in place did not fit at the level she was at so there was nothing else to do except wait for the inevitable.

Again, I looked into her destiny, and it was not her time yet; once more I told her she was not due for death, and we will start working on her levels to make it acceptable for the standing protocols to allow the surgery. After two sessions, not only were we able to stop the progress but the levels reversed five points. According to the protocols for surgery, to be a viable solution she must drop the levels another thirty points. I have to keep variations on the cleansings just like antibiotics to much of the same thing the medicine stops working.

This is where we are. I don't just know how it will turn out, but the first cleansings look promising and I feel she will overcome yet again and fulfill her destiny of living another ten to fifteen years. Oh yeah, she is not a young woman, so even her years are not on her side. She is a therapist, so she is used to working with the mind making what we are doing much easier as she keeps a positive mental attitude. I know the worse is still ahead. When we get to the point she can be operated, we will shift to a healing type of cleanse to strengthen her body after the operation. I told her there are no guarantees in something this advanced, and no matter the person's destiny, if you stand in front of a bus, you will die. So it is with deceases like cancer. I told her I can clean her to give the best chance and the fact that her destiny showed her living longer can affect the outcome, but in cases like this, she is taking a chance. She agreed and continued the sessions with the understanding that it could still go either way. She told me during one of the sessions that it's better than the other option, just to wait for the moment and die. She told me that hope is the one thing a person can never loose. I agreed, and we continued working on the problem.

A client came over for a cleansing. She has been my client for many years, and this was the very first time her deceased father showed up. He approached in a way that she would recognize. After a few words from him, she was convinced that it was in fact him. He then proceeded to speak to her about some regrets, and again she knew what he was talking about. He reminded her of a day when he felt like he was having a seizure and he had never had one before or since. He told her after death he realized it was his uncle attempting to channel through him to heal him but no one understood. I also told her it was a man in uniform like a general who had come to get him upon his passing, and she recognized him as her uncle, her father's brother. He also apologized for an incident he had with her mother while she was in a home. She had a seizure because he came to close to her. He really only wanted to help, but like him, she rejected the energy in the form of seizure. Well, definitely she did a lot of crying but released many emotional bottlenecks related to her father who in her youth had been a great dad and as he aged changed.

Several years ago, I cleansed my friend's mother. During that cleansing I told her about her ex-husband, my friend's father. I told her he would end up in a wheelchair, and the woman he married would take his money and run, in essence leave him during his time of need. As it turned out, he just e-mailed me that his father had an aneurism and ended up in a wheelchair. He also confirmed how his father's new wife ran out with over $100,000 in cash and jewels. I e-mailed him back and told him how sorry I was to hear about his father but to remember that when his father was advised of what was going to happen, he did not want help and did not want to hear it.

This was an interesting reading. I got a call from an old client. I had not heard from him in about five years. He started by telling me about his new relationship and how five years prior I had predicted her arrival in his life. He read what he wrote down five years before: blonde, from a faraway land with an accent, well, you get the idea. I had described her in great detail, and at the time, he was dating a blonde and he asked if she was it. I told him that this woman I was describing would arrive years later. When he met her, he recognized my prediction and received confirmation. I told him about the woman he was with at the time then and how she was great just not for him. I went into details as to why she would drag him down. I discussed her past as I saw it and other things he was not aware of. He also paid for the blonde to get read by me as she was curious who this man was that could predict the future.

She called, and I tried to take the reading in a direction different where she would have expected. I knew she was thinking it was all a con or at the least he set her up so I spoke of things he did not know of and in great details previous situations and other things my client had no knowledge of. At the end she told me she would be referring me to many if not all of her friends so I could help them. I thanked her because this is how I get business, referrals I told her. It was 10:00 p.m., and she was the last reading of the night, so a few minutes later, my client called and told me how in awe she was over the reading and then he told me he confronted the girlfriend and she confirmed all I had told him. She was very freaked out that a complete stranger could know so much about her. He thanked me for all my council and told me I would be hearing from him soon. Another thing I had predicted of the woman he would meet many years later, I saw many boxes, and once he met her, she told him of the shipping company she owned.

There are many things that can happen during a cleansing or reading. Always remember when I do a cleansing there is no way of truly cleansing without a reading. What I mean is during the process of a cleansing, I always end up reading the subject and the people closest around, so this next story should be of no surprise. I went to Boca Raton to cleanse two clients at the same home: one was a visitor and the other the owner. I started with the visitor. As usual I gave her some idea of what I was going to do and why, and then I started and told her a few things like if she had urinary track problems or bladder problems and she said no. I also told her about an eye issue and that she needed to go to the eye doctor. I also told her that she was thinking of purchasing a red car and to be careful because it had its mileage setback. She said no to every single thing I had told her. As I continued, she realized I was speaking about her niece who lived in New York and said she remembered being told recently that her niece had a bladder issue of some kind, and she was not sure about the rest including the purchase of a car. As far as she knew, the niece had a car she liked already. We finished and she left. As I was cleansing the other person, the friend I had just cleansed called me. I took the call since her friend was okay with it, and we were wondering what had happened.

She was so excited and amazed; every single thing I had told her about her niece was true. I told her that since she really had nothing going on with her, they took me to someone important to her that had many issues. She was amazed, but none more than the niece when she confirmed the purchase of a vintage Mercedes Benz that had very low miles, and she thought it would be a good investment. She was now mad as she told my client where was I last week when she bought the car. The aunt laughed because her niece was a police officer, and she should have known better. My client was so amazed not only about the cleansing but how the spirits knew that there was nothing wrong with her and took it to someone who, as she puts it, her only living relative and someone very close to her. I was glad it all worked out, and she told me her niece would call and schedule an appointment with me.

This client came to me very distraught. She was having money problems. She said her husband had a security job with the government, and he could lose his job because they also were losing a property and it was affecting his credit. I told her not to worry that this would not happen. This was her main concern at the time. Several weeks later, she called for a follow up where she confirmed they were not going to fire him because of his worsening credit. She was interested now in figuring out why she was feeling poorly and if there was a way to better their financial situation. I told her she needed to come see me for a cleansing, so she scheduled it. When she arrived, I told her not to worry, but there would be a minor in and out health procedure and that there were no other problems with her health. Then all of a sudden, a spirit arrived: a woman who slapped her across the face telling her to toughen up and stop whining. I told her what I had witnessed, and she immediately identified the woman as her deceased mother. She explained that only once in her life had she been slapped, and it was her mother, and she used almost the same words as when she was slapped by her for real years before. The spirit of her grandfather also arrived, and I gave her a weird name. She confirmed it was her father's father, her grandfather. Once I was done with the cleansing, she felt empowered and ready to go forward and get her life back on track.

Most feel that as a person passes it will take a while before they can be contacted. I don't agree as we are as diverse from one another so are spirits. I had a case where a mother brought her son to see me. He was in his thirties, and his spouse had passed of a tragic vehicle accident a year before. I told the mother as I tell all that come to me to communicate with a specific soul. It's not up to me, but the spirit must choose to manifest. Fortunately this one was willing and able as I told the mother to bring him for a cleansing; as part of that process, I read the person anyway. Someone like this that has not moved on from a tragic death can always benefit from a good cleanse of energy. So I began and the spirit was very chatty. She started from his tooth that needed fixing to the fact that he took too long in taking one of their children to the doctor with a urinary tract infection. He looked at me with amazement as he confirmed that had just happened, and yes, the doctor told him he should have come earlier and it would have been fixed earlier. She told him many intimate things including to tell her best friend by name that she needed to lose a few pounds. He explained that the name I have him was indeed of her best friend, but her extra weight was she had given birth a few months prior to that moment. Anyway I wanted to affirm that a spirit can be contacted right away if it chooses to and it's up to the spirit. Oh yeah, he had told me in the past he saw another medium who had told him that the death was supposed to be for him. I told him that life and death was in the hands of God and the person who told him this was wrong and he did not have to worry as I saw a long life.

Karmic Complications

I would like to offer this food for thought to all those who believe that life is more complicated than most believe. Most of us know a small portion of the big picture. I say most to be kind, the majority of humanity go on with their mundane existence concerned with the everyday things and seldom take three steps back to look at their big picture let along the person next to them. So with this I will tell you a story of one of my clients that will bring you in to a reality seldom thought of but always there. She came to me for a reading and cleansing of energy, at the time she had no idea what was to manifest. After giving her information that covered the names of family and former lovers and many other pinpointed events in her life she opened her mind to more. This journey we were to undertake was over months and several cleanings and specialized releases of other things from previous lives. She had lived a life where success had taken her to the tip and let her fall far several times. She questioned why, at this point I asked her to review not only her situation but her family, blood family that is. She recounted all that she remembered as far back as her great grandparents; a very similar pattern started to occur. It was not her who was suffering these things but her entire blood line as far back as she could recall. We continued to look back until it was identified that the affected bloodline was strictly from the mothers side as she could identify all the divorces and these unexplainable ups and down on the careers of only that side of the family. She recalls all the good relationships from the father's side way back to the grand and great grandparents.

We discussed how subtle all these occurrences that most in the family had not put it together as we were discussing. All divorced, all go to the top only to fall multiple times and so on it continued; I told her we needed to do a ritual that would stop this with her and then another that would prevent any further occurrences in her own progeny. She asked a simple question, why; not so simple an answer as I began to explain that there is more to heaven and earth than most can fathom. For example I explained the soul decides the life to come into and what things that it is to accomplish not silly things like the food to eat or the clothing to wear but how they will grow and what it will accomplish for the greater good of those whose life the soul is to touch. Well this is fine and dandy, but what if, oh yea, what if, simple words with unpredictable outcomes. If somewhere in the deep past of the blood line the soul is to incorporate there was a curse placed on an ancestor. A curse that would forever more affect all who carried the D.N.A of that ancestor who was originally cursed.

In this case this is exactly what had occurred; as I delved deep into the person's past and the soul's purpose I realized that her soul had success and accomplishment as part of this life. Unfortunately the soul came to reap this into a family that had a curse put upon them. Curses are seldom part of the plan but like many things in life can have a bad effect on the mix. Let's say we are taking an antibiotic but this particular dose will not work well with liquor and the person drinks the outcome might just be to lessen the effect of the antibiotic or it can have and adverse effect like damaging the kidneys. So it is with the path of life, if you sower the mix the outcomes are often unpredictable and never good.

I saw how this curse had affected my client and in particular her brother, all confirmed by her. I began my campaign to put right what once had been put wrong. I told her to come to my place for this release of the curse. You must understand that ritual is not something I'm fond of, if I could give each of my clients a pill to fix the problem I would. Imagine if I put you through hoops to find the things you needed and then to do a multitude of things to fix the problem. I think this stress might be worse than the problem so a pill will be a great thing. Most of the time I keep my fixes simple in this case it was not that difficult but there were several things that needed to happen. I required nine ribbons of different colors and I had to prepare a pan with water and some herbs; leave overnight so the energy of the moon and the sun will have infused its energies upon this mix. I also needed to have 5 different waters in the mix, for example rain, tap, ocean, river and well water. The ritual was to be done after I had cleansed her and she had done some home cleansings I had prescribed. Then on the day I would tie her up with all these ribbons and blind fold her with one. I would cut these ribbons and place them in a bag along with the scissors she had brought me. I cleaned her again just to make sure it looked good, and then instructed her to go to a cemetery with a gallon of water and a bouquet of flowers; she was to find a grave that was abandoned and clean it, place the flowers and dig a hole on the side. Speak to the spirits of the cemetery asking as she tended to this abandoned grave if they would tend to her request. As she buried these ribbons with the scissors that cut them may the curse they lifted go and stay in the cemetery forever without ever harming another living person. We are now in the proses of cleanings the children as she puts it to make sure I don't see it and a good cleaning can only help so I agreed and in time I will cleanse all her children.

Chapter 4

Exorcisms and Haunting

My first exorcism was a wild ride. I had no idea it could be so freaky, only in the movies had I seen such weirdness. Nothing like I thought it would be, these things are not of the same plane as spirits and much more energy to them, malevolent energy. I first read this woman about seven years ago; she called as they all do, referred by a friend or family member. I tell them not to tell me anything of their problems and I begin. By the time I'm done a good percentage of the reason for the call usually comes out, and then I tell them if there was anything I left out that they wished to discuss this was the time to ask. This could be about friends, family, anything. When I began with this woman, I was thrown off by how she repelled me; I was having trouble getting through to her. I began by telling her that her life had been slowly changing and not for the better over the last five years.

She acknowledged my statement and continued to listen. I told her she had a spirit that had to do with the law or justice. She again said yes and explained she was an attorney. I continued to tell her of her loneliness and weird dreams. She again agreed with me. I told her of her family member who passed within the last three years of an aneurism. Again she said that was her mother and how she died was of an aneurism as I had said. I told her that although things had been going wrong with her after her mother's death, they skyrocketed in the wrong direction within no time flat.

I had asked her if her mother was a very religious woman. She said yes and explained how she would go to church at least twice a week. I ask her if she did. The woman said that it was not her thing. I told her how her mother would pray for her as she felt something was wrong, and in my opinion, this was partly why she had died. She did not quite understand. I explained she felt as if she was under some sort of spiritual assault but of a level I had not experienced before. She took note of my words and told me that she had been feeling as if she was under attack but did not know from where or who.

We finished the reading discussing men and how no relationship seemed to work. I told her how good-looking she is and that it did not make sense as she was a package. Smart, good-looking, nice, a professional and a kind person; she agreed but had no answer as to why this was happening. She did acknowledge that it had been about five years since things began to go wrong as I had previously stated. She began to cry over the phone. I knew then that if I did not intervene, she would spiral into a dark precipice that she might never recover from. I told her of my cleansings but was not sure how effective it would be just with one.

You must understand, in 90 percent of the time, one cleanse is all a person needs to get them back on track. I really believed that in this case it might not be enough. No idea of how right I was, as we scheduled the appointment, she sounded positive about doing this. I explained that the first one I would like to do in her home as usually this is where negative energy grounds itself. As usual I prayed and asked my spirits to go a day before to get the lay of the land as it were and soften the blow for me when I arrive. For the first time one of my spirits told me several things to do to prepare and protect myself. He instructed me to prepare in a way I had never before done.

I'm a warrior. Fear is not part of the equation; caution, however is, so I did as I was told and I'm so glad. I don't know what I thought but prepared I was not; when I arrived, the house felt evil. I don't use that word because I think in terms of positive and negative energy. This, however, felt different. There was a malignant stench, maybe not one that she or anyone else could perceive, but if you understand energy, you know it's flow and this was murky, full of venom, dark thoughts emanating from the inside of this home. I received all this, and I had not entered the home; I became a bit hesitant. When she opened the door, she gave me strength as I saw in her face her need and desires to have me there.

She was placing her hopes on my arrival, and I could not fail her. I immediately invoked my spirits, angels, and archangels. All in God's name, you must always begin your prayers in God's name, to set the tempo as positive as possible. Now I felt more like me, filled with confidence and ready to take on anything or so I thought. I started by giving her a bath in a gallon jug I had prepared. It was full of herbs and other ingredients that I won't get into; remember when I do one of these baths I tailor it to the person. I told her that I would be cleaning the energy in the home, and she was to go to the bathroom and pour this concoction over her body from the head on down.

She agreed and very excited left toward the bathroom; I started to burn some sage and also some church incense to get the ambiance flowing. Well, it took me over five minutes just to get the carbon to light; I use carbon that is ready light, so one little match, and it starts. I like this better than those little sticks as they really put on a show of smoke. The show is not for the clients but for the energy. It's letting whatever is around the stagnancy is over and all energy will flow. No matter where in the home I would go the energy was the same, bad!

I finally finished and thought I had missed something because although I had felt the bad energy, I never found the source of the problem. It's kind of like you smell shit, but if you don't find the source, no matter how much perfume you throw into the room, soon it will come back stinky again. As I was deep in thought, the lady came back, and I knew she had done it as her body and hair still looked wet. I asked her how it felt. She said, "I can't explain, but I feel somehow lighter." I said good, and I asked her to go into the backyard with me.

I could feel her. I knew there was something there, but I was unable to see what it was. I can usually see spirits or at the very least where the stuff is coming from but not this. I was a bit baffled, but I figured that whatever it was must be in her, and I would get rid of the intruder when I cleaned her. The bath was just to loosen it up and make the job easier.

I began by a gunpowder, camphor and sulfur mix, the way I use it can vary, and maybe I won't use one or another ingredient. This explosive mix usually does the trick.

I created my symbols on the ground. I told her after it burns she should use some sort of cleanser immediately or at least the same day, so it would not create a stain. She did not seem to be concerned with stains but with her issue and fixing it. After I created my symbols I asked her to step into the center and then I enclosed her in the circle by closing the little area I had left open for her to pass through. You see if you close it before and she steps over it, whatever was with her could stay out and then get back in or reattach after I clean her and she steps out; by cleaning her in this way, it will be torn from inside her.

Remember in the case of these types of cleansings all things leave her; however, the good always comes back as it belongs with her and the intrusive energies go elsewhere for easier pickings. If a thief is looking for a house to rob, they will look for the open door or window, not with the house locked or with alarm. So it is with these types of entities they look for the unguarded, the unprotected, and the turbulent to call their new home. When you start cleaning up your energy, they soon leave and find an easier host to inhabit.

If I had not mentioned, I read the burn in cigars, so as I light and start to smoke, the way it burns lets me know what is going on. So I started to light the cigar and lit the stuff I laid all around her on fire. As a match it ran its course all through the signs I had painted and if you have ever seen fire it burns differently with different ingredients. I always use very similar ingredients, so I was used to seeing it burn. This time, however, the burn was very slow, and the color was completely different. As it ran its course, I looked at her and could see an image that was not her own.

I felt my spirits agitated at the external expression not her own coming from her face. I immediately started to pray and summon all my energies to assist me in what was coming. When the fire extinguished, she could no longer sustain her body with her feet and started to collapse. I ran to her and held her and helped her to a chair. I took out the plants I had brought and doused them in the mix I had prepared and started to clean her energies by making passes of the plants all around her body. I would even hit her with the plants.

After I was done, I placed the plants in front of her and asked her to stand and stomp on all the plants as if she was stomping on all that blocked her life. She regained her strength and stomped on the plants like if there were cockroaches. I asked her to step away and poured alcohol on the plants and set them on fire. I asked her to cross over the plants while on fire over and over, back and forth for a few minutes. By the time the fire had extinguished, she looked and felt better. I no longer saw the face emanating from her own face. I took out a long machete with some markings on it. I added gunpowder and other ingredients and asked her to stand over it facing in the same direction as the machete. She did. I told her as I stood behind her that as I lit the machete and the fire moved, she should keep still so as not to burn her accidentally. The fire went through her legs and out the front; then; I felt another release, I felt better but it was not over yet.

I told her there would be a need for her to do a second cleanse. This time, however, it would have to be in the ocean. She was in a mood to finish this and agreed, so we set it up for the following morning at dawn. We met, and she had purchased the ingredients. I told her and she brought everything along with her. I had told her to rest the rest of the day and get a good night sleep. She told me she slept great, and the alarm was the only reason she awoke. She had gone to sleep at 8:00 p.m. and awoke at six-thirty in the morning. She had told me it was unheard of for her to sleep more than six hours straight.

She cleaned herself with the fruits and the other ingredients and entered the ocean to clean herself of all the fruits she used to clean her body. After she left, the water she dried off and looked at me with a fresh look. I looked carefully at her and told her your problems are over, and I believe that her future would now progress without the episodes she had been experiencing. She smiled and told me, "You know I believe you." She hugged and kissed me and told me she did not know how to thank me. I just smiled and told her this is what I do, so just recommend me and that would be all the thanks I needed.

Over the years I've gotten over a dozen calls from people she recommended. I only heard from her again a couple of years ago because she was going to get married and wanted to check if all was good with her direction. The reading was great, and she is now married to a nice accountant. Imagine that, a lawyer and an accountant. Good for them. I had told her that within two years she would get pregnant, so I'm sure soon enough I will get another call from her to check on the pregnancy.

There was an occasion where I had to go clear a home of some energy that surely did not belong with the family living there. Over the years there have subsequently been several homes or structures I should say harboring very negative or even viral energy, but this one scenario took the prize. I had been reading a woman over several years and always one relative came up in the reading, not from her but my own energies would gravitate to her. Finally one reading she commented that her cousin had been told of me and was eager for a reading.

It was a few days later she called and make her payment, scheduled the reading a few days later. We discussed all the weird things that happen in her home on a regular basis. She had a priest over to bless the home, and on another occasion, a group came from the same church to sing and pray in hopes that the nasty feeling in the home would go away. Guess what, it did not change a thing. Prayer does have power. Don't get me wrong. Unfortunately this case was way beyond a one-day prayer group or a priest just to come by and bless the home with holy water.

I gave her some guidance for things she could do herself and for her family and then she was to call me for the actual cleansing. A cleansing that I told her might have to have several parts to it for the home and those who lived in the property. I told her to make sure there was no one else present when I arrived, except those who dwell in the home. I explained to her that she did not want any confusion, and it could take on a life of its own and waste my time cleaning the visitors instead of the real problem, a problem I had told her was within the home even before she and her family moved in.

As with any job, the more you do it, the better you get at it. This was my very first haunting, so not just an attachment or some king of spell or witchcraft. This was an actual haunting. The presence had been in the property for over forty years. I asked the family to do research, and sure enough many families had lived in the house and none stayed over three to five years. This type of turnaround was not very common as the home was large, in a good neighborhood, so the initial investment was sizable and not to be easily discarded.

All right let's get to the details. I had instructed the woman to have all in the home do the salt and sugar bath. This type of cleanse is not particularly strong but it does clean the aura of the person doing it. It goes like this: After you take your normal shower, stay wet and scrub your entire body from head to toe with salt, a defoliation of sorts, and then wash the salt from the body. Then take brown sugar and do the same procedure again then wash the sugar off the body, then dry off. I told her as a whole the family should have a good night sleep that night as most do. Then I asked her to have the kids take an apple cider vinegar bath. This bath goes like this: you would fill the tub with water and then add three gallons of the stuff into the tub already full of water. The children were to strip and get in. They needed to get the whole body wet and stay in there for at least ten minutes. I told her they must dunk the head and get the face head and hair wet. They were to do this several times while in the tub. The trick to this bath is they must not dry off. So I told her to let them brush the hair and teeth after they get out and sleep with that odor on them. They could take a shower in the morning and wash it off from their bodies. The overnight is all that is needed, and after all they would smell like a salad.

You can do this bath for anyone, but I prefer the old or young and the results are amazing. Anyway back to the preparations, she asked me what else she needed to do. I asked what type of floor; she told me tile. I instructed her to clean the floor with nothing but regular white vinegar, and as she mopped it, she should not dry it but leave it on the floor so it would evaporate. I told her to do it in the morning so she could open the windows and allow it to dry off. I explained to her that to even sprinkle vinegar out the front door.

She had written it all down and agreed to take care of all these things before I arrived in a couple of days. The day before I was to go, I did my prayers and sent my spirits to work on the property before I ever set foot there. It does help, and sometimes hard energy takes a tool so anything we can do to diminish the body's receipt of these turbulent energies the better. So by the time I arrived, the house seemed to be more manageable or so I thought. Usually other worldly energies do not manifest physically, yeah right not there.

Everything had been done to prepare, and my arrival seemed to be as if nothing had been done. The home smelled bad as if dead people had been left to rot in the property. The client did tell me the entire family felt better from the things I had directed them to do. So maybe at some level a little loss of grip had occurred. I was sure if I did nothing, it would get back to however it was before my arrival soon after things done lost its energy.

I asked everybody out and did my rituals; I lit the place from the center outward with gunpowder, camphor, and sulfur, my usual heavy-hitting cleansing. I can tell you whatever was living there was not happy. As I was creating my symbols at every door in the home out to the front and rear, they were pushing back. I got a headache and at one point even had to stop and went to the bathroom with diarrhea. I had brought a friend as I felt maybe some channeling would be required. As I proceeded, one of the energies took control of my body and projectile vomited all over the wall of the home. My friend was able to free me from this spirit. That's right, it was a spirit and just one of the workers of the main energy that was causing the problem in the home.

Once I was done with the initial pass, I asked my friend to sage the home and also burn some church incense. I continued to clean with some well-chosen plants and my special aroma that I wet them with to give it an extra push as I passed them through each room of the home. We were both doing our prayers and demanding all that did not belong be gone. I expressed in a very harsh way that I would bottle the entities and not allow them to roam free if they stayed. Bottling is not a very easy thing to do so I was more bluffing than anything else but sometimes that is all that it takes with bullies.

By the time we were done more than three hours had passed and I could feel a break in the flow of negative energy. I then proceeded outside to clean the family as they patiently waited in the garden. I had made each a special bath to be poured on their body in the shower. They were to just dry off and come back outside. Then I used the plants and cigars on them as a thermometer, you know a way to make sure what I had done worked. All but the teen daughter showed free of this energy. I spoke with her as I cleaned her and asked if something had happened within the last two years, something the family was not aware of.

She came clean and explained she got pregnant and had an abortion. I counseled her and asked her to allow me to bring the mother to discuss this, and she was so scared that she said okay. I had to do an additional thing to her, and after I felt she had released what she was holding on to. I told her she would have no problems conceiving in the future so not to worry and she and the mother hugged each other. At the end I left contented that what had been there for so many years had broken its hold on the home.

I told the lady she had to do what I had asked them to do before my arrival the following week and then all should be fine. Over the years she has called for readings, no subsequent cleansings needed to be done. I've cleaned different members of the family; but for other reasons, one was doing badly in school the other had been caught with marijuana in the car, and yet another one had lost a job. All very mundane and normal family stuff over the span of five years no more problems, and they have been living there seven years more than any family since the home had been built.

I had a situation: a woman with multiple personalities or so everyone thought. Guess what, she only had one the rest were free loading spirits. She was a medium with the softest touch I had ever experienced. She was easy to penetrate. She could be in a place, have a drink, and as her cognitive abilities lowered, she would be tapped by any spirit in the area. She is crazy. She does not have a clue and thinks she has some sort of multiple personality disorder. At least that is what doctors have been drilling into her mind for as long as she could remember. They are just in awe that she is still functional; by this I mean keep a job and finished school with this handicap as they call it.

Until she got to me. She was recommended to me by another client that I had helped with a haunted car, but that is another story for another time. So when she called, I gave her a reading, and in the reading, so many things came out relating to her family history and none of it was of crazy people or any mental disorders. Her diseased aunt came through asking me to help her, to free her from this obvious problem in her life. I told the aunt that it was up to the niece what I would do or not do so don't be so bossy. I explained to her what the aunt said. She laughed and told me that was her way, a bit bossy and tell you like it is personality.

After we started to discuss the options, I told her what she needed was not just a simple cleansing. She, I was certain, did not have multiple personality disorder as she had been diagnosed. I told her it would be a process, and there was no guarantee. This after all was her natural state; perhaps a little training with her abilities will help her to control them. So I told her it would be several months' worth of work, and she would have to do as I instructed. I would not be cheap, but if she was willing, she would probably master the ability to control her channeling: to only when she wanted to allow it in to her life and not when the energies choose.

She agreed. Without a second thought, she said after all the years that I've wasted with no results and all the money she had wasted what is a few months and some money. So we began to work. I sent her to do some of my regular home remedies for a week or so before we stepped up our work. I took her to the beach after dark. As a matter of fact on a full moon at midnight. She was to clean her body with lemons, from head to toe. She would follow it by cleaning her body with five yellow soft papayas, crushed from her head down scrubbing her body with each papaya.

She would have to enter the ocean afterward and clean every inch of her body free from the lemon and the papayas. She had to make sure her hair was free of all the fruit that was in there, after she gets out she would dry off and home she went. As predicted she had a wonderful night sleep, she called me the next day to tell me she slept twelve hours. Not uncommon for this type of cleanse, I've had people that when they do similar cleansings cannot even drive for a while. The energy exchange is such that they are spent for a while until the new and fresh energy recharges the aura. Remember any cleansing clears negative energy from the person, when that energy is great it takes a while for the aura to replenish with fresh energy.

Okay, then she would have to sweat her clothes for a day and then strip, take some bloody meat chunks she bought from the supermarket, and clean her sweaty body. She was to place all the chunks into a brown paper bag; she would then take a shower and dry off. Get dressed and take the brown bag to a railroad track where she was to dump the bag. I had given her a special perfume she was to use regularly to change the frequency of her aura. This is not done easily, so she had to pour all over her body regularly.

There was an array of things I did for her and had her done for the next two months, along with some ritualistic cleansings and prayers. Well, within two months, she had ceased to have the episodes she had been suffering from most of her life. She was pleased with her progress. As of today, I've heard from her sporadically as she needed readings for business advice. Oh yes, she started her own business and got married all in a span of three years. Her life was free of the possessions; she knows she has to maintain a regiment of energy clearings on a regular basis to keep her clean.

Most earthbound spirits are just lost souls wanting attention and to get their message through or asking for redemption from mistakes they committed while with their earthly bodies. Guess what, forgiveness is and was always theirs. As they depart a guilty mind can hold them back, I had a case that a woman passed and she had told so many lies that after she passed she stayed with the family in hopes to make amends. She caused such disharmony within her family that mother did not speak to son and sister to sister.

All this and more she did to get attention, while in the afterlife she could not or would not pass to the other side until her self-imposed punishment was complete. The first time I went to clean the family I told them that this would not be a simple cleaning but would take many as the woman who was haunting them was not ready to move on. Once I explained who she was some of the family even told me to discard her soul that they did not care to help her as she had done many wrong things to almost everyone while she lived.

They agreed to do as I suggested after many hours of speaking with them; she was hung up on so many things I had to figure out what to do so she would stop bothering. Finally I decided instead of cleaning the living and their home, it would be more fruitful and beneficial to the soul to get it back on track. After about the fifth cleaning of the soul, it decided that maybe I was right and moved on, from that day, that moment the ambiance of the home felt differently and the family was so in awe for the next two years they would ask me to come and clean them again just in case. Look I cannot help if the spirit does not cooperate, so therapy was key in this haunting.

The energy of a place can have life of its own; I can relate a case where a client would have a property that loved them so much that it would not let them go. I started with the husband and then cleaned the place. I told him from the beginning that we can try to appease the place but if we cannot convince it that another family would be better suited then he would be or could be stuck with the property. This was a very healthy man in his late thirties who owned this beautiful ranch. After he put the place for sale, he threw out his back and even needed surgery.

I entered the picture and tried to negotiate with the land to let them go and another one can come and life there. I did several cleanings to bring buyers. Guess what, I moved the energies and many qualified and overqualified people came to look at this beautiful property. None bought as expected the land did not want them to leave. This is an incredible example of a thing keeping a hold of a human and not allowing them to do something just because the property in this case thought or believed that this family was best for it. To date they still live there. Many changes have occurred and the people, especially the husband was given opportunities to keep the land by opening doors to new and impressive income, while still allowing him to have a life on the ranch.

I've seen many types of homes and offices. Over the years typically the energy is stagnant from people that lived there before, and when the new owners moved in, they never bothered to cleanse the place free of any leftover energies from the previous owners. I believe that energy does not necessarily go away when you leave a place. Echoes of all sorts of experiences and occurrences seem to imbed into the place and can affect the new people to the property.

You have seen this over and over in movies and haunted places, for some reason old places seem to keep memories, especially places where great emotions were a constant. If you go to an old hospital or an asylum for the mentally disturbed, if you have visited some of the old castles in Europe, you know what I mean. Right in your own hometown, there was always the haunted house or abandoned building. One of the greatest conduits of spiritual energy is smoke. This is why most burn incense in the homes to cleanse and when you sage a home I also clears old energies. Another conduit is fog or humidity; this is why some entities come out in the evening.

Back to the story. I was called to this store. The people had purchased the building, and as I stated previously, they never cleaned the energy from past situations in the building. After I met with them, they explained that although they had several other properties, this one has constant problems. Not only would things break but electronics would go wild with no other cause. I asked if it happens when there were storms or any other changes to the ambiance. They had electricians and other specialist in the building, but as they stated, this does not account for things breaking. The man explained how portraits would be broken when they arrive in the morning. I asked to explain, and he took me to the closet where they had some of the items.

It was such a large variety that it could not be explained by any physical manifestation. I say this because the year before I arrived at a home where they thought it was spirits, but there was a factory near the area that was causing shockwaves that was even cracking the walls and floors of other properties. This was different, vases falling from tables; I saw the portraits and the class were cracked as if hit by something. Sometimes it is what people call ghosts or—as it is commonly talked about—ghosts from the past affecting today. So with that in mind, this place had a combination of ghosts or echoes of things long since passed and a few spirits that were causing havoc.

Ghosts some can just be over and over repetitions of pivotal events in the life of the soul, or it can be an actual imprint or rewind reel like a replay of an event. So in either case, it's not doing much more than what it does daily or weekly or monthly or yearly. It depends on the event; for example, if it was an incident that occurred during a war, and then it will repeat that incident at the location during the time and date that it occurred over and over probably for eternity.

Back to our story, by this time, I had discovered that it was not one but many different things causing all the problems. I told them it would take about three different cleansings to fix the problem but not to hold me to that number. They agreed, and the first thing I did was clean the inside of the local and bind it from more apparitions. Then I set out in the yard and bound the outside to prevent more stray visitors from coming into the property. Last but not least I cleaned the owners of the place as they were probably affected by all this stuff. It all took over several weeks to get the job done, but I've read for them over the phone and since that date no more problems other than people fumbling and bumbling as people do.

There are many types of spirits and not all can be channeled and even the ones that can't be channeled by any medium. So is the story I'm going to tell you about one of these scenarios; I have friends that do what I do, not many but a few. Much like most of you have friends from your industries, maybe not great friends, but its common sense that we all gravitate with people that do what we do for work. So it is with most people in most industries, doctors have friends in the medical profession; teachers with other teachers and so on.

So spirits will find people in the world of the living, our world that they find an affinity with. Not necessarily work wise but energy wise.

Remember most spirits are looking for help or vindication of some sort. It was during one of my readings that I found an attachment with one of my clients; this was not your normal attachment as this spirit was well aware of what it was doing. He was the exception to the rule, so someone or a couple of some ones summoned or used this soul that was not so lost but enjoyed attaining things just like the living by bargaining with it.

I don't know what it accepted, and I did not care to find out. This spirit was interfering in a big way in the life of one of my clients. She is a very nice lady, a professional who was going downhill during a time where she should have been going up. After carefully looking at her over the phone and the inexplicable reasons she would not move forward in most aspects, I finally detected the energy of this malicious soul. Once I was able to identify it was not one of her protections and this took me two readings to decipher; it was pretending to be a good spirit there to help her and to me he was representing himself as one of her protections.

As I said, it knew what it was doing and was there for the reason of placing her life on hold, forever as far as I was able to detect. Once identified I queried him as to why he was so foolishly wasting his time there and indebting himself in the scheme of his own immortal soul. He was good, and it took me a while to get a clear reading from him. After it was clear and I had no doubt that he was there to hurt her, I told the client that I needed to do three cleanings. She thought that was quite expensive, but after I told her what I had seen, she had no problem going through with my idea.

Not only did I detail what had been happening to her but I also told her where all this was going in her life. I told her what I had seen as to where her life should be and where it was going because of this troublesome entity. We scheduled a clearing with another person; either I or he would channel the soul and give it some therapy. You must understand not every spirit can be channeled by just any medium. There has to be some sort of affinity, energy wise, so happily my friend was able to tune it. I was not looking forward to channel such a manipulative soul. We end up with some of that energy for a bit, and it feels bad. Imagine if you are a good person but start to have very dark thoughts, thought to deal with, exactly. So as he took on the entity, I spoke with it, and it dialoged back, very confused. It really thought that making bargains with the living would empower him to get stronger. It does not work that way. Maybe if the people are good at what they do, they might give some sort of offering that will temporarily empower the spirit. Like any quick fix, there are always repercussions and so it is with this sort of stuff.

After a long talk with the spirit, it looked as if it was going to release the hold it had on the lady; no such luck it was playing with me. It was then that I realized that the soul was here to stay or I would have to brute force remove it from the side of this woman. When my friend came out of the trance, he was disgusted with the energy and was able to give me some insight. With most trances done by people who are also mentally connected, he was able to sense what was really in the mind of the soul.

Whoever had created this bargain was able to identify the soul by name; they were able to know its life before death and offered some ritual sacrifices and other windfalls to entice the entity. They were able to promise by name. They would empower the spirit to visit his wife. She and he had divorced as he was not a much better human being while he was with the living. So basically they promised that if he did this act against the woman they would be able to connect him to his former wife so he could live with her as her husband even while he was dead.

There are different types of souls and mediums. The completely gone ones: these are the people that when a soul takes over their body, they have no recall of anything that happens during the episode. This type of medium usually is the best trance medium but not very helpful in scenarios like the one we had encountered. As I said, the medium that is also in semicontrol of the body while the spirit inhabits. It will have residual impressions of the spirit after the episode is done. So my friend was able with detail give me a good idea of what was going on in the mind of this trickster.

After this attempt, I was able to tell the woman with more certainty that with time I would be able to rid her of this troublesome spirit. She agreed, and we continued. During the next encounter I came loaded for action and summoned my heavy hitter spirits. I would do some rituals to dislodge the intruder from her, and they would rip him apart and deposit the soul in a location where he would no longer be able to harm her or anyone else. Kind of like solitary confinement for the soul, with no chance for redemption or moving on. Hey, sometimes you have to do what you have to for the greater good, so as I told another friend, if you don't like it, try being in the innocent shoes of the woman in question then tell me another story.

Everything went according to plans as I ripped the hold from this spirit and my own spirits took it away. The lady told me she could feel like something being torn from her body and then a very different feeling like emptiness. You must realize even if the soul did not belong, it was taking up space and its energy was part of who this woman was. So as with any thing tangible or not, when you take part of something out, something else must replace it to make it complete again.

So it was in this case, and we scheduled another cleansing just to incorporate the pieces back together again, this time with good energy. I did a beautiful ritual to summon positive energy to her side, and the hole was plugged. It had been about nine months before I heard from her again. This reading was totally different, and she was a totally different person. Her energy vibrated with happiness. She told me how within a few days of the last cleanse she was already sleeping better and had desire to work out and go out with her friends. Soon after a relationship began, and she said it had been six good months with that new man in her life. I told her how much more her life would change until it was caught up with where it was supposed to be.

Imagine if this had not taken place. This woman would have never moved forward, and if it continued she would have fallen into a deep depression and maybe even an early death. I belief that death is not the greatest loss in life. It's what often dies within us while we are supposed to be living. So my message is to always turn a corner, always open another door, never give up, never surrender. As sure as there is night, I guarantee there will be a morning. Hopelessness is never a solution. Try and try again. If you fail, it's just another way to learn you were on the wrong track. I guarantee if you keep on, you will open the right door, the door that will give you the bright destiny that is your divine right. Determine happiness from within and not from around. Most gain it from others temporarily; in truth it always came from within!

I was called once by a woman from another state. She explained that she was not sure what she needed; I explained that a reading could possibly clear up some things and then we could take it to the next level. She agreed as it made sense to her. She made her payment and called to schedule. I gave her the appointment within two days, and when she called, the start was—let's just say—explosive. The first energy to manifest was nasty; it started by telling me to get out and never return. I asked her if she had been experiencing night terrors; she said yes. I asked her if it was a tall man with long fingernails. I continued to describe the entity I had seen: the nasty one. She told me yes. I told her if he had long messy hair and a slender face. She was startled but agreed. She said how I could know what her dream looked like; I explained that there was an entity that was coming into her dreams and possibly into other aspects of her waking life. She got more nervous. I told her not to worry—the process first is one of discovery and then one of figuring out how to put her life back on track.

As I continued talking with her over the phone, the visions became more present, and she started to manifest feelings of fear and apprehension. I told her this was all normal for the situation she was going through. She asked me what situation I was speaking of; I told her she was being spiritually assaulted from a dimension not of this world. She was not a believer in anything, this included God, so I had to open that door that swings both ways as we spoke to allow these hidden things to come out and manifest in the day light instead of in her dreams and the deep recesses of her mind.

I explained that one of things that I felt was ashes of a dead person in her vicinity; she told me that in her closet she was keeping the ashes of her grandmother. I told her that if she loved her, she needed to get rid of the ashes, that those ashes are nothing but a magnet for any and all spiritual energy in the area. As I tuned in even deeper, I told her that there was something else at play here. She asked what I was talking about.

I explained that there was a door opened that allowed something to come through, something not of this world. What, she asked; I explained that there could be a number of ways that this could have happened.

I told her with my experience this could be accomplished by the use of the Ouija board; I did not think she would fit since she did not really believe. To my surprise both my suppositions were wrong. She explained that she had some friends that would come over, and they would play the Ouija board game on a regular basis. She said that nothing of substance ever happened, and she was not sure if what they did was real to begin with but some of the friends liked it and after a glass of wine it was more fun. I've gotten from the Internet several of the common designs for your inspection. I do not believe it's ever a good idea to open a channel of communication like this as you never know for sure who is on the other side. Once you develop spiritually, tools like this might become of interest to you, but just make sure you are developed enough spiritually that you know, by feeling or sensing or seeing what or who you are actually in contact with before it becomes a bad experience as it is with many who play regularly.

This is an image form the Wikimedia Commons. This image is in the public domain because its copyright has expired.	This is an image form the Wikimedia Commons. This work has been released into the public domain by its author, Mijail0711

Again, that entity came to me and told me to stay out or I would regret it. This was not the first entity to threaten me, so with limited concern, I continued. I explained to her that she should do several things; get rid of the ashes and never use the Ouija board again. I further recommended she speak with the friends and ask them if they had experienced any weird things. She agreed to do so, and we continued. I asked her if she had scratched her left leg recently. She, again, very surprised told me that she had backed out of the way of someone walking out of an elevator, and she scratched the back of her leg on something behind her.

I asked her to remember if she turned around and if she really saw that had scratched her; she thought for a moment and then vaguely recalled a round garbage can behind her. She did not make much out of nothing and assumed something loose must have scratched her. She asked why I had asked her. I explained that at the time she was scratched, the thing I had felt was behind her and I saw it scratch her with his long nails. She freaked out and asked me what she needed to do to fix this problem; I told her for now she needed to do the things I had asked her and get back to me.

It was no more than a week that she called for a second reading; she told me that she did as I had asked. There were four people besides her that had played the board game and only one had experienced weird occurrences. I explained that it was her house that they played with the board, so she had become the center of the episodes. By now she was really concerned, and justifiably so, as I continued the reading, that entity came to me again and told me that I needed to get out and to do it quickly before something happened to me. I explained to her all the entity was saying to me. I told her I felt it had a plan and it would not be good. I gave her an array of cleansings she could do and for the other person suffering similar situations.

I believe in the power of prayer. Here is a very simple one I do. Of course you may modify the reasons for summoning, but you will get the general idea. I reach many realms, but the one I feel most comfortable in is the angelic real, so it is for this purpose that I use this prayer. "In God's name I invoke the Angelic Realm. I pray to the angels and archangels of the divine commission, asking for assistance. I ask, come to me in this my hour of need, grant me your protection from all not of the light. I ask for enlightenment. May your divine intervention fortify my will and give warmth to my soul as I traverse this human existence. May I find my way to peace of mind and soul. This I request of you my angels and archangels as always in God's name!"

I recommended her to come and see me as what she needed was some hands on work with me. She explained that she just did not have the money to take off from work and travel to another state to get the help she needed but asked to keep on giving her the help through advice and she would do everything to the letter of what I said. I made sure it this reading that it was the one entity and nothing else working in the background I had not seen before. After we finished I told her that we will start with the things I recommended and we would speak again in a couple of weeks.

She called for another reading three weeks later; she was upbeat as most of the weirdness that had been happening had considerably diminished in frequency and strength. I knew the thing was still around as it was not as tough sounding as the first to encounters, but I could feel it still in her home. So without causing her any discomfort, I changed the frequency of the work she needed to do on her home and her person. She felt much better, and her friend was free of the impulses that had been driving her to anger and that emotional rollercoaster. It had retreated to its entry point, at my clients house, we recapped she had gotten rid of the ashes and as I recommended burnt the board game. She had done each of the things I recommended she do.

I told her next thing to do. She thought it was a bit weird but decided how much weirder than what she was going through. I told her this should finish what needed to be done, and she—if done correctly—should be fine. I continued to tell her as long as she stayed away from all the board games and any other type of fun that covered dealing with the other side. She told me without missing a beat, "You can count on it," and asked me when she needed to call me again. I explained to her that if she does it right, it might not be necessary to call me again. She told me how about in a few months. I said okay, and she did call me about three months later. Not only was everything good in her life, but she had a new awareness about the afterlife and spirituality in general.

I recently heard from her, she sent me an e-mail after she ordered and read my new book, *Life and Beyond*; she found several of the cleansings I had her do in the book. She was grateful for me and for this new book; she told me in the e-mail she knows how many people in need can now get my help from the writings in my book. I was pleased how she ordered the book and especially for the review she gave it, in either case I was happy to hear from her and that her life had moved on as it was meant to do.

Dark Souls

Over the years I've experienced many strange things; even by my standards weird to me might be off the hook for most of you so here it goes. I had to help a person go into the light. The daughter is my client, and the mother was in hospice; she called me one day for a reading and as we started I was shown a life at its end and peril of losing its way. I told her what I had seen she understood better than I did and explained to me about her mother and how she was holding on. The doctors had told her that her mother was long passed her time, and they did not understand what was keeping her here.

I told her that what I can do for her is go and visit the mother and talk to her and see if I get an idea of why she is holding on. I told her there are no guarantees but only that if is truly her time I might be able to get to her and help her cross over. I asked her if there was anything about the mother I should know as it pertained to her wanting to hold on. She explained that she had a good life, and as far as she knew, there was nothing for her to still do here on earth. I continued the reading, and at the end, she made an appointment with me to meet with the mother at the location she was being cared for. The fear of life is the favorite disease of the miserable until it manifests into a physical reality.

The day was Thursday afternoon. The location was far off from my home, so I did not want to make it too late as traffic would delay my return at least an hour. Anyway I arrived and called the daughter to meet me in the lobby. She came right away, and we headed for the mother's room. As I was walking I felt a large group of spirits in the area. I then remembered this was a Hauspie center, and all the folks there were going to pass in a short period and all the souls I was sensing were probably there to help them to pass to the other side.

We arrived to the room, and I was surprised to say the least, the soul that was there with her was not a good one, it was a dark soul. I was surprised because she was a good person and she had a good life and her time was up. I pretended not to see anything but took the time to indirectly speak to the soul. I told my client that the key to the spirits evolution is moving on passed this realm. I explained how we are here for a short period, and then if the mission was complete or not, the soul must move on to remember all the things it had chosen to do and realize how many they did not and why. This is a learning planet, so with each lifetime we learn more about our real life, our spiritual life.

I explained again with the goal of having the spirits in the room listen, so I continued explaining to the daughter that as a spirit passes, it will go to the astral place where all souls travel where their veil is lifted and they remember everything about themselves. They remember all previous lives and all the souls they were connected to here on earth. The reason for their existence and why they choose the life they did. There is a divine plan; part of that plan is keeping this secret. Can you imagine if you knew why you were here? The soul would not learn as they would do what expected and the emotional maturity would not be improved. In the light there is forgiveness, love, and understanding; and I continued on and on in hopes to move this dark soul back into the light.

The darkness exists if for no other reason but to realize the light is the right place for all things spirit, so after about a fifteen-minute lecture, the daughter asked if I would help her mother to cross into that wonderful place. Well, I guess I convinced the client, but did I convince the dark soul? Unfortunately the next action showed me the soul was there to confuse and even keep her here and move her into a bad place. He leaned over and whispered something to her. She moved, and I could see her soul was wrestles and scared. I told her that the reason her mother had not passed was that there was an entity in the room scaring her from the light.

At that moment the soul looked up, and we exchanged glances. I smiled and I could see he was angry. I could feel his negative will; I could feel the negative energy he harbors inside of his soul. So it begins, that soul is there to divert the mother's soul from achieving the goal of all souls to enter the kingdom of heaven. I still thought to myself why this was happening to the mother, so I asked the daughter some questions. Remember the mother was in hospice and had been catatonic for other four months. I got some good feedback but nothing that gave me a clue as to the reason this spirit was coveted by the darkness.

I tried to speak to the soul in the room, but it looked at me perplexed as to my arrival and I guess wondering why I was interfering with whatever he was up to. He left as easy as he had arrived, just disappeared. I know that a spirit can and has the ability to make itself invisible to people like me. Assuming he was still there but invisible, I told my client that her mother needed energy work. She agreed, and I came back another day with my equipment to clean her energy in hopes to detach whatever was attracting this spirit to her. I could not have been further from the reality of the situation as I concluded the cleanse. The spirit smiled, and there was no or very little change to the energy of the mother.

After studying the way this spirit was working with the mother, I realized it was working toward a much more insidious plan. It wants to cause the soul to come with him when the death of the body comes. I told the daughter that this would not be an easy cleanse. I explained what I thought I had discovered and how this was something not common to my experience. I told her there would be no guarantee of what I could do for the mother as this was uncharted territory. She said she did not care if there was a chance I can help her cross and move her into the light she would do it. I like making money, I have a family and a home and all the bells and whistles, so I have to do plenty of readings and cleanings to pay the bills but I've never, never told anyone they needed something they didn't. I can tell you from all my clients that most of the time I tell them what to do and they can fix the problems themselves. I believe that people need me when things are complicated or when they had no desire to do for themselves and would rather pay for the service.

When I got home, I had a powwow with some of my spirit protectors. I was really lost as to what to do, like you when you have to learn something new you need an education on how to do it. No one knows how to rebuild engines. You must read and take some classes to really know how to fix them. Unfortunately I don't have this, so I depend on my spirits to guide me and show me how to help the clients that come to me for help. I definitely learned some stuff I never thought about before; for example, there are groups of these dark light souls, and their jobs are to corrupt new free spirits.

I learned that these souls are like us except they have been corrupted to work toward one goal, to increase in numbers the about of dark spirits that roam our planet. Why, I asked, they explained to me that in order to rock the boat, if I may use this analogy, there has to be enough of them so numbers are the solution. Unfortunately they excel at bringing out doubt, and if they can convince a soul with such light like my client's mother, this would truly be a win for that dark lighter.

I have to find a way to reach the lady in a state that makes it impossible for me to have a conversation with her. So I will begin by speaking to her on life and the afterlife. I also told my client that she should read to her. I told her to take my book and read it to her, anything to help her come to terms with the fact that going to the light is the proper evolution to the soul. Since she had not purchased the book, I gave her a copy and asked her to read to her and she would also learn as the mother did.

I told her I would come by next week to begin. She got the book and started to read to the mother and found the book interesting for her as well. I visited the mother and spoke with her. When I spoke, there were spirits that came and left, and I explained to them to help me. I kept on speaking with the mother about life and death and how the afterlife was a very important part of the process. She could tell I was listening, or at the very least I thought so as I spoke to her about certain sensitive topics she would flinch.

She looked as if she was in REM sleep. She, I believe, was processing all of what I was telling her. Unfortunately the dark spirit was not far behind, and I could see as it gave its own agenda to the mother. I was not sure if she could understand me or him, but if this is truly what this spirit does, then I suppose that he knew what to do to reach the person. I had not been privy to this type of spirit in the past or at the very least. I was not aware of the ramifications of an entity that corrupted the natural order of a spirits evolution after the death of the physical body.

Now I was really frustrated. I thought I had seen most things, but I had just become aware of a whole new view of what can happen during the transition between life and death. I decided that evening to again confer with my spirits and pray for an answer to deal with this new issue. I was shown a different view than I had thought of before. There are souls that cause chaos in what is already an emotionally stressful moment, the moment of death. This type of spirit does nothing but take advantage of the soul's confusion to further draw it away from the path of enlightenment.

So back to this scenario: The mother was fearful of death as she was not sure what would be waiting if anything for her. I imagine she is not far from how most souls feel just before their time comes, and the anxiety of the moment can often create confusion. This is what these souls take advantage of. I told all this to the daughter, my client, and let her know I would be going back to the mother's room to further help her stay the course and accept that she will go to a good place, a place of light, freedom, love, and understanding. I revisited the room and spoke with her, or at her, not sure if she was really listening to my words, but I feel that even in a coma, the spirit will hear the words.

I tighten up the room, spiritually speaking, to try and prevent that spirit with an agenda from approaching the woman. Over the next few days I did not perceive this entity in the room although I'm sure that like a dog wanting a bone, he was not far away, and sooner or later, he would find a way back in to the room. After all there are only so many things

I could do in a place like this. I tried to summon the spirit guide and protectors of the woman. I figure that the more help I got for her, the better it would be and the safer I could make her.

The problem was that really her time had come and gone. It was only sheer will that was keeping the soul attached to her body. So help from the other side to keep her alive was not in the cards. I need to figure out how to get to her; otherwise this spirit would corrupt what would be a beautiful moment, and she will miss the boat as it were. I will continue to think while working on a solution maybe looking into this spirit and what it represents would be a better use of my time and maybe this will give me the answers I need.

I meditated and prayed that evening and was shown a whole new view on the moment of death, so it's not as easy as choice for the soul. There are relatives that often come and help the spirit transition. Death itself has a hand; the spirit guide and protectors can also help at the moment and prepare the soul for the change. These asshole souls that find some benefit toward increasing their ranks and at this point I'm open, who knows what else is out there interfering with this change.

I decided to dream on it and see if I got a clear picture on what my next step would be to help this lady make her change and help her go in the right direction. While I was asleep, I traveled to the location and was able to see the soul at rest inside the body and the spirit wanting to pervert the change just outside the door to the room. I approached it, and to my surprise, he was able to see me and interact with me. I asked it why any soul would willingly cause so much damage to their spirit as he was causing to his.

I was happy when I realized this spirit tried to recruit me to his side. He laid it out to me as he knew it. He told me that there are groups like his all over the world. I asked him to run by what benefit there would be for me to do what he did when I died. He interrupted and told me I could start right now just work for them. I ask who they are; he was a bit vague, but suffice it to say, there was a hierarchy to this organization, who was on top of this food chain he was not telling. Good thing about being alive my energy was high compared to dead souls and so I could definitely overpower him if things got ugly.

No such thing, he was very accommodating as he continued to explain that since they did not have so many rules as does the light side, I would be compensated in ways that on my current path would not happen. I asked him what ways. He told me that he would make something happen to me so I would realize that doing business with them could change my life if not more. He continued to say that if I did this for them when my time to go happened, I would have moved up in the organization and as a soul the benefits would be immense. I—not having the problem to be dead—had no problem in entering the room and was able to reach the woman. Although she was out, her soul was very much receptive to my input; who would have believed that all this was happening in the background of the real or living world?

I explained to her that her daughter was very concerned at how she was holding on and told her about the astral plane and how she would recover from any physical ailments from this life and as a free spirit it was her goal to go to God's side where the soul will remember all things from this and every other life. Where she will be shown why she choose this life and all the other people she choose to share it with. After some therapy, she seemed content to move on, and my out of body experience was done. I awoke in my own bed, and if what had happened was good, I should call my client to meet her at the mother's room and it should not be long before she passes.

I called the daughter and asked her to meet me at the mother's room. I told her what had happened at night, and if I got through to the mother, I expected her to pass very soon. We arrived almost at the same time and walked in together. As we were walking in to the room, the mother had her eyes open and she had a smile on her face. The daughter reached for her hand, and they held each other for a few moments and the mother at peace closed her eyes and died. It was a very interesting case where I learned that there is more to this death than what I thought.

I've often thought of the scenario that occurred and that spirit with an agenda. As of these writings, it has not happened again. I'm sure it happens more often than I can fathom; after all I'm one person in a small area of this big world, but at least I'm now aware and may be able to assist when it occurs again or at least keep an eye out. As I reflect back to other times where I've run into darkened spirits, I wonder if they started out like this woman and were seduced to roam with an agenda to corrupt other souls. All good questions, I'm sure with time, I will learn more of this, and I hope to be able to find the key that breaks the hold or the allure that draws so many souls to serve a master other than God's free will.

Some haunts are not of current times but often intrude on current time situations. This was the case in this situation I found myself in; I was called by a good client and asked me some questions as she was worried about a good friend. She gave me some details of things that were happening with the lady in question and asked me if those seemed to be typical in haunting. I explained that although one of the common things in haunting is a spirit, like there are many differences between people there are also with spirits, so yes there are some typical things but also huge differences. Everyone has wants or needs so do spirits. Remember a grounded spirit is nothing but a person without a body.

One of the not common things is for a spirit to follow the people from one place to another unless they are haunting the person and not the location. She had told me her friend had moved from place to place over the last two years, and the weirdness as she called it seemed to follow her. Even when her husband left her, it still seemed to follow her wherever she moved to. I told her to send her to me and I would see what I could do. I told her to have her friend call me to schedule a reading, or if she preferred to get right to it, a cleansing sounded more appropriate in this scenario.

A few days later the friend called, and she told me who she was and who recommended me. I made an appointment for her. I told her from what I was told a cleansing would probably be more appropriate than a reading. I explained that when I do a cleanse, I usually see what is going on, similar to a reading. So why waste time and money if cleanings was what she needed? She agreed and I gave her a date to come and see me.

She agreed, and then I changed my mind and told her it would be better if I visited where she lived. I explained how it's often better if I visit where the person lives. There might be other things that can lead me to a solution for the person.

She was waiting for me. As I was getting close, she called me and told me she had to leave. I said, "Wait, wait! What is going on?" She explained as she was getting in her car that as she was sitting watching TV waiting for me, the TV changed channels and the volume turned to the max and she got scared. I asked if anything else happened. She asked or yelled, "What else do you need?" Then she said all right. As she walked out the front door, the TV just turned off. She said forget it and hung up on me. I called the client who originally called me and explained what had just happened. I asked her to call her and try and get her to give this another chance. She agreed and hung up. The next call I got was from her, and she said her friend was very upset if I would give her some time she can calm her down. I told her to call me back and take her to her house and I would meet them there. She thought it was a great idea, so I asked her for the address. I never remember addresses, too many people, and I think it was over a year since I had given her a cleansing, maybe even did it at my place.

Finally she called back. She met her friend at a coffee shop, she calmed her down, and the friend agreed to go back to her house where I was to meet them. It really got interesting then. I got there before they did, and I could already feel the war drums beating. As I was summoning my spiritual support, I felt they knew it would be a difficult situation to overcome. I was getting ready to help this woman, and one of my spirits told me to make sure I gave myself an aura boost. I did one of the meditation exercises from my first book and I felt better.

As I opened my eyes, the ladies pulled in. I exited my car and greeted them. I have to tell you as I walked up to them, the new client had all around her a dark aura that moved as if it was alive and not of her own soul. As if without being possessed, she was being manipulated, whatever this was owned her body and soul. I greeted them, and we entered the home. It felt clean, so this is a plus. I would only be fighting one thing and not from two fronts. I asked the lady of the house if she could give me a deep pot for me to prepare a bath for the friend I was to clean. I started unloading the stuff I had brought from my home in the house, and the lady gave me a big cooking pot. I took out a mixture I had prepared earlier and poured it into the pot, filled the rest with water, and mixed it in good.

I made sure before I began that I had everything I was going to need for this cleanse. I told the lady to go into the bathroom and take off her clothing and pour all the contents of the pot over her body. She took it with her; I figure the softer I made her energies, the easier it would be to detach whatever had a hold on her. I told the friend whose home we were in that probably it would be better if she gave us some alone time maybe go to the market. She looked at me a bit concerned as I've cleaned her before and did not do half the things I was preparing to do to the friend.

As her friend walked out of the bath, the lady grabbed her purse and told her she would go to the market to pick up a few things but she and I should feel at home while she was gone. I thanked her and asked the friend to come outside with me. I prepared a cocktail of gunpowder, camphor, and sulfur and made some weird designs on the cement floor. I could tell she was curious, so I told her that these were specific signs asking for a resolution to her situation and a banishment of the intruder entities. I asked her to get in the middle of the circle and then I closed it off with the rest of the mixture. I began my chanting and lit the whole thing on fire. I told her she could move around in the circle but under no circumstances would she step out of it.

I saw her close her eyes as this big plume of smoke engulfed her. She was scared, but this needed to happen in order to release the hold on whatever this was. After she was done I asked her to come over to me. I gestured her to sit on a chair I had placed under a tree toward the back of the yard. She did, and I started to clean her with a cigar. I would speak to her to get her mind off what I was doing and also I had a small container burning incense burning under the chair toward the front or toward her feet. I was beginning to get to her and that stifling energy she was carrying with her. I poured from another container on the back of her neck another concoction I had prepared, and it was cold so she who had her eyes closed jumped from the chair.

I sat her back down and told her just as she was not expecting this neither was the bad energy. I told her this was all part of the plan to secure her energies were free of whatever this was. I continued to clean her with cigar, and I also cleaned her with some plants I had put together. I kept looking at her, and I knew that her demeanor and energies were getting better. She felt somehow softer and more open to whatever. I asked her that if she had gotten a headache. She told me that after the big gunpowder thing, she got a bad headache. I told her to close her eyes, and I took out of her that headache. She told me she felt better immediately.

I had asked her to take off her sandals for all this to connect her to nature from the bottoms of her feet, also had placed the branches I cleaned her with under her feet. She told me she felt better, asking me how much longer and if she could bathe after this event. I told her that a shower is just as essential as cleaning her energies. Remember if you stink, the least of your problems would be spiritual, so smelling good is always primary. By the time I was done, she felt like sleeping, so I told her enough and go home. I asked her to call me in the morning to let me know how she felt sleeping in her house.

Next day she called to let me know she had slept fifteen hours, something she had not done in over ten years, so I was pleased and believed the energy harming her was gone. She asked me if she could see me in another month for a follow-up cleanse. I told her that that sounded about right and waved good-bye to her. She was so excited that she kept repeating how good it feels doing God's work.

The Mother

I have a client that I've cleaned a few times. She asked me to go and see her mother at the home where she was at. It was a center or elderly living facility, very plush and comfortable place with a gated community type of place the mother had her own apartment with one-bedroom and bath. I was impressed by how well she lived and how clean everything was. After I arrived, the mother told me that the daughter had asked her to sit with me. She told me how the daughter had received help from me as her son-in-law had passed. I was able to communicate and give her daughter some closure and some personal messages as he had died rather unexpectedly.

After the introductions were made, I asked her about a bad toothache and she said that it was true that a crown she had was bothering and she had not even been able to eat from that side of her mouth. I told her about several other issues like the high blood pressure and asked why she was taking two medications for the same problem. She gave me some explanation. I did not understand and asked her to speak to her doctor about eliminating one of the two pills. I told her she felt very dehydrated, and I believed only one pill was necessary. I discussed several other health concerns and without any question from her expressed how she still had many years to go. She asked me if I was sure. Well, I said if you stand in front of a bus, you will die, but karma has her living many years at least another three to five. Considering she was eighty-nine that was indeed a long time.

A spirit arrived—female, older, and with the *initial c* in the first name. Remember I get names, but even if I get the name wrong, the first initial and the sex would be correct. So I told her a spirit that was a relative approached me and she said it was her mother. I told her how she wanted her to know how badly she felt her life with her had been without as much love as she should have given her. I saw several kids and she confirmed that the mother had if I remember six kids. Where are the two I asked; she told me that her mother had been married twice. I asked her about a spirit around her who showed her a ring and had not been dead even a year yet. She confirmed it was her ex-husband who had passed; she continued to tell me how he and she had been divorced many years. Also I asked her who the European spirit was. She could not remember but pointed out that her sister lived in Italy but was not dead. We continued with that sister it was later when I spoke with the daughter and my client that she confirmed that probably the European spirit was that of a man she was briefly with after divorcing her father.

I confirmed something that happened while I was with the mother that had me confused the spirit of her deceased father the mother's ex-husband told me he would be bringing her to the other side. I told her that I tried to convince the father that it was not his ex-wife's time and he was not thinking correctly. He expressed his dissatisfaction as he just wanted him to move on. Nothing I did or said could sway the spirit from his quest to help the ex-wife along to the other side. My client said, "Oh my god, this is my fault. I asked why she would think so. She said that often she would speak to her dad asking him to get her the mother in line or to give her some light as she was a lot of work and a very difficult person to get along with. She feels after what I said that the father could have gotten the wrong message and he might have thought the daughter asked him to take her into the light. I also told the daughter he felt betrayed by her. She said yes but was not willing to elaborate.

I told my client that a mass at her home for the father might do the trick, but before she should get three relatives who loved the father to do a church mass at three different churches. She agreed and we left it at that. We also agreed I would call the mother and give her a serious cleansing for that dark energy around her aura. I had discussed with the mother about my book and how I serve as a spiritual counselor or some people call me a life coach so she would be easy to convince to allow me to clean her energy. We scheduled the house mass for the following Wednesday, and I would call the mother Tuesday to coordinate the cleansing.

The day came, and I brought with me two other people to help me. It was my hope the father would make his presence known and answer the question of why he wanted to take his ex-wife and mother to the daughter with him. The two ladies started to do the house cleanse and then my client. I had been there before, so I wanted fresh eyes to see what there was to see. They were on target with what they were seeing; we sat at the table and started some prayer in order to set the ambiance for the deceased father to speak with us. As I started to concentrate, he made appearance through me and showed us how I had misunderstood what I had seen before at the mother's home.

He cleared up my misconception that it was he who wanted to take the mother's soul to heaven before her time. In fact what he showed was darkness attached to her that he was attempting to dislodge in order to free her from that burden. It was this darkness or dark soul that he was trying to take to heaven. He explained that he no longer had anything to do with her mother but her request asking him to help with the difficult mother that prompted him to go near her. Once there he realized that entity could be the cause of all the problems with the daughter and attempted to take it away. He was unable to succeed so with this new knowledge we would schedule a return visit to the mother and I would try and take out that spirit causing some difficulties.

I had a man call me and ask me for help. He explained that he had seen another like me in the past but no results after three attempts, so I was recommended as a person who could handle as he called it heavy stuff. I agreed to see him and scheduled an appointment. I told him to come in jeans and clothing. He would not mind if it got dirty or broken. He agreed, and on the day of the appointment, he got lost for over an hour could not find my home. I live in a very easy area to find, and there are some very well-known landmarks around the area. I told him as I was giving him further directions that this type of problem is common with people with bad energy, and the reason is usually barring them having poor directional skills that an entity would be disrupting their mind to prevent the help from arriving. Remember whatever was attached was comfortable doing their thing and did not want someone like me to disrupt or fix the problem being caused.

Finally after an hour and fifteen minutes, the person arrived all frustrated. Once he arrived he stated he had passed by the entrance several times and just did not see it. I gave him some water, and we walked out back to start. To say the least he was right it was a difficult situation. This is a person, well, a nurse, who in the last year had lost two jobs and been arrested. Part of the problem he had court in two weeks, so we had plenty to do on this day. After taking off the primary spirit causing the problems, I did a spell, so court would go well for him. Then I told him about some probiotics, and he had to megadose with them for about a month then tone it down to what the bottle said. Two pills with each meal, and he was to eat three meals a day. I explained there had been some physical damage done to the digestive tract and this would put things back in good working order.

I told him he would be feeling better right away but he was to return in a month for a follow up as this was very strong energy and I wanted to make sure it did not return. I was sure it would not but just for good measure. After all in a year he even lost his home so this damage was horrible and I wanted his true path to reassert itself so we finished the cleaning and I walked him back to the car. He called the next day, just to tell me that it had been the first good night sleep he had in over three months and he was grateful. I reminded him of the probiotics and some other thing I had told him to do.

I had to do a very different type of cleaning; the attachment was at the chakra point of the body, so I had to pull this attachment out with some cups and a bottle. The spell itself was not so complicated. I just don't do it very often. The person was going through a very bad depression, and the attachment was not letting go through the traditional or more common ways. Some of these entities are very smart, and this one had figured out we could not easily unhook it from the chakra point of the body. So I used a technique similar to the ancient Chinese acupuncturist but with a spiritual twist. I lined up some wide mouth cups and placed them along the area of the attachment. I placed a dollar coin and a cotton ball wet with regular rubbing alcohol. Lit the cotton on fire and place the wide mouth glass over it to cover it and attached to the body. As the flame extinguished, the vacuum created sucked the skin into the cup; half of the cup was filled with flesh. The person got a bit nervous, but I quickly calmed her down, I explained that this process would release the area of the attachment and she would soon feel better.

I was done fifteen minutes later and finished cleaning her with other more traditional methods in her case a big napkin was used to clean off her aura of any residual effects from this entity. She left already feeling better, but it was the next day when she called me that I was sure the detachment had occurred and it was a success. She called to tell me she got up from a full night sleep and cleaned the entire house. Something she had not done in over three months. She could not stop talking about the change and how something like that could have been the cause of her depression. I told her that my feelings are a good percentage of people's problems are related to attachments or negative energy so if we work on our energy more regularly, perhaps people would not have to come and see me as often. I recommended she purchase my book, *Life and Beyond*, or this one when it comes out as they would offer many recipes for maintenance and prevention of this energy from ever attaching. She agreed and said she would order the kindle version as she loved that type of media.

Chapter 5

Solutions to Most Situations

I don't care what the problem is; as long as we live, there is a way to resolve any problem. When I say resolve, it might not be what you think of as a resolution, so let's clarify. If you get fired, I might not be able to get your job back; however, a new start some other place is definitely possible. If you read my previous book, you saw so many examples of situations where people without jobs often for years resolved the problem often in less than a month.

Thinking outside the confines of a box is what most people need to learn. Come on, be realistic. If a company closes the doors, you must look elsewhere for a new job. If a relationship ends, I can help get it back on track if that is the best for your life path. More often than not all you are is hurt because they cut you lose. Look at the big picture, and let's work on opening new doors to better relationships. I can guarantee there is someone out there for each of us. I've heard about the other half and many other ways to describe that special someone out there for each of us. I hate to break it to you there is many possible partners with successful outcomes out there for each of us.

Keep an open mind, and any magic we do together will have a much more satisfactory outcome. If you come to me for an impossible relationship, there is no such thing. However if that person you yearn for is in a committed relationship that is not an impossible relationship that is bad karma for you, and I will not be part of it. If on the other hand your husband or wife was taken from you by a younger or more successful con person, then come and talk to me. If it's in your destiny to get them back, I will make it happen for you. Even then, nothing is necessarily for the best. Even and if your time with your spouse ran its course and you have been given a way out to start a new adventure in life, I will also let you know what is coming is better.

With the first book I wrote, *Life and Beyond*, I gave detailed basic information on how to grow spiritually and then some practical application on the matter. In this book I would like to take it a step forward and put together all the things I separately taught in *Life and Beyond*. Let's consider you did all the meditation and spiritual development instruction I gave in the book and now are mature and ready for the next steps in your spiritual evolution. If not I would highly recommend to go back and read it and practice all the instruction before proceeding to the advanced lessons in this book.

Let's begin. There are only finite areas where we as humans need advancement or an edge. One that is without doubt is health. This area will become more important once there are any health issues. So we can work on this area by preventing health issues in our lives. Let's talk about different things that can be done to keep us tip top. I'm of the belief that if we are healthy of mind, then the body will be healthier than if we are going through emotional issues. Most health issues that people get are directly or indirectly caused by emotional turmoil. The second is hereditary. Those are also areas we can work with. Again if all else is good, then keeping up with health is not difficult at all, even hereditary diseases.

Stay fit physically—good weight. Cardiovascular health is very important for any age group, so if we are physically healthy, our spiritual development will also be easier as the spirit will work within the confines of the health of the individual. In other words if you are not healthy, then the spirit will only go so far. I can give you a personal example: a good friend of mine Elsa; she is a fantastic psychic and spiritual counselor. When I first met her, she had just got the onset of diabetes. All her life, she had the gift and never needed to do card readings to divinize. After a few years, she could no longer do the reading without cards. It was just too hard on the body.

It's like any other muscle. If you are not good physically, the sport you practice will suffer to some degree. She can still do readings, and her information is good, but that direct connection throughout the reading is too exhausting for her. I myself can do readings with or without the cards. I've learned to divinize with different spirits, and some just talk to me and others work within the confines of the cards I use. If you look below are a couple of examples of my cards. I'm proud to say they are not common, and the entire deck is only thirty-six cards unlike most of the common tarot or the Spanish cards or many others that have many more cards in the deck.

Cards:

Rider, Clover, Ship, House, Tree, Clouds, Snake, Coffin, Flowers, Scythe, Whip, Bird, Child, Fox, Bear, Star, Stork, Dog, Tower, Garden, Mountain, Road, Mouse, Heart, Ring, Book, Letter, Man, Woman, Lily, Sun, Moon, Key, Fish, Anchor, Cross

Above are names of some of the cards that I use. The back design of these cards depicts each of the cards in the deck; I hope you see what a friendly bunch I work with. The original deck was used in the nineteenth century, and among the people I read with was Napoleon. So I hope to continue to give this beautiful deck with its illustrious past justice.

So remember that with mental activity comes the need to stay fit. I make an effort to work out at least three days a week. I'm fortunate my wife likes to exercise, just another activity for us to do things together. I do more lifting than cardio but a good balance I think. I definitely do not want to get to a time where health issues prevent from giving my clients 110 percent each and every time they need my services. For me it's all about being of help and making a difference as some of my clients say I'm a warrior for God. So if I am to war against negative forces, my body must be fit to trance all the energy necessary to triumph. We are the vessels that all energy must pass through in order to manifest. Energy from other realms needs a host to manifest. The better the vessel, the better the manifestation.

In order to channel we must be in touch with our body, release control to other worldly thoughts that touch our minds. Remember, with control we can curve how much we allow the spirits to channel. Over the years when I've been sick and needed to work, the spirit would come close and even channel completely, and during those couple of hours, I did not feel any of my physical maladies—a bad cold, fever, aches, and pains all go away. I would complain if they can do this temporarily why not completely. They explained that going through these things was part of the human condition. I can, however, help others with many other sickness or maladies or even diseases.

There have been times where I've needed to clean a client that had problems in a relationship and as a side-effect clean their lungs from bronchitis. I've been able to get rid of migraines for others and many other maladies clients have been suffering from. Imagine if you have a headache and I placed slices of potato all around your head, forehead, and temples; and within minutes, the headache leaves you. Often I've grabbed some tap water in a cup and placed my hand over it and pray to the water to energize it, asked the client to drink it, and a fever leaves them. Or they had problems with a sore throat, and immediately, if not within hours, the sore throat leaves them.

Within each of us is unharnessed—the potential to tap into universal energy. This energy has been here since the beginning of time and will be here long after we are gone from this existence. So tapping it is a big plus. How? By sheer willpower. We have inside us a sleeper that needs to awaken. How? By activating parts of the brain that are now dormant. Belief is essential to manifesting and summoning up these powers. Yes, powers that are at our disposal.

Think back how often you have been so excited, and there was an adrenalin flow that gave you that elated feeling—a feeling you would have liked to harness again and again but were unsuccessful in every attempt. Proper use of the brain and body can allow this to happen over and over. It's just the beginning to opening doors to other worldly energies. Once you learn to call on these extra powers in your body, by activation of the adrenalin flow, the flow that only happens in extreme distress or emotional elation. Then and only then can you begin to take the steps necessary to tapping into those universal energies all around us.

Let's begin: calling on that adrenalin flow is as simple as imagination. Since you have practiced all my exercises from my first book, you are practiced on visualization and meditation techniques. Now we must take it to the next level by invocating those energies. Visualize yourself in a circle, then a bubble, a golden bubble. Once there, create a protective flow of energy, so only what you want will enter. Remember once you open doors, they swing both ways, and you don't always know what is on the other side.

Do your prayers and celebrate life. Celebrate the universe and all its mysteries as just doors ready to be opened. Emotional maturity is essential to develop spiritually. We must be responsible for our actions and how our actions affect others. Let's flow, go, and reach our goals and exceed them by tapping into the knowledge of the universe. That divine knowledge that through the ages a select few has been able to tap into and grow exponentially.

As we start the exercises, we must leap beyond what is and embrace what was, is, and will be as in the here and now. What does this mean? Forget time and understand that all that was, is, and will be has already occurred; and we can veer through that veneer to see the answers. Here is the trick; once we see the most prevalent outcome of any situation, we can change it if we choose. With the emotional maturity we spoke of earlier is how we judge what should be changed and what will affect an entire time line if we do.

I like or enjoy giving out remedies from the typical home. Why? Simply because there is a better chance you will do it if it's already there. The bottom line of my remedies is to help others. Yes, in spite of themselves and their narrow views of life in general. Believe me if life squeezes you enough, you will reach for all sorts of things to get help, so why not simple effective solutions? In the past I've spoken of baking soda. It's a good cleanser. You can get a plastic container and add a couple of cup full of let's say arm and hammer baking soda. Fill with some water and mix until you get a nice paste solution, then you get in your shower, and normal shower will do. Without getting dried off, just bring in the past and defoliate the entire body from head to toe. After you have thoroughly done this, just turn on the shower and wash it off. How many of us have had or suffer from acid indigestion. Just add one-half tablespoonful into an 8 oz. glass of water. Drink it and it will at the very least neutralize that excess acid. Why don't the companies advertise this? You guessed it, no money to be made. Hey, just try it. I believe you will find it rewarding.

Take a glass of water and add to large tablespoonful and mix and then gargle. It will ease throat or mouth discomfort. Feel that carpet is a bit musty, just sprinkle all over the carpet and leave on for at least a day or two. When you vacuum it out, you will find some of the odor if not all will be gone. Drinking is no less effective but in much smaller doses. I say one-fourth teaspoon in an 8 oz. glass of water just before bed, and it will level out any acidic tendencies your body might have. In the paste form above, you may even try it for rashes or any other skin irritation. Look it's not for everyone, but my results have proven it to be an inexpensive solution, readily available to all.

I want you to recall one of my favorite baths to do: the apple cider vinegar. Spoke of it in my first book and briefly in this one, but did you know that apple cider vinegar is also good for what ails you from the inside out? For example, I like to offer this simple but very effective remedy that might better if not cure a number of maladies. Each and every morning, you may take a glass of warm water or hot, your preference and add a big tablespoonful of pure apple cider vinegar. Drink it. It will do the body good. You may also do the same in the evening before bed. Let's cover some of the things that it can help—digestive tract issues, allergies, arthritis. Women have told me they add a bit to their hair to add shine, and I'm sure many other things I have not covered. If you are truly interested, I'm sure you can go on the web and do a search, it's truly a wonder. Oh yeah, I almost forgot. As a kid I was told to put it on bites, mosquito, ant, bee stings, etc.; and it will ease the pain of the bite. I've had several clients that had cancer; I recommend a cocktail that neutralizes the acid in the body, this helping neutralize the body thus making the environment for the cancer to flourish not so comfortable. Here is the simple home recipe: Again 8 oz. glass of water one-quarter teaspoonful of baking soda, a green lime but only after it has turned mostly yellow. Mix well. Remember if you have low blood pressure, monitor as lemons can lower it as well. Then a daily dose of vitamin c, take four 500 milligram pills throughout the day. Take the drink: one in the morning and one in the evening.

There are many natural cures as I have discussed not only for spiritual reasons like lemons. I briefly covered how to do a cleansing with lemons in a previous chapter. Did you know you can use them for many other things? If you mix baking soda and lemons together, they can definitely clean most of your plastic containers of any stuck on stuff. They are so acidy that you can kill germs with them. If you use them on fruits, you can keep them from getting that brown color longer. If you drink one lemon in the morning, preferably before breakfast and wait at least thirty minutes before drinking or eating anything else, you may not only have most of your vitamin c but also burn fat. Have some common sense. Remember it tends to be acidic, so if you are going to include milk, don't drink a lemon on that day as it my ruin your milk. Don't get rid of your lemons after use, stick them at the bottoms of your garbage area, like in the bathrooms or the kitchens. It will deodorize bad odors. Squeeze lemons into most things; it will serve as an antioxidant, like tea. Add lemon juice to it, and it will increase its antioxidant properties.

Earlier I spoke about a body cleanse with lemons. If you are going to take a shower, take at least three cut lemons and scrub your entire scalp with them. Apart from cleaning off dandruff, it will make your hair shiny and cleanse any spiritual negative energy you might have as an attachment. Then do your regular shower, not forgetting to wash your hair normally. It usually won't take long for the lemon to have its effect, so do the lemon on the head. Wash the body then wash the hair normally; by then, the lemon did its work. That is how strong lemons are. Want another cleanse? On a plastic container add salt, any type will do, then add or squeeze five lemons into that container, mix well, and scrub the body. The results are marvelous. Don't forget as always to wash off because it is so strong it could cause a rash if left on for too long a period. Have some common sense. If you are allergic to any of the things I speak of in this book, don't use it. I know I've said what an acidic thing lemons can be, but if you get one that is very ripe and add it to some hot or warm water like tea, it might just help you with some digestive issues. In other words, flush your body of extra acid or even constipation.

I'm often asked how I do the medical stuff. I tell them as with everything there is a beginning. I have with me a spirit that gives me medical information, so this is an important aid. With this I can tell you that most people can become medically intuitive. It's an exercise like any other. I would remind you what I've stated before we can all walk and run but not at the same pace or speed. What I mean is some people are very fast and very good at what they do, so it is with this. Here I will outline some of the exercises I did to start my ability. I would always ask for the person's name and date of birth, and then I would separate myself and create a blank canvas, like an x-ray machine. I have a couple of people I've help developed because of their memories; they like the machine to look gray or dark and for the areas of problem to highlight as darker. Remember it's all about you, so use the technique that is easiest for you to visualize. I simply serve as a guide, a spark of an idea or direction.

So on with the lesson. Say the name and birthday of the person out loud or in your mind to bring in the picture of the person. After you get an outline or silhouette, start filling in the areas of problem or organs that need your attention. Don't analyze all; this should happen in seconds. If you use your reasoning mind, you will blow the whole thing. It's all about allowing your extrasensory perception to kick in, and it does not work if you analyze. If you analyze, go to medical school and become a doctor. This is about tapping into that information the universes puts out and allowing it into your mind and field of perception.

I like to scan from top to bottom and then back up; however, at this time, I just kind of see a picture, and automatically it fills in the areas of problem. In the first book I discuss how to read the aura and perceive color and a little on chakras, so if you have not read, I suggest you do as I do not want to be repetitive. The objective is for you to visualize areas of the body that need work or have deficiencies. You can see everything in your inner eye, so do not think limits. They are only imposed by your own limitations. Do they really exist, or have you imposed them upon yourself. Fly as high as you want and look down, and you will see the earth. Look around and you can see the universe; it is this mind-set that will separate you from those who analyze everything and thus allow you to see the truth that is already out there for all that can tap into it. Once you get good, you may do this with a picture of the person or ask questions. The key is for you to make sure of what you see before passing the information. If you have no doubt, you will always see the truth. Doubt is the killer of perception. Your first would be your best view. Once you let in your subconscious, you can be sure the information will be skewed.

Karma Dilemma

To affect an entire time line we affect the lives of many, not just us or for our benefit, you must consider the ripple effect that changes can cause, so your decision must be based on the common good and not just yours. Let's take an example. A few years ago I was asked to help a guilty man from his sentence. The person had been found guilty, and the prosecutor wanted the maximum sentence of thirty years. I was moved by the daughter's request and love for her father. I asked her how she planned to get the case overturned. She said the attorney had been asking for a thirty-day extension to do some research and statements from New York City. Remember I live in Miami and the case in question was from here.

After looking into the possible outcomes, I saw that he would be freed earlier than she thought; however, it was not my call to make, and I told her I would help her get the extra time for the attorney. Within a few days, the judge's chambers reached out to the attorney and asked for two months since they apparently could not find the case file on the girl's father. I simply made it temporarily invisible to all eyes, but it was still there. After the time, the mitigating circumstances the attorney looked for were found and the sentence was much, much lighter, enough so that the father has long since been released.

Imagine a second set of possibilities. It was a drug case if I had not mentioned it. The father was a very powerful person in that world, a world that the daughter had nothing to do with. In this scenario, his release would have caused him to grow and kill or destroy the lives of hundreds if not thousands. This is the emotional maturity I spoke of, and it is one of the things you will have to deal with as you explore and gain a measure of control over these powers. This time it was a clear-cut answer, and how about the next when you have a vested interest in the outcome? Can you truly stay detached and make your decisions based on the greater good?

Unfortunately humanity is not ready, and most would simply abuse the information for their benefit. Many years ago I had to make a decision where my information could save a life or allow nature to take its course and by that route prevent later in life bad things from happening. It was a case where the woman was pregnant and could come with some defects the baby that is. After her reading, she asked if I could do something to help or she would have to have an abortion, an abortion that she did not want to have.

She was with a man whom she loved, and her religious beliefs would be in question if she had the abortion. I looked and believed that while the baby was a fetus, I can in fact change some of the DNA and help the possibly deformed child fix itself from the womb. I was also shown that the child in the future would become a criminal and cause great harm to many people. That scenario still haunts me to date. I choose to help the woman, and the baby was born, a baby boy as predicted in my vision. I never told the woman of this premonition, but I believed and still believe today I can change that. I've kept counseling her over the years and believe to be guiding her to prevent that forecasted future.

It's still a possibility, but with every year that passes, I can see that the solid future is becoming less of a certainty. I clean her at least once a year and read her probably twice a year, plenty of times to keep me in the loop of the child and thus enhancing my opportunities to change that premonition. It was the child's strongest possibilities if born but since subsequent energy work has been done to change that future. I feel another two or three years, and even before the child becomes ten years of age, I can eliminate that once concrete future. As I said, all these years it's haunted me, my decision to intervene for the love of a mother.

I hope with time, he grows to be a good person and prominent addition to the community. Time will tell, and every time she calls, I'm reminded of that moment, thus making every other decision I've made since much more cautious. The attitude I took was not cavalier, but I felt for an individual and did not pay heed to the future of the many. I've struggled with this and still do; fortunately it has tempered me and my subsequent decisions in other circumstances. I've always decided on the side of caution as I like to sleep at night and still make decisions, but I have without exception sided on the cautious side of life.

I have never told that mother about all this, and it is my hope that she someday can purchase the book and read these words. Then she will understand why all these years I've tried to guide her toward all the cleansings she has done for her son and why I always tell her to try and keep him free of negative people and situations in his young life. I still feel responsible for that possible outcome. It is no longer the only or even the strongest future for the kid, but it is still there. My hopes are that with time together, we will be able to completely take that window of possibility from the big picture of his life.

My visions of the future are always shown to me in terms of the strongest windows of possibilities; I believe we have multiple destinies, not just one. With every move we make we can make slight modifications, but the big picture stays on track; in other words, if a person was supposed to wear the uniform of a military man, we can change his education even his major but destiny will have and imposes all possible outcomes geared toward the predestined.

Over the years many have asked me about karma, so with this story I just told you, I can confirm that the overall determining force of life is what the spirit chooses to come and do on this world. In the cases of a person that came to suffer, no matter what the family does, that destiny will attempt to be fulfilled. So it is with a child who continues to go into a bad path, in spite of the great upbringing and advice, what was written will try to fulfill itself. I believe that knowledge is power, so if I or someone else can see a future filled with problems, energy can be thrown at this destiny in attempts to change it.

Everything can be changed. With time and constant effort, most things can be changed or, at the very least, softened. So in the case of someone who is supposed to die from a sickness, if within time or early enough the manipulation can often soften that sickness or that negative or dark path that the soul was destined to bear. It's not easy to change and not always successful even with ample time. Many things come into play when this is attempted. Faith, consistency, environment, love, and many other factors can affect the outcome. I tell some of my clients that have children, and they come out so different that their part affects only so far as their path goes.

For example I have a woman who has three children. They were all reared in a happy home with father and mother. They were given every chance to go on and become well balanced and successful members of society, yet one died in a traffic accident and the other two are in jail. I told her that we would have to do separate readings to look into each of the karmas of the children and what I described was how each life had gone. It was not any fault from the family but the path chosen by the souls that caused their lives to go wrong.

In the case of her friend and the person who recommended me to her, she got a reading many years before, and it came up that the middle daughter would or could get pregnant early; I believe I gave her an age of sixteen. She took action and changed that destiny. The time came and she saw it moving into the direction I had foretold, so she worked and worked some through magic some through circumstances and the time where she was to get pregnant passed and so that path of life was avoided. I had also told her that the eldest was to get into a car accident that could cause him to break some bones. I told her that the accident was to happen on the summer of his twenty-first birthday. It was partially because it happened as I had foretold that she took action with the girls and prevented that path for her.

There are many ways to change things. Mostly I'm of the mind that through energy work, we can soften most things if not eliminate them all together. I give many remedies and most are simple. Some are to bring positive things into our lives, and some are to clear negative energy and divert strong negative influences from affecting our life path. If you take the time to read this book in detail as the first book, there are many types of ways you can change destiny. Remember, most is really not changing destiny; most is simply to bring life to the positive extreme or away from the most negative side. They are after all two sides of the same coin. You can either let the toss of the coin choose or take action and do your best to move destiny to the best side.

My favorite place for a cleansing is the ocean or water in a general sense. I've cleansed my energy in the ocean, rivers, lakes, well water, any place that water runs is good for me. That is not to say it works the same for all. Of all the places I do cleansings for others, only the ocean do I partake with the client as this is such a great place for my energies to release and replenish. So it is with energy, so make sure if you choose to do cleansings on your own, what you choose will actually be good for you. In my first book, I teach some techniques on divination with coconuts. The reality is you can use anything; for example, take four quarters or four fifty-cent pieces or even a dollar coin. Make sure you clean them of extraneous energies by just placing them in your hand and put your hand under running water.

After you cleansed the coins, you bring them close to your lips and say, With these coins, I as for the truth, so I do not want a truth from a lie or a lie from a truth, give me your answer to my question, a truthful answer and nothing else." Cup your hands together and ask your question; shake them over your head and drop them. Look to see how they fell.

If two coins show head, it's yes to your question.
If four coins show head, it's yes to your question.

If three coins show head, then the answer is maybe. Ask again and only
accept two or four head as an answer.
If you get three showing tail, it's no to your question.
If you get four showing tail, the answer is no to your question.

In a pinch or a quickie as I like to call it, anything can work if you
just prepare it or endow it with the right energy. So remember, anything
is possible. Look for solutions to your problems. The tools are all around
you. I've done some weird spells over the years. One of the ones I've
done many times is one of the weirdest ones. I first saw the spell done by
a friend, and one of my spirits told me it's a good spell. Learn it and use
it and gave me some modifications for my personal use and to help my
own clients.

You never know where you might find a nugget, so I worked it and
I have given it to many clients over the years. It's a simple spell. I had
once a client who the son left the mother and had not reached out to her
in several years. I told her the spell to do, and in less than six months,
the son started to call her until they reunited. So from years of nothing,
within six months, the son had returned to the mother, and the family
had reunited.

Now for the spell, get yourself a nice big green papaya. Place it
sideways like a boat, slice it lengthwise, so one side is bigger but you can
get into its center. Clear all the seeds or a good amount at least, and then
get a photocopy of the picture the person you want to work on. I like to
clear the seeds as I do a very similar spell with the seeds to help a person
get pregnant, but that is for another story. Remember make the copy
black-and-white, the less chemicals the better. So once you cut out the
picture, place face up inside the papaya and bring it close and peel inside
until you cover the picture. Recover the top of the papaya and wrap it
with a yellow ribbon. Place it in a shoe box and cover it. Keep it until it
rots. You may place it outside or any place hot, so it rots quicker. When it
finally does, take it to running water like a river or canal. Open the box,
and empty the rotten contents into the running water.

This spell is supposed to clear the way between two people; so if there is something in the way—pride, magic, envy, and jealousy—whatever it will, clear the way for two people to continue. Remember it will work if it's supposed to be, if not it will do nothing. So don't do it just because you know it, don't abuse magic. Use it wisely. Remember there are always consequences once we step outside the natural order of destiny.

If you are into writing, this might be a good one for you. Buy a nice watermelon and take it home. Wash it and use your hands. Your wish is important, so as you wash it, you are cleaning it of any other energy. Cut a hole from the top of the watermelon, three inches wide, like you are making a circle. Take that top off and carve the inside to at least four inches deep. Take a brown paper, like the kind they would give you at a corner store or a gas station to hold a beer. Anyway get a brown paper bag and tear it open. The idea is you will write on this paper with pencil, your letter to the universe. Be truthful for your wish to come true, don't write nonsense or that is all you will get.

After you wrote your letter, fold it up and place it inside the watermelon inside the whole you carved up, and then add some honey over the paper and close it back up with the top you had cut earlier. Get a blue ribbon or any blue cloth and wrap the watermelon up so as to make sure that top did not fall off. Take it to the ocean and place it on the water and say, "As I have written my request inside this watermelon that I offer to this ocean, may it be well received and my request be answered." I have faith in the grandeur of the ocean and all its wonders. May I see the answer and my faith validated? Look I give you some guidance. Once you embark on these types of spells, you are in the control seat. Say what you want as it pertains to what you wrote and requested.

This has no limitations, so if your wish is well received, you will get back a reply in the form of result based on what you asked for in the enclosed letter. I like the closer to nature, so brown paper and pencil is closer than white paper and pen or computer printout. The more you put into your request, the more likely it will be that you get the answer you wanted. Over the years of giving this recipe, I've heard the results and oftentimes within days. I recently had a client who was told they would be fired and the family only had him as the source of income.

I told him to do this spell. They had called on Friday, and they did it that same evening. The meeting was on Tuesday, and the answer came in the form of a reversal from the owner of the company. He point-blank told my client that he had the weekend to sleep on his decision and after mulling it over decided his service to the company was of sufficient value and would look for cost cutting in other areas. He called right away and thanked me; he told me that the watermelon was so simple, why other people did not know of this wonderful thing. I explained that I was told to give him that recipe, but all things are not for everyone. What had worked with him might not be the right recipe.

I like fruit cleansings. For someone who has had much mental anguish or torments, I would recommend a cleansing with pears. You know if you have eaten them, they are generally hard, so make sure yours are soft before you attempt this. You can buy sixteen pears but leave them in the trunk of the car. This can accelerate their softening, it does for me. So anyway you let it get soft, and then you go to the ocean and sit by the edge of the water, crush each of the pears on the head. As you do, cleanse the rest of the body as you rub it from head to toe. Do the same for each of the pears until all sixteen are used. Once done just get into the ocean and wash all the pears from your body. It's fantastic to clear turbulent mental energies from you; I'm sure once you try, you will soon see the difference.

This is a prayer that I like to do every once in a while. Let's take a week and say it out loud every day twice a day. My preference is in the morning before I start any activities and then as the day progresses at any time I find a free moment. Always ask God to illuminate your thought before you start so as to have the best chance to be well received.

This is a prayer to the Saint of Faraway (Alejo)

Oh, my glorious Saint Alejo, you who have the power to remove all the evil that surrounds the chosen of the Lord. Remove all evil from my surrounding. I ask that far from me you place my enemies. Keep me away from Satan, liars, accidents, and sorcery, also from sin; and finally, Saint Alejo, keep me safe and away from those who come to me to hurt me or to cause me any harm. Put me so far from the wicked so as they will never see me. So mote it be!

Saint Alejo, you that keep away bad thoughts from mortals, keep away those bad thoughts from me, and the fools that would come to do me harm, bring me close to the Lord so that with his divine grace he might cover me with all his divine good, reserve for me a seat in the shade of the Holy Spirit. In the name of God, so mote it be!

It's a cool prayer, and you will find that most of the little inconveniences and obstacles that might be going on around you will subside or altogether disappears. I suggest you do it repeatedly three times every day for seven days and then you can just give it three to six months depending on how turbulent your life is and do it again for seven days. When you read it, do it consecutively three times, any time of the day or night is fine. For my taste I like to do it in the morning before I leave my home or drive anywhere. This is just my preference. For example, my wife likes to do it in the evening before she goes to sleep.

Easy Fixes

I like to find quick solutions when the energies go out of whack, so in this chapter, I will give you many home-type remedies not only for immediate fixes but some permanent solutions to protect yourself your home and prepare for the next time it's needed. Some you can make ready and will last until you need it next time. Let's do some prep work. So get fire water; aguardiente is the Latin name for sugarcane liquor. Get the strongest that would be 150 percent proof. The stronger the liquor the better. If you can't find my favorite, any will do. Again just make sure it's strong like rum for example.

So you got the hard liquor, next add dried star anise. You can find in most supermarkets in the area where you can find the cinnamon sticks. Place at least nine in the liquor. It does not matter if the mouth is small, you have to break it to get it inside. You must leave for at least five days before you use. Remember it has to give its essence to the liquor. It's very concentrated, so if you pour a small amount into say an empty Coke bottle like a two litter, the amount you put of this mix into the bottle is like one eighth of the bottle filled. The rest is just plain water. You can pour after a shower from the head on down then dry off or just at any time you need pour down the head and dry off.

If you are planning to move into a new home, you can do this simple ritual. Create a mix of brown granulated sugar, salt, and rice. Then walk the home on the outside; as you exit the front door, you start toward the left. As you sprinkle against the wall of the house all around the home until you get all the way to the front door, remember throw the handful at the wall near the base of the home. Say the salt is to cure any negative energy in the home. May hostility leave the home for ver. The sugar is to sweeten the home; may it bring love and good thoughts to our lives. Finally the rice is to open the home for chairing the gift of abundance to receive with grace all the good wishes and harmony in our new home.

Then you are to go inside, and at the doorway of each room, take a handful of this mix and toss it inside each room of the home repeating the statement above. As you finish and are walking out the front door, you may throw out the front door the remainder of the mixture. Remember most of the house cleansings rituals will work best in done before you move in to the home or apartment.

You may find your natural colors as described through astrology or Chinese astrology. Each science has its own way to divinize these colors that would be good energy for you. There is nothing you cannot change, so as you develop, you can prefer a color and indeed make it your favorite outside of the once these two ways of looking at life might determine for you.

There are many ways to protect our homes. An alarm is a good one against thieves. What about a spiritual assault? These can happen more often than a thief, so why not learn a couple of techniques to block it from your personal space? You can get red devil brand lye or pot ash. It comes in a can and you can make holes on the top, plenty of them, then dig four holes one at each corner of your home on the outside. Once you dug the holes, you may place each of the cans inside the holes. Let's continue. Cover each hole after you drop the can opened side down, and that is all you have to do to keep the home safe from that jealousy, or envy, or just plain not liking you or another family member.

You can place in the front or rear of the yard; this is a windmill that with air can move energy. Try and make it red and white, so as it increases in speed, its energy will help propel that negative energy elsewhere. Consider this windmill an air protection, so on windy days, you will get more of it than on days of no wind. Hey, nothing is constant; all we are looking for is that always something is going on. Remember you can clean with just about anything, so as you leave the house, get an apple and pass it around your body, back of neck chest, face, arms, and legs then just toss it out the window toward any corner you pass by. Try and never leave things you clean yourself with close to home unless told to do so. It's always better if this energy is dispersed away from the home.

Salt can be used for good or bad. I like good as bad always has a possible rebound effect. So let's talk about the good effects of salt and how to prepare it. I like to use a white candle, soak it with olive oil, and a little salt. Rub your hands on the candle and infuse the wish or desire on it. Get a white bowl and fill bowl with salt. Place the candle in the center of a white bowl. As you light the candle, ask as the candle's energy burns may it infuse onto it the power to "repeat your wish or desire that you infused upon the candle as you rubbed it" and then use it appropriately. You can use this empowered salt over and over until it runs out. The good thing about this is you can empower the salt for just about anything you want it to do for you. The more pure the oil you use, the better, and with this exercise instead of salt, you may use brown granulated sugar or even cinnamon powder. Look, it's all about intent. When you find something that you have an affinity with, this is often more potent than any standard I could write. I feel no one wants things to work more than the person in need, so if you believe in the effects of cinnamon, then by all means use it.

Chapter 6

Eastern and Western Signs Astrology

The Stars

Feng Shui   **Yin / Jang**

The Twelve Signs

RAT OX TIGER RABBIT DRAGON SNAKE HORSE SHEEP MONKEY ROOSTER DOG PIG

Again in this book, I would like to cover a bit on oriental astrology. In my first book, I spoke about feng shui in some detail. In this one, I would like to use the astrological equivalent of our own. It's largely based on the moon and its cycles. Don't get me wrong. It uses the heavens, but the moon has a much more profound impact than anyone other than the heavenly body. For example this study uses the year, month, and day, not to mention the time of birth much as our own astrology.

They use the year as the dominant sign. Combined with the animal and the element, it gives a very accurate description of the individual. The month of birth speaks of intimate relationships; it is also the ascendant sign, the animal ruling the month. The ascendant sign animal ruling the time of birth describes the person on how he or she sees her or his self and relates inwardly, and it is said it can either enhance or subdue the dominant sign in the astrological chart. You must remember something about the oriental astrological chart. It's not based on our month, and rather it's based on the moon's cycle, so the month can start on a totally different day than ours.

Oriental astrology has their own belief system; for example, soul mates, does not have to be related to love exclusively. It could be best friend, parent, sibling, child—whatever the relationship that is supposed to support or follow from a previous life. Karmic combatants, does not mean they are coming together in this life to fight but to make better what they were unable to do in that previous life.

There are equivalents as are in many things, so it is with these two types of astrology. I will below give you some examples of one animal sign in Chinese astrology that might be similar in our western astrology: Aries and dragon, Taurus and snake, Gemini and horse, Cancer and sheep, Leo and monkey, Virgo and rooster, Libra and dog, Scorpio and pig, Sagittarius and rat. I like before making assumptions when doing a reading to find three signs in common before I say this is true or that is not.

What I mean by this is as above the Libra sign and the dog sign might have similarities; however, before I say they would be a good match, I would find at least two other good matches to say yes or no. I go to this because I do many reading that in part I'm asked about a relationship and if I see it's a good one or not. I don't just answer yes or no. I try to quantify my answer and explain why. Again using as an example, the Libra sign and the dog, let's say one has in its month the animal horse and the other the goat. In the area of soul mates, the goat is the soul mate of the horse. Before I move on, I remembered someone asked me today about broken things. I said get rid of them; no matter what they are, they took an energy hit on your behalf, and fixing them is not an option.

Are you getting the idea? I would still like to find one in another, so in this case again, let's say the Libra person was born at 4:00 a.m. and the dog person was born at noon. Between these two hours, 4:00 a.m. is the animal sign between 3 and 5:00 a.m. and is ruled by the tiger while the person born at noon is within the hours of 11:00 a.m. and 1:00 p.m., the hours ruled by the horse. In the Chinese method, these two signs are considered friends and free spirits. There are my three aces as they say to complete what I require before I say they would most probably be good matches for a relationship. Don't get me wrong. I still do a reading and allow the cards to do their part, and my spirits are very chatty, so they will also give their take on the situation.

If on the other hand, three of the answers were wrong or stated that they were karmic enemies or just plain enemies, then I would tell them the probability that the relationship would work is not in their favor. Remember what I give is an educated opinion. No one should overrule free will, and this is after all the most important thing we have been endowed with, the ability to choose. Always choose your path based on more than one opinion as I do with my readings. No one person has all the answers so as many people in power do. They surround themselves by smart and live people, people that can give a valuable opinion. This is the key word, *opinion*; at the end of the day, you have to make the tough choice. If you don't, the choice makes you.

Look, you can divinate many things in life, but there are general characteristics you can follow. For example, I'm often asked, "Is my man faithful?" My answer is "I would have to look at the person on a case by case," but as a general rule, here are some basic traits to the signs.

If you are a *rat*, don't expect much until he settles down. Even then make sure you discus the rules of your relationship. monogamy for example, and he will surely love you without any detours. They generally like a few close friends although socializing is not out of the question. Family is most important.

The *ox*, on the other hand, is one of the faithful types. As long as you are taking good care of your man, nothing to worry about with this sign. A bit of an introvert, family over friends unless considers a friend like family.

The *tiger* in general if getting the extra attention they tend to need will stay put; however, if not, they will look for it elsewhere. They like company but will only keep you in their inner circle if you show to be a true friend.

Rabbits are not known for jumping out of relationships unless you do. If he feels you are not true, then all bets are off; remember they are cautious, so they usually stay faithful. They keep a tight knit group of friends to keep up with the intellectual side as well as cultural identity.

The *dragon,* if enough ego boost, can go off the reservation sort of speaking. If, however, you keep the pilot light on in the bedroom, he will most likely stay faithful. Only a select few or one will truly know their inner heart.

Most snakes will wonder if they are sure of themselves and their relationships; however, they will stay with no more than looking around. Like the chameleon, they travel in different circles, and if you look carefully, no one person knows everything about them.

If a horse is your fancy, make sure you can keep up. They need to stay stimulated; otherwise boredom will set in, and they will quickly look for greener pastures. They tend to like open-minded and practical friends, don't like complications.

The *sheep,* if not vested, will stray, so make sure if you want or have one, they are firmly grounded in the relationship. Oh, just a reminder. This year 2012, the star of romance shines on the sheep. They like all kinds of people and get along with most but tight group only who share their philosophies and views on life.

Most *monkeys* that fool around is because they get to believe their own stuff. In other words, they act up, and if the other person goes with it, the monkey might mistake it for sexual innuendo and into another bed they will go. Get in with this sign, you must have an intellectual side. They need stimulation of the mental kind.

The *rooster* is a bit kinky on the sexual side, so if he is fed in your bedroom, then he will most likely stay there; otherwise that erotic side might make him wander off. They like stimulation and value loyalty, so these types will look for other intellectual types to fly alongside of.

The *dog* is not a cheater, but don't push his buttons. If he feels cornered or cheated, he will be open to the possibilities. Loyalty is key, and only those who have proven themselves will truly get in.

Pigs are, well, prone to skirting the edges. They will stray if easy access and a perceived chance they will not get into trouble arise. If you are good to them, they value you, but even if an old and trusted friend, if betrayed, out you go.

The wind chime. This topic can be a book on to itself. Here I just want to make you aware they are very useful, so read on and put these simple rules to good use. Proper application is important, so let's get to it. They can be made from just about anything, and they are. Some of the more popular are bamboo, copper, stainless steel. Most are tube form and hollow in the middle to allow the vibration and chi to flow through them. There are two main reasons to use them, to get rid of or ward off bad energy or to attract it. Also we must know the period in time we are in to use the right number of tubes now, and for the next few years, you will do well to use six, seven, eight, nine to attract and five rod to scatter the negative chi.

South, east, and southeast of the home or business should use wood element. Remember to do some research and see what element is best for each corner. Again, remember, combine this with what you want to attain. Bring in good chi or scatter negative energy. Feng shui is a study not just to do because you heard wind chimes are good or bad. If properly applied, it can make a huge impact on your future. You can combine the elements and numbers. For example, in a wood area, and you want to control the negative energy, you can place red carpet or red bulb and make sure your wind chimes are metal and with five rods. *Why* you ask. Simple. Metal controls wood and fire burns wood. The red carpet or red bulb will serve as a substitute to the heat of fire, thus starving the negative energy that might be flowing in that area.

Let's take a brief look of the elements and how they work. Wood produces fire, fire produces earth, earth produces metal, metal produces water, and finally water produces wood. If you walk or look the other way, each element reduces the other; for example, wood reduces water. I think you get the idea, so depending on what you need is what you use. So for example in the south, the element *wood* rules, so if you want to enhance that area, you would use a water feature. If you are in a water area and want to get rid of negative energy, you would use a wood chime as this element reduces water, thus diminishing the effectiveness of the negative element in that area. If for example you have a child out of control, maybe you need to apply the brakes or control on him or her. So let's say their room is in an area of the house that the element is water or the child has strong water element, you could use the earth element to control and not reduce the person. One takes away the other just tones down. Remember earth is a natural barrier to water, so it can slow down its flow but not suck it up like wood would. I hope you get the concept; if not, there are plenty of books on the subject in the bookstores or libraries.

Let's look at it from a romance point of view and remember no absolutes, so these are general rules. If you apply my philosophies to these trends, I always say find as a minimum three or more trends to make a judgment. In other words, don't just say because one trend said this should be a certain way, you blindly follow. Find at least three trends that match before you can begin to give it some serious thought. Even then trust your judgment and your other senses before making a decision. Here are some other general trends to look at when making judgments about relationships.

- Water can extinguish fire, so a water sign should dislike a fire sign.
- Wood can break the earth, so a wood sign should dislike an earth sign.
- Fire can melt metal, so a fire sign should dislike a metal sign.
- Earth can make water disappear, so an earth sign should dislike a water sign.
- Metal can break wood, so a metal sign should dislike wood.

Don't narrow your learning to just tradition. Eastern philosophy also looks at the extremities like hands and feet and head. For as long as I could remember, I heard about hand reading, but later I found about the other extremities and how powerful a tool they can be. The key to learning is not to get stuck with any one idea and discard the others. I've always thought the more I learn, the better I would be to divinate for the person looking for answers. Even when I use some of the diagnostic methods like iridology or looking at the tongue, eyes, lips, and all the rest together, the client or person you look at will get the full gambit of your expertise and less of a chance you can miss something.

I'm often asked why is it that I keep on bumping with the wrong person. It's all about the programming you have given your subconscious mind. So let's start with some simple techniques. On a piece of paper, write down your idea of the right man or woman. I won't tell you because that is as unique as each of us, so write down some characteristics: tall, nice smile, good talker, blue yes, great lover. Well, I think you get the idea. Once you write these things down that are dear to your heart's desire, start on the new moon until the full moon each and every month. Wishing that is, read each characteristic to yourself out loud. Feel that person manifested in your life and happy together. I guarantee you that if you do this as I've described every day, you will within a year or less achieve or manifest your new reality and the right someone will be in your life.

If you want to clean your home of turbulent or negative vibrations, just buy a smudge stick, and as you burn it, invoke the spirits of the home as you walk through each bedroom invoke the guardian spirits of the person who sleeps there. Explain that you wish for peace for the person and you are pacifying the room of all negative energy. After you do the entire home, make sure you check in the bedrooms if the person or persons there are sleeping with their head pointing in an auspicious direction. In my first book, *Life and Beyond*, I created the chart to look at that. If you do not wish to purchase the book, I'm sure you can go to a local bookstore and look for this in one of the books there.

I believe that pictures are worth a thousand words and properly placed a portrait can fill any gap in your home. In the exterior of the home, you may create abundance by simply placing bird food in whatever is the abundance sector for your home on a particular month or year. As the birds come in for a landing, they do double duty, not only with their flapping wings clear the area of negative chi, but also, as they land, they will bring with them new opportunity for wealth and abundance. Everyone today is obsessed with wealth in a monetary sense, but come on, there are other reasons we can be wealthy: a good relationship, health, friendship, love, and on and on. So depending on what you wish to activate is where you would place the bird food. There are tons of sites out there that show areas of abundance and what they can do if activated.

With feng shui you can use symbols to activate reality, so if you want to activate fire, use red bulb or red rug. If you want to activate mountain energy, get a picture or portrait of a mountain and place it on the applicable wall. Water elements are no different. Get a picture of a waterfall, and there you go. So why not for relationships, having distance or issues with your partner? Stop it with the lone pictures and replace with happy, smiling loving together portraits. Find the area of the home for love and put a picture of you both, there tie it up with a red ribbon to light a fire or reignite your relationship fires. No matter what the reasons, there could be some haters that are throwing negative energy at your love. This type of stuff will work just as well for any type of romantic problems; as long as there is love, there is hope. You can also get one of those statues of the lovers wrapped in love's embrace and add your names to the images, and if you happen to have gold chains, wrap it around the couple to bind the relationship. This will help in shielding you guys from any negative external energy.

Let's cover some basic ways to improve your life: at work, home, play, and other ways. Some would say today it's prudent to start with work because of the money crunch that many are going through in these tough times, so be it. If you work indoors and have a desk, let's begin by not having it close to the entrance. The farther into the office, the better and not facing the front door. Besides this, having a desk close to the entrance to the bathroom is also a negative space. If your desk is hit by a poison arrow, poison arrows are any sharp corner or pointed surface. If you look overhead, try and not have any exposed column over your head. Keep your back away from the entrance to the office; it can bring betrayal or backstabbing.

You may have your back against a wall as long as your view is open to the office and not on a narrow path. The wall behind you should have a picture or portrait of a mountain for support. If any of these are not possible, then you can apply some cures to lessen the effects. Any time you want to block negative, you may use a big leafy plant. There are others, but you may have to do some research. If you go to a meeting and have to sit at a big table, don't have your body face any of the corners or pointed areas as this will debilitate your position to others in the meeting. To maximize energy for business, check where the good flow is for the month or year and place a water feature. As a general rule, place abundance signifiers on the west of the office, so you can place a golden chest or another money signifier and fill with coin. It's all about money.

Let's light up the good luck everywhere. Get yourself some simple ten to twenty gallon aquariums and place them in the auspicious area of your home and work. One for each should be more than enough. This is freshwater and should not be very expensive. I personally like goldfish. Get eight red and one black. Don't feed live foods as this can create negative karma. Remember you are killing something alive, so keep it to frozen or any other type of food. I like my aquarium mobile. Let's say I can move it monthly at work and yearly at home. Must stay on top of where the good luck will be the next month. There are many books you can look for in bookstores that will keep you up-to-date.

Let's activate some dragon magic, so if you have dragons in your home or work space, let's place them to look east. Once you have your dragon's facing east, pick a dragon day and dragon time. Their time is seven to nine in the morning, and get a red coloring ink. Color the eyes of the dragon in red; remember to have them looking east and preferable in the living room or close to the front door. Never place your dragon in the bathroom or in a closet, although many have them in the bedroom I say this creates an imbalance, remember we want the bedroom calm and quiet for sleep.

Let's look toward our future now. If you have children and they need a bit of calming down, try and not have their bedroom doors face a bathroom or stairs. Either one of these can cause the child to act up. If you cannot change this, then add a metal wind chime in front of the bedroom door. Make sure it's on the outside of the bedroom, so when the door closes it stays outside. Make sure they are in one of their positive directions with relation to the backboard of the bed. Do not let them sleep on the floor or on a water bed. If possible avoid a window. Have their bed rest against a solid wall. Just remember they should have support and the entire previous example make their night's sleep restless. Make sure there are no exposed beams over the bed. If you remember any beams over, you can cause a feeling of being trapped. Whatever the problems you are having with your child, always check for energy problems. More often than not, it's bad energy and not bad child the cause of their misbehavior.

Find below the five elements or more accurately the five changes as unlike western astrology that are linked to the building blocks of matter, the Chinese believe they're ever-changing forces or energies. their ever-changing forms of life force. You will see how each is linked to the cycles of nature and the color and planets that they are associated with.

木 Wood The East （東）
Springtime　（春）　Azure Dragon （青龍）
The planet Jupiter　（木星）　The color green （緑）
Liver (Chinese medicine) （肝）　and gall bladder (Chinese medicine)
　　（胆）
Nervous system and eyes / flavor sour / honest / anger / affected by wind

火 Fire The South （南）
Summer（夏）　Vermilion Bird/Vermilion Phoenix（朱雀）
The planet Mars（火星）　The color red （赤）
Circulatory system and heart (Chinese medicine)　（心）　and small
　　intestine（小肠）
Tongue / flavor bitter / polite / happy / affected by heat
土　Earth Center （中）
Change of seasons (the last month of the season) The Yellow Dragon
　　（黄龙）
The planet Saturn（土星）　The color yellow （黄）

Rat (zodiac) 鼠（子）Digestive system, spleen (Chinese medicine) （脾）, and stomach (Chinese medicine)（胃）

Mouth and muscle / flavor sweet / promises /worry / affected by wetness

金 Metal The West（西）

Autumn（秋）White Tiger (Chinese constellation)（白虎）

The planet Venus（金星）The color white（白）

Respiratory system and lung (Chinese medicine)（肺）and large intestine(大肠)

Skin and nose / flavor spicy / renown / sad / affected by dryness

水 Water The North （北）

Winter（冬）koi[citation needed]/Snake and tortoise（玄武）

The planet Mercury（水星）The color black（黑）

Skeletal（骨）, urinary bladder and kidney (Chinese medicine)（肾）

Ears and excretory / flavor salty / gentle / fear / affected by cold

Astrology

It's widely accepted as the astrological standard in the west, the twelve sun signs. What most don't realize and this is where there is some confusion, often people with the same signs are very different. Every bit of change can change the signs, so dividing the signs into three can narrow down the accuracy for these people. For example, we can take Virgo, not only can we divide them into three types of Virgo's, we can also separate female Virgo's from male ones. There are some very definitive differences within each sign, and if properly looked at, we can find a much more accurate view of each.

The first third of Virgo usually falls from August 23 to September 2. This type of Virgo can get on others nerves, often excessive sarcasm, you get the idea. They are sharp as whips mentally, but emotionally, they need to put it together. From the third of September to about the twelfth, you may find a person that enjoys their sensuality. They will like the stability of home and are grounded for the most part in reality. If they start something, they usually finish it. The third type of Virgo finishes from about the thirteenth to the twenty-fourth of September. These are usually the ones that like culture and looking good. They know how to behave in every situation. Let's just say these are the ones you can take out and will always make you look good; they have the combination of brains and the beauty to pull it all together. The sexual difference is another issue altogether. Women Virgos are much different than their male counterparts. They are very moody and will not show it except in their private life. To most they always have it together. Women as a whole can pull this off but don't be fooled. You do them wrong and you can expect repercussions. Always remember Virgo must learn to tone down. If not broken, don't need to fix it.

Libra, like all the other signs, has this duality that can make the world scratch their heads. Again don't count them as one sign. To truly know a sign, you must break it down further than the month. If you break to the three parts again, you may see the differences. You were not able to identify with the general characteristics. Let's take the twenty-fourth to October 3, I like to say they are the kids as they need like most kids' attention, and if not received, they will like kids act up. Very creative, so if open to this, they can become very successful. Just don't expect things to be perfect or they will find nothing but disappointments in relationships. From the fourth till the thirteenth of October, they are the charmers and hard to resist when they turn on that intangible charm. Let them be free, and you will have a great life. Tie them down, and they will drown without the freedom to become and explore. The last part of Libra will if in love give all and make you happy. If not in a loving relationship will pack and move on although their straight to hold on might make the decision process longer than it should, but they do not generally look back when gone. Men Libra is much more indecisive than they should be, for the masculine side in them is tempered by their tiptoe attitudes. They are a bit womanizing when it comes to the opposite sex. They like what they like and often can forget their obligations for a quick and dirty romance. No need to change things. Remember what you see is what you get and if not okay then move on!

You can also look at the month; for example, the ones born to January will usually do well with earth tone colors. As with earth, they need to ground and grow; if they learn self-control, they will avoid the pitfalls of open mouth and insert foot. They tend to be tenacious with their desires; also they need to keep an eye on their teeth as they might need to take supplements. Let's look at August. This month will do well with sunflowers in the home. I would like to recommend they get a coral horn. This item can be ordered through jewelry stores. It's a small item you can place on a necklace or wrist or ankle bracelet. It will with time dissolve as it is natural but will also serve as a protection of sorts. This month can do well wearing or surrounding themselves with the color of coral or orange as it will help with their enjoyment process, their creative or artistic juices must flow. It will do well if they wear some gold on their person as in general they will like the good life and status.

As you have seen, there are different ways we can analyze people. Using some standard means, you can size up a person using nothing but a birthday. Keep in mind some of the above examples are just examples, and in order to do a comprehensive analysis, you must have as much information as possible. These are trends, and I always suggest using three different mediums in order to find the truth of a thing. Don't just settle on something because they might just be having a bad day. Look into their makeup and analyze. I suggest starting with your own sign and your own makeup. After all no one knows you better than yourself, and if while in the analysis process you find out a few new things about yourself, so be it. Learning is how we improve and unless you are closed off improvement is what life is all about.

Let's look at the most asked question. What's my best lover or are we compatible, sexuality, and so on. Let's begin by stating that Venus has nothing to do with sex. It's all about the love; this is the most misdiagnosed question, so if we are to talk of sex, for either male or female, Mars is your planet, the drive, desire, intensity—all has to do with Mars, so I will give a brief on each sign and how to best describe them astrologically according to that type of intimacy. Don't blame me if it does not work. There are infinite possibilities and these are just the most common. If you want to look in detail, call me for a reading, and we can compare spiritually speaking what's up. You can also use some simple techniques like the sign opposite yours on the wheel is said to be a most compatible sign to you. Again just another indicator, you must always look in detail the big picture, and you can truly only do this with a one-on-one reading.

Aries is the initiator, and he will want to pursue and be pursued. This Sun or Mars placement will have abundant sexual energy. Loves winning, hates losing, although they can be on the fence to see what happens just to be on the winning side.

Taurus is the most sensual sign of the zodiac and will want to be cuddled and caressed. This sign will have great endurance in the bedroom. They believe in having it all and hate it when others do the same.

Gemini is the most versatile sign of the zodiac and will enjoy variety in sex. If you're interested in someone with the Sun or Mars in Gemini, keep things fun! He or she will also step up when needed; otherwise this sign will be fine having others do the heavy lifting. Loves freedom to do, to be, but make sure if you have one give them plenty of love and attention lest they go looking elsewhere.

Cancer is the nurturer and will be protective sexually. Once they feel safe, however, they have an unsurpassed intuition to know what their partner needs. Love family or familiar environments, needs tender loving care from those around them!

Leo is the performer and wants to be adored and respected. This sign will shower you with love and playful sex. Will go above and beyond to captivate but can slack off once the goal is achieved; always give to this sign and in return you will receive!

Virgo is the perfectionist. You'll need to be cleaned and groomed for this sign to make a move, and you will also have to provide mental stimulation. Some need order, but it's not necessarily what most has branded this sign as. Just the same they need to know, for them having enough information to make informed decisions is a must!

Libra is romantic. This sign will go out of the way to please a partner and will want nothing but class and elegance. Appreciates relationships where they are appreciated but does not flourish if people around them are vulgar or nasty!

Scorpio is intense. This sign will want powerful lovemaking and may want to own you in and out of the bedroom. They need to be moved emotionally, intensity drives them, hates cheap or superficial feelings, and if continued will get stung by the Scorpio stinger!

Sagittarius is the adventurous lover. This sign wants to explore together and looks for a spiritual connection with sex. They love optimism but loathe depressive people. Don't bring this sign down or out you will be!

Capricorn is the ambitious lover who wants to control every aspect of sex. There are "rules" for this sign, and they must be followed. Order is the name of their game, hates to have their time wasted, in other words keep your promises!

Aquarius is the experimenter and wants to enjoy a relationship without losing his freedom or individuality over it. He may be kinky in bed. They follow the beat of their own drums with irreverence for what others want. Unfortunately, they feel their way is the best way!

Pisces is the sensitive lover who wants to meld with you completely. This sign truly wants two souls to become one. Two types in most signs in this one she can either be smooth or she can be a complainer. If it's the latter, run as it usually does not get better. Love the elegance in life. If you are riffraff, veer off, for this sign will not tolerate loud buffoons!

Cleansings

Let's talk about some abundance type cleansings. If you are stuck, then this might be an easy cleanse to open roads to abundance. The ingredients: a big red cloth, break it down into pieces; how many of, you say. Well, that will depend on several things. I would like you to make this calculation. Take your birth year; I'll give you an example. If it is 1961, you will always take the last two digits; in this case 6 + 1 = 7, so you will make seven bags. If it's 1989, then you will add 8 + 9 = 17; always bring to single digit so 1 + 7 = 8, so you make eight bags. Now that you know how to work out how many bags, then you will fill each bag with these ingredients. Get fresh parsley from the supermarket: honey and yellow cornmeal (make sure it's the course, not powdery one). Fill each bag with all three ingredients; tie it until you close the rag like a pouch.

Now that you have all the pouches, let's get to the next part, using a large container like a big Tupperware. Add water cornmeal, parsley, and honey. Mix it together and then rub all over from the elbows to the hands, from the knees to the feet. Now wash with water until your extremities are free from this combo. Take each of the bags one at a time and pass it rubbing your body from head to feet. Once you have pass each of your bags around your body, get in your vehicle and away from your home or areas you pass by every day. Find streets with at least three open roads and toss each bag in a different one until you are done. So if you have seven bags, you must toss one at each of seven different street corners.

If you wish to get abundance into your life, inject it with a process with nature. Get some dried corn husks. Even if not dried, you can buy some fresh corn husks from the supermarket and place it outside to dry quickly with the heat of the sun. Once completely dry, slice in round slices until you are done. Place the dried slices in some sort of pan with about one-half inch of water at the bottom. Make sure it's a big pan so you can place the rounded cuts flat in the water. As the corn starts to grow into a small tree, let's say at least four to five inches, you may transplant them into the ground. Remember the corn must be very dry, or else it will not grow into a tree, so again once you have about four to five inches in height, you can plant them in the ground. Make a nice area to grow the corn as it will grow big. Corn trees are at least five to six feet in height. As you grow them, talk to them and say symbolically as they grow, so will get your abundance, "As the corn is grown once the tree is fully grown, my abundance grow and bear fruit." If it's a business you want from the beginning, let it be known to the universe that as you grow this crop, your business will yield a successful crop. Tend the garden to keep the plants growing, and when they bear new corn, make a good meal from it and give thanks. This is a spell creating a pact with the universe—that is you tend to nature so will nature's energies tend to your abundance.

There are infinite ways to clean your energy, your home, your family, so as with my first book and earlier in this one. Just use common sense. I had a lady e-mail me that she did a cleansing in my previous book that incorporated cinnamon, and she got a rash. For goodness sake, if you are allergic to the substance, don't use it. There are always variations to the themes, so if it calls for cinnamon, and you have a problem with it, then use brown sugar. For example, in the case of replacement, if cinnamon is powdery, use the powdered sugar. Try and keep the general idea and just replace the ingredient. If the cleanse calls for a salt scrub but you have high blood pressure, use common sense and don't use that particular cleanse. After all you want a benefit, not a detriment as a result of what you do. There are many types of talisman that people can use to protect themselves. For example, the very popular cross. People wear it all over, have it in the home. Can it help, do you believe? If so, then the answer is yes. I feel that intent is just as important as the actual ritual or talisman you wear or place in the home.

I was asked the other day if placing a picture of white doves over the front door, representative of the Holy Spirit, can serve as a source of protection. Again, do you believe? If so, then the answer is yes. These energies are all around us, if we through prayer or thought pull them, then more often than not, they will come. You can do on behalf of another, I do it all the time, when I'm asked to do a remote cleansing, a friend or relative will come to me, and I will through them reach the person in question and the results are felt. Distance does not matter, so they can be in another country and still feel the benefits. As a general rule as with intent, I would ask the person asking to think of whomever they want me to help, and I engage them in conversation about this person, to bring them into thought, and through this thought, I can reach the right person. I've done this on a regular basis when I'm asked to help, but the person is not near enough to come see me. I get them to e-mail me a picture with name and birthday, and I print it out, and through the picture I can accomplish the same thing.

I've gone into these explanations because in my first book, I gave plenty of recipes and many people have e-mailed me if they can use them to help others. The answer is yes. There is no difference between you and I, except I've developed this wonderful relationship with the other side. With this bond comes a certain amount of protection not only for myself but for those I help. This is why I can help, and in some extraordinary cases of very dark energy, it does not affect me and I'm able to help those in need. So with this I remind you not to put the cart before the horse. What I mean is get yourself to a good level, a level where you are comfortable with your particular energies and summoning of your spirit helpers. It is them after all that have your backs, with this abilities you can accomplish many often thought of as incredible things.

I would really appreciate those who go on and develop these talents to a level that an impact others to keep me informed as many times I'm asked to do things that require more than one person, and I can always use the help. For example, it's not always enough to clean energy but to physically channel a spirit to get it to cross over. I can do the channel but another person is necessary to speak and awaken this soul from the mist currently found in. In my area I have plenty, but I travel and it's often difficult if not impossible to find a true medium to assist in this endeavor. For example as of this writing I find myself on a plane headed for NY City. I know at least one scenario where it would be helpful to physically channel a spirit that is obsessed with a particular person. I will do my best, but as I've stated it's often best to allow this spirit to make a physical manifestation with a body to have an interactive chat and get it on board with the idea of moving on.

Religion

There are some amazing similarities with religions of the world; they have a very similar playbook. One is to get people to believe in their idea of God, another is to expand their belief system, third, convert believers of anything else to their system, the system that will take people closer to the one and only God. Oh yeah, and this is only the good stuff. How about the way they keep believers indoctrinated? If you deviate from their belief system, the fear is you will not go to heaven or whatever they call heaven. Not only used on their own believers, but these believers are taught that any other religion or belief system is wrong. Further most are taught to take an active role to explain why their belief system is the right one and why any other is the wrong road to God.

I don't want to trash any one religion, but most have had in their history some violence in a sense they have stayed in power by killing or in some other violent way getting rid of all those who oppose that particular belief system. More people have been killed by religious wars or zealots than most wars in the history of humanity. Incredible but true, and they all preach peace in one way or another as long as it's their way and diminishing any obstacles to free to belief in any and all possible religions. So I needed to express my own belief of freedom of belief without persecution because one or more do not have the same beliefs. With this I would ask you to keep an open mind. No matter what your beliefs are, to at the very least, allow your neighbor to live with the same freedom you have.

Most religions preach dogma. Unfortunately things that were true a thousand years ago might not be right today, so this is why spirit is so fluid. The spirit will speak on today for today and not what was hundreds of years before. This is why most organized religion sensors spirit; it cannot be contained to whatever dogmatic view that organized religion has. I have personally experiences the pushiness of some of these beliefs as I've been woken up on Sunday morning with people preaching one thing or another, even after thanking them, but letting them know I had no interest, they continued to tell me if I wanted to go to heaven and how their belief was the one, that would take me there. On one occasion I simply shut the door. What is this zealot belief that must be spread like the plague? Folks, I can tell you without doubt that belief is something personal, and the more you understand, the better you can decide what to believe in so no being pushed or prodded or blackmailed with heaven to believe in something is not the right way.

Many religions in the world have opposing views on evil. Some believe it is part of the world, and we must live with it. Others believe it is here but does not need to be part of the world. Dogma dictates truth for most religions. What truth is real and just part of someone's idea of reality from many hundreds of years past. These and many other topics for conversations will be with us as long as humans exist. The construct of religion is in diversity. If all perceived the same, it would seize to function with its foundation in conflict between theological ideas the idea of one thought would disarm most religions. Even with the major ones in the world today, their concept is not of the individual but the community belief, that the belief in one correct belief is the overriding concept of religion.

Chapter 7

My Spirits

I have never spoken of the spirits that work with me in detail; they gave me permission, so in this chapter, I will cover each one: how they help me and why they are here. I will give you detail of their previous lives—how and why they arrived to be here with me and what they bring as experience. Each of us has spirit helpers and one guardian angel or spirit guide. I will use mine as examples but have no doubt you have them as well.

The Samurai

The very first spirit that came to me was one that rarely comes through. He was a samurai, and his life was a very lonely one. This was the life he chose to appear to me. The first time he came, he channeled through me. He spoke and said simply I walk alone, expressing how he lived as a killer for hire. He was often hired to get rid of bad influences attacking local villages. As he explained once he got rid of the ruffians that were destroying the different villages. He must leave after collecting his money a good night sleep and a good meal. He explained that if he stayed long enough, he would become that witch he was hired to get rid of.

As he explained in detail, the life he choose as a samurai would lead him to travel the country doing one job after another: some for food and housing, some for money, others for good company for a while; but he must never stay to long, for he feared becoming that witch he despised. He grew up in a small town and saw much abuse by sword wielding villains. So he swore as a child to grow up to protect the ones who needed protection. He did not realize that what he had become had no future as a husband or farmer. He was a stone killer, and as an assassin, his one talent was to kill. He was very good at it, and the only reason he had survived was by never becoming comfortable in any one location.

In the eleven years or so that I have been working with my spirits and helping others, he has only channeled twice and appeared to me another three times. He has told me that in a time of great need he will come and give me the strength to overcome any and all obstacles in a spiritual realm. So I asked him if he could explain why he chooses this particular lifetime to manifest to me. He explained by stating that I'd chosen the path of the warrior. What do you mean, I asked. He explained that it is the smallest percentage of the people that can work in the spiritual world that choose the warrior's way. He explain that the folks that choose to work toward maintaining balance in the spiritual world choose a difficult path and this particular lifetime he choose is the one where he can help me the most with.

He took me to one of the instances that he was hired to fend off a group of thugs causing trouble in a small village in the middle of the mountains. This place was so remote that whatever law existed at that time would only visit the village once a year and only if needed. One of the villagers was sent out to find someone that could get rid of these people. Once the local arrived at the nearby village, he was told of this samurai who would help those who needed. He explained they were not rich and would pay with what they had. The other villagers explained that he takes food, shelter, and anything else worth his deed; so they told him were to find the samurai. They had last heard he had gone to a nearby village near a great lake, so the villager headed there in hopes that the great samurai could be found and talk him into aiding them.

After a few days of travel, the villager arrived at the town, much bigger than their small village and with some trouble was able to find the samurai having a meal and drink at a local tavern. He did not know how to approach the samurai who seemed to be in trawled with the meal and a drink; finally he gathered the strength and approach. The samurai looked up and asked if this was important enough to disturb his dining.

The villager, terrified, backed up and waited outside the place until the samurai was done and leaving.

The samurai saw the villager and asked what it was he wanted. The villager explained the situation and how they would be able to pay with hospitality. The samurai said he would do it for one week's worth of service to him. The villager was happy and agreed. They went to where he had his bag, and they headed for the village. Along the way, the details were explained to the samurai. He was only interested in the food and housing and other hospitality, women to be exact. In this time, part of being hospitable to a man who visits is the loan of a woman, so he being a single man would expect no less as part of his payment.

Several days passed, he was also told of the nine men who had for months being able to take their food, women, and killing any who stood in their way. He said not to worry about those he would take care of their problem one way or another. They arrived the village, was in an uproar as they knew that the bad men who were destroying their way of life would soon be gone. Right away the villager met with the elders and explained the payment method. The elders gestured to the villager to begin to make the samurai comfortable, and they took him to a home for comfort. The dinner was served. His bed was made and asked if there was anything else he would need.

The samurai walked over to the bed and lifted the sheets. The villager understood, and soon an older woman brought a young woman over. She was dressed in typical dress with a veil over her face. The samurai walked over to her and lifted the veil; he then looked at the older woman and gestured with a nod of his satisfaction with the woman. The old woman bowed and moved away. He took the hand of the woman and asked her if she wanted to eat. She said yes; after all, the meals he was being served were those fit for a king, and she was hungry.

After they finished, they walked over to a wooden tub, and she bathed him and serviced his needs. She had already been cleaned and prepared for him, so he took her, and they went to bed. He enjoyed an evening with her and slept the rest of the night. In the morning she had breakfast ready for him as he arose and walked over to the meal.

She bowed to him and served him a complete breakfast. He told her she could leave now. He put on all his garments and began to warm up for his day of action; he recalled the village elders telling him that on precisely this day, those bad men would usually arrive, creating havoc in the village.

As predicted after the morning activities, the group of marauders arrived, as usual pushing people around. They were calling for food and gold. He stood in the middle of what was a street during those times in the middle of this very small town. They stood, and their leader approached, asked what he wanted. He explained that this was their town and there was no room for more, so he should keep on walking and they would not kill him. He smiled and explained how he was hired to get rid of them, so unfortunately, they would have to deal with him. He walked back to his group and told the first four to go and kill the stranger.

Well, all hell broke loose, and one by one, he killed the four like they were not even there. At the end, he turned back toward the five remaining bad guys and without breaking a sweat asked who is next. The leader signaled to the rest, and they all approached him. This time with more caution, they surrounded the samurai and attacked in tandem. With the same eased as the first four, he dispatched the remaining hooligans.

That day he was a God in this town that for months these people were causing great physical and emotional harm. That evening he was served another spectacular meal and warm bath to clean up after his work of the day. The evening fell, and after he retired to his temporary housing, he was brought a beautiful young woman for his comfort. It was on this day that he realized he could never stay for long after he completed his mission. As the woman who brought the lady in question turned to leave, he pulled her back in and had both of them on that evening. As it happened, the woman in question was the wife of the mayor or the main person in the village. There was no question about his abilities, and no one in the village said a word. It was at that moment he realized that if he was not careful, easily become that witch he fights. He could become the bad guy, and it was a slippery slope. He never wanted to see again.

From that moment on, he was always careful never to cross the line; he would take on the jobs and clear out within a day or two of accomplishing his task. There were over the years many jobs, and in the area he worked, he became a celebrity for good. He never forgot that one job where he let his guard down and momentarily became one of the bad guys. He tells me to always do my job and take no more or no less than what I charge. He always warns me that with power comes responsibility and weakness is human. Never put myself in situations where things could get out of hand. In other words, all that call me for help are just people in need and I'm never to let it become more. He tells me the flesh is weak, and no matter the intentions, any one can slip if we ride to close to that edge. I've been told since he was the first and did not stay as my circle comes to completion, he will also be the last to come in and close the inner group that will ultimately work with me. So far he's not, so I imagine there are more to come. With development, there is always more.

The Healer

The doctor, I call him that, all these spirits have names, but they do this just for me, making it easier to deal with all of them in the day to day with what I do. Remember they are but lights in the afterlife, so all they represent including a specific lifetime is for our benefit and not necessary for this type of spirit. This type of spirit has gone through certain evolution and is on the path to enlightenment. That is right; all protector spirits are still spirits on a path for enlightenment and as part of this path is working with a living person like me. It's not to say that the everyday person that can't see or hear anything does not have their own set of protectors. I speak of the ones like mine who are not here just to help their charge but in a broad canvas help all in need on this plane.

So back to the doc. He is a very humble man. He chose to manifest with me in the form of a traveler. He would go from town to town and help all in need. He always wore white as he puts it. It's a clear color, allowing no negative energy to become strong enough to manifest. He loved to clean with plants; he would prepare herbal baths for people. He believes in all kinds of remedies, including modern science, so as with many cases I've worked on, he usually offers enhancements to existing medications to help in the healing process of patients. Remember I'm not a doctor, so I never give advice other than to enhance today's modern medicine, and as with all my clients that need this, I always refer to their doctor to get blood work and diagnosis.

During the lifetime he chose to work with me, he learned valuable lessons in the shortcomings of medicine. Hence he is very happy to be working with me in this time where there have been so many advancements in medicine. He's given me many messages about health and upcoming health issues. I will give you one that recently occurred. A friend of my wife was over with her husband. I let her know she really needed to see the gynecologist, she asked why. I let her know that there was a cyst. I did not see it as bad, but it needed to be addressed. As usual I gave my disclaimer. I'm not a doctor or do I practice medicine. I give messages and very often a heads-up as what is to come in health type issues, never sidetracking standard medical practices and that is why I'm sending her to the female doctor.

She said okay, and I knew she was wondering what the heck I was talking about; it was a few weeks later when my wife called to chat when she was told the friend had gone and the doctor detected a huge cyst. In fact she was told the hysterectomy was in order although it was not malignant. She told my wife that I had told her not to worry that it would not be bad. She told her that a hysterectomy was bad; I was in the house, so my wife walked over and explained what she was being told. I told her to tell her friend that I did not see such a thing, but I guess anything was possible.

When she hung up, we spoke of it, and I told her still did not see such an operation. She explained that her friend was very worried and the date for the hysterectomy was scheduled in a couple of weeks. I told her to tell the friend of a simple cleansing she can do in her own home, but I did not foresee a problem. As a matter of fact I still did not see what she was scheduled for. We did not speak of this again, and a few days after the operation, she called to so how her friend was. Guess what the friend told her after she was in the operating room? The doctor changed his mind and told her after careful inspection he did not see the necessity to do this very extensive operation, and it was not done. The cyst was removed and all is well with her.

I stuck to my guns as this medical spirit like anyone is not God and mistakes are made. He kept insisting in his original diagnosis, so I continued to say what he was telling me. If I don't believe, how can I teach others to believe? This particular spirit is very good at sizing up medical scenarios and—like anyone—can make mistakes or miss something. The way he explains it to me, there are many things that we are not meant to suffer; however, because of our lifestyles, often things that are not destined happen and not expected. It is in these cases, he explains that we can help the most. Remember the divine plan is something that usually overrides other things in our life path.

He was a traveling healer, going from town to town. Over the years he learned as much as he taught. He told me how no matter where the need took him, humans, were are not that different, and I should look at people as just that, people. Never let my own shortcomings and narrow views of people as they refer to society or race or color interfere. The human factor, broken down, he believes our values are not very so different; don't just hear the need but analyze what comes behind. Partly because of this advice, I've fine-tuned how I do my work and can read over the phone.

Yes, I do personal readings in groups only. Throughout the years I've fine-tuned this way of reading over the phone. I can give you thousands of examples where personal readings have thrown me off; suffice to tell you, I can get into the reading much quicker over the phone. The spirits that work with me give me the same advice over the phone. I diminish the human factor. I don't see or let most of the senses affect me. Even the voice over the phone is not as bad as seeing the entire package. Some can come across a bit guarded over the phone, but at least the sarcastic look or the defensive posture doesn't amplify.

I've done many readings where I've temporarily lost my sight by how the client is dressed or how much perfume or makeup, even the person's physical appearance can disrupt my view of the person. I have learned that eliminating all the impute can help the reading by shortening the time it takes for me to tune in to the person I'm working with. The information will not be lessened in this way or will it be better in person. It does help me get on with the client's needs and answer all their questions without the delays in getting through the physical stuff that each person can bring.

When the plan goes bad, then it becomes quite possible to place that person's life back on track through energy work. We are the captains of our own destiny and, like any driver, can often crash or go into a lake by making some boneheaded mistakes. So it is with life, keeping an open mind can help us move through difficult times and into the silver lining side of life. Remember if there is good, there is bad. If there is light, there is darkness, so we need to learn to navigate. As they say, when we are not flowing, it's best to stay under a rock. What that means to me, nothing out of the necessary; stay to the basics as no matter how difficult, with a little work, sooner or later life finds its balance. Even when a person is not good, there is a lesson. If they are not a good example, they can serve us by being a horrible warning of what we can become if we delve into the darkness instead of the light.

As part of my readings, I give people advice and information about relatives and people close to them, people of value, emotionally or materially as partners or work-related stuff. The healer gave a woman a message about one of her close friends that someone close to her in the family had or would get diabetes. After the reading and many days later, she e-mailed me that the friend could not confirm as she told her as far as she knew there was no one in the family with diabetes or a blood sugar problem. It was several months later that she text me with a confirmation. Her friend had taken her young children, twins if I remember correctly, to the doctor on a regular checkup, and the doctor told her that one of them had the onset of diabetes. No one is God on this earth, but this particular spirit has a good 90 percent accuracy with the diagnosis that he gives the people. Remember the further away the question, the harder it is to get to them. What I mean is if you ask about yourself, the accuracy is much better even of predicting possible medical issues as it is to when you ask about friends or family. It all goes through you.

This reminds me of a lady whom I read, and she asked me of her sister. Almost everything I told her about the sister was related to her. Although she asked about the sister's health, it was her who had most of the issues. We talked about thyroid, lung issues, constipation—everything I mentioned was about the person I was speaking about. Finally at the end, I told her to let's switch to her and then try the sister again. After the spirit was done with her and we tried again, there were no problems with identifying the sister and her medical issues. By the same token, if the person with the problems is a spouse, they will take me there although the person might be asking about themselves. Bottom line they are here to be of help and will gravitate the reading to the one who is of need.

Remember this is why it's important to do it privately. When I've done a reading with a husband and wife on the phone, even without knowing, I started to talk about the spouse who was listening and not about the client. Somewhere along the way, the client told me that everything was about the spouse and I asked if he was close to her. She acknowledged that he was listening on the other line. That does not work very well for me, so if you want, you are welcome to record, but one person at a time is how I do best. Remember as it is I'm doing most of these readings on the phone and the same way the communications must be clear to talk to someone for me the energy must be clear. In other words more than one energy can throw me off.

It's funny in an interesting way, when he works with me, I often feel my hands and face warm and hot; he has so much energy that I have to let it pass through or it gets very hot for me. He does this to allow me to help others without depleting my own energies. I learned early on to tap into the universal reserve. This energy is everywhere and available to all who knows or learns to tap into it. Never fear what is part of the whole of everything. Along with taping into raw power, this is the easiest to do.

Once you get better, you can tap into universal knowledge. Remember it's available, but you must understand that knowledge is power, so you must be at peace with yourself to truly understand what is being given to you.

The Inca Priest

Along the way of development, there were many different spirits that came and made their presence known to me. Amongst those that I recall is an Inca priest. Yeah, with sun worshiping and everything. He first manifested. I thought he was just a spirit that was with someone else. As I do readings and cleanings, sometimes spirits of light present themselves in an attempt to help the person they are with. But no this was one of the many spirits that assist me in my development and help of others. So as he first came to me, he had or was adorned with gold everywhere, most significantly was the golden bracelet's he had on each of his forearms. He worked in what looked like a pyramid, and they were devout worshipers of the sun god. They offered up many human sacrifices. I guess it did not do them much good as their civilization collapsed. Hey, I was not there, so who I'm I to judge as to what really happened to those people. His job while with me is to help me with my skills as a spell master; they did so many incantations and others things to gain power over others and the elements. Although he is still there, I don't see much of him these days. There are other that made themselves known and many we've yet to see or meet. He has offered many suggestions that to this date I practice; for example, he believed in the power of sound or different vibrations. He also showed me the concept of using different colors to modify even emotions.

The Magician (as My Wife Calls Him)

He is the spirit that speaks to me of the mind. He believes that we should all strive to be less emotional and work with the concept of the analytical mind. He has on several occasions channeled through me as they all have. When I sit with my wife and they take turns channeling, it's always interesting they speak with her and answers her questions and explain the process to which they are bound to. For example he came from another realm and the world he came from was on the fast path to enlightenment by purging themselves of emotions.

His race was for thousands of years attempting to leave all emotions behind. They created many beautiful things. They were able to find interstellar travel; eventually they were able to use a large portion of their brains and tap into many areas of life with their overdeveloped senses and raw brain power. As he explained there was a world geared to excel in all aspect of learning. They were not interested in war, conquest, or borders. It was an open society.

With the centuries their society became in tune to such a degree that all could hear the thoughts of the others—a tipping point when all thoughts became one—and with this thought, they would reach out into the cosmos and touch worlds light years from them. This is how they started to probe distant parts of their own galaxy; it was faster and more effective than sending probes. So when they located other life, a manned vessel would leave for the place. They would tap into certain life-forms to start to guide them toward the day they would physically arrive.

I guess if I were to give you what I thought was comparable, I would use from the show *Star Trek* Spock. He was the Vulcan who his people had purged emotions. This is a very loose comparison. Remember I've never seen him, just his experiences and his life as it was while he lived. He said that ours is one of the worlds they probed, and as far as I can tell, I believe they also sent a probe here to make contact. It's hard to know how far in the past this was, or maybe it's to come in the future. His messages to me are of a different type, and his guidance is to help me be more about mind power.

One key element to his teachings that has stuck to me was that he wants me to realize that emotions are necessary to leap beyond a certain point in any society. He explained that their civilization once achieving total emotional control, or at least to a level they were unable to dream of a future like a fantasy they became a world or a race on hold. He explained to me that when there was nothing logical still to learn, they realized they needed that emotional portion of their original makeup to go to the next level of their evolution. They needed the god particle as I call it belief that—is or not, does it or not—simple ability to leap into the unknown became difficult if not impossible.

Back to the magic guy as my wife calls him, he like any advanced being would seem like magic what he does. He can do many things with his mind, something that he tells we are capable of as well. Remember from his story of his people: it took them thousands of years to grow mentally, but again we have a similar capability and thus why they showed interest in our race as a people. He tends to isolate with his messages. Remember I work with a group of spirits each brings his or her own brand of experience and knowledge.

He tells that what we do now with magic spells, material things as he calls it, is archaic; what he promotes is working on improving the mind. He tells that with a fine-tuned mind, we are capable of doing 100 percent more productive time than we are currently with our current way of doing things. He explains that most of the things we allow to happen because we are weak-minded would be eliminated. He gave me one example: Right at the time he was giving me this talk, he told me that my thirst for munchies was not helping me with my health. He explained that with time it would become a problem, and I should learn to control my impulses better.

We talked about a case I was working on; this client was having problems getting some money from one of his clients. He showed me alternatively how to reach out and get the man to pay the money without doing my usual material type of spells. Well, folks, I did it, and I had done my spell a few weeks before without results. After working as he showed, I got results for my client within a few days. I have to tell you it was mentally draining, and like most work, it was specific to that scenario. We as a people are lazy when it comes to mental exercises, so if you use many of the exercises in my first book, then I can assure you that major improvements will show themselves to you with time.

I believe he as a soul does not come from the same tree as do other souls that come from earth. His soul is of another completely different branch. He has given me enough information so as to allow me to understand why he is here with me helping me expand my mental abilities. Although he professes working with the mind, one of his lessons gave me some insight as to his people and the why of their eventual stagnation while on the fast path to enlightenment through mental growth. He was very candid in his explanation. As people, they had achieved wonders all through their mental development, which took them to incredible achievements. They fell short of their next step.

The one thing that took them to those heights also has stalled their growth—their emotions, that part of who they were, they purged became an important component to their next step. Their people had lost the leap to cross from logic to the unknown. They had lost the ability to dream of illogical ways to become more than they were. For all their knowledge and abilities, the one thing they now needed to grow beyond their logical confines was gone. So part of the lesson he taught me is not to leave behind any part of who we are as we were given this in order to grow. Yes, emotions can delay our growth, but when we achieve the same wonders as they had, we will be able to dream to the next part of our evolution, beyond logic, beyond belief. We will be able to leap from our physical bodies to that of energy. This step they were unable to belief in therefore unable to step into. He tells me it is the natural evolution of all souls, to live in this world of material learning without the bounds of a physical body. He is not telling me they would become souls. The soul will still exist within the noncorporeal energy incarnation. They would be able to travel as energy everywhere without the need of rockets and such.

This is our future as long as we stay focus on growth and not make the same mistakes they did. Yes, in the beginning, it was fruitful, and I'm sure huge shortcuts as they avoided many of the mistakes we are and will continue to make, but the end game will be extraordinary compared to their limited growth. I asked why not mix with us as a people; I'm sure our offspring will have some measure of emotions. He told me that option has been studied over the last thousand years. I asked how long they had been tapping on us. He said since we became cohesive as a people, so over one thousand years I asked. He said yes.

Here is my own opinion of this spirit. From the exchange, when he channels through me, what I mean is he speaks through me, but our minds are in touch and the communications is not strictly one way. I can sense his thoughts not just his words coming out of my mouth, so I feel they took great strides by avoiding all the wars and other side effects of emotion out of their equation. However I can tell as a raise they ran into many walls as part of emotion is leaping beyond what is into what would to them be just fantasy.

So many times in their evolution to find the answers of their existence and the why of existence itself, they could not take the leap of what if. What if we were able to teleport just because our minds made it so? What if we were magic? They could not quantify these things, so they did not believe them possible. To me that is the truth of existence. I'm sure as our own science has thought that there is a fifth dimension, there could be countless others we cannot rationally come by, but we can dream and speculate. These simple ideas or dreams or fantasies as you want to name them were beyond the intellect of logic.

So in many ways they are not as advanced as we are today. Maybe our science is not close to theirs, but we will get there. They can't imagine beyond their science so that roadblock will eventually stop their evolution. I sense they look at us and other places in this universe and question why. Why what you say, how we can dream of things that are not logical and cannot be logically explained; however, I know they feel this must be part of the solution because their advancement as a people had halted many thousands of years ago.

Yes, they learn about other people and places and ideas. Unfortunately they cannot grow beyond what can be proven true. So I think at some level they will or have tried to help us along so they can eventually piggyback on our insatiable flights of fantasy into a reality that escapes their intellect. I know from bits and pieces of information. I've felt we are not the only planet they are experimenting with. With care not to allow us to leave emotions behind. I feel they have been moving us along and will continue until our intellect is at a level they can observe growth. They have not experienced other thousands of years. I hope in their quest for more information, they don't move us so far and fast along that we cannot keep up emotionally with our science.

As he said on a couple of occasions, we are very young and need tending to or else we would be lost in this gigantic universe of questions. So my opinion is we are being guided to serve their purpose of understanding by our ideas and abstract reality to take them into uncharted emotional realms of reality. Like many science fiction movies, we have always thought if we can imagine it we can make it so. What or when will they think enough and begin to fear that we may actually outshine them and what will they do if that day came. Just some food for thought, I try not to think of this as we are still thousands of years behind them and many thousands more before they question this if ever.

The Therapist

He brings an internal peace. When he comes, I settle down. No matter what the situation, the clarity of thought I feel is a feeling hard to bring to words. I could be in an argument or any other situation, and as he approaches, my conversation and tone changes. It's almost like I become another person; in a sense, I do, I'm still there but my view of things change. I have been discussing a situation that has taken a turn for the violent, and as this spirit comes close, my control over the situation increases exponentially. I ask him why he does not lend a hand more often; he explains as so many others do, this is my life and it must contain all of life. If it's too easy, I won't learn to grow beyond my current limitations. It's frustrating how the knowledge that there is an easier solution and being limited to the parameters the universe has laid out. Granted I could push the issue and probably change the rules of energy flow at least temporarily. I step back to this internal argument and realize I preach flow; we must follow the flow of least resistance for the greater good. As humans we must evolve beyond our own petty differences. Yes, even mine must be placed in the back burner of society. Hey, after all I'm only human, with a little extra help from some friends, but I the person am still passing through this world doing my part as the universe sees fit.

All this reasoning is part of what that spirit brings to me. The reasoning mind cannot be subdued by erratic thoughts, so keeping focus and perspective is essential. Not all of us have a built-in therapist, even with one human nature often rears its emotional head and steps in the pitfall that is emotions. I'm glad that humanity has learned to step up and open its mind and heart to reach beyond what is real to what was thought to be unreal. The more we move toward this spiritual evolution that is beginning, the more people start the flow to enlightenment and leave chaos behind.

There is a ritual that spiritists can do. This ritual requires other spiritists with evolved senses; the more evolved spiritually, the better for the person to be initiated into this elite club. So the first thing before a person should take on this initiation they must evolve spiritually. My first book gives many techniques to grow spiritually. The more we attract the spirits that help us the better we can find our spiritual path, and any in this path knows with knowledge comes power and commitment. Anyway back to it, this ritual requires at least six other people with spiritual maturity. The ultimate goal is to define of all the spirits that accompany the person—the one that will take the mantle of leadership among the rest. The people in the group will each have specific abilities that will allow them to see each of the spirits that accompany the initiate.

So a circle is created as each of the people helping will take a position around the person in the middle. One chair for the person to be initiated and the others sit in a circle around him or her; a cleaning of energy is done on the person, and lots of white flowers are placed everywhere in the room. This is to be done. Prayers are initiated to start the flow of energy, so as all the people involved start in prayer. In unison the energy in the place is exponentially increased. All focus their prayers on the person in the middle, placing positive energy to surround the person. The person in the middle has one role to focus on the spirits

LIGHT AND THE DARKNESS

that accompany him or her and summon them to assist in this important event to a spiritist.

With prayers flowing in the room, all kinds of spirits make presence. We hope the right one will take the mantle of authority over the rest and order in the spiritual realm will settle over the person's spiritual path. The group surrounding will attempt to make sure that the right spirits are there. They will give their opinions as to what they see. The key person in the middle will usually start to channel all the spirits that come to make themselves known. It's with these visits that hierarchy will begin to be settled, even amongst them some take the lead and others are just happy to be able to help the living.

So as the process continues and more spirits manifest through the person in the middle, a better view of their spiritual evolution. This ritual should only be done with someone who can channel and is able to communicate with at the very least two of the spirits that accompany them. So try and understand if you do it. Before you are ready, you will only shortchange yourself. The more of your spiritual growth happens before this is attempted, the better outcome and a better chance that the right spirit will be chosen as your spirit guide amongst the known spirits.

I've assisted in a number of these and can tell you many were done prematurely. When my coronation of spirits was done—coronation is the name given in this ceremony—it was an incredible feeling. I had all my close friends there; eleven other spiritists assisted in my ceremony, and until I had channeled at least ten of the ones that came and lots of prayer no one spirit took the mantle of leader. Once one of the spirits came forth the rest took their place. For me it was a much evolved moment as all these spirits that manifested through me came to order as it were. As the spirit that is to become the head of the group is channeled through the medium, he gives his message or messages, then each of the mediums stands and takes some white petals from the many flowers surrounding this event and dousing them in a pan full of perfumed essences, mixes them good, and walks over to the medium in the middle and sprinkles all these petals over his or her head.

As the medium does this, he prays for the person and the spirit as they join may it be fruitful. Each of the mediums does a very similar ritual, with their own prayers of welcome into this spiritual community, offering many blessings and all that they can give in the way of positive white light. The idea is to consecrate this bonding that had occur and fortify it between the person and the spirit, always giving blessings and light to all the spirits that attended this event. Asking that as this group matures together and work each day with this medium, may their bond become stronger and full of universal light.

There is a lot more to this coronation that what I have described, but I feel you get the idea for the ceremony. Much like us as humans as spirits in a group this also has need for order, and like us, they also have a sort of ranking system, so once this is determined all goes as usual. Not much changes in the day-to-day activities of these spirits, but when the need arises and decisions need to be made, the order has been established. This is not to say the others don't have their say. As a matter of fact, the main spirit in my group more than ever lets the others do their thing. I think he understands that their own evolution is part of the growth process, and as he had been as much by us as his counterparts decided upon to be the leader of sorts, then he must by definition have not only my back but the backs of those who choose him as the head of the table.

The therapist is great. No matter where I am, even if not doing a reading, he can come in and help me in the day-to-day communications with people. He can generally come in and settle things down; even if what I'm doing is not working well with him, it usually ends amicably. I remember one time the guy who used to cut the lawn for us was giving me a hard time about being prompt. He would tell me he was coming the next day and show up several days late. I had a conversation with him, and I was going to fire him. While the therapist came in, he changed his tone and explained that he was taking in too much work and he was sorry. I knew he was there because the lawn guy was getting a bit defensive, and as soon as I felt his energy, the man calmed down and changed his demeanor. I thought that was very cool, not only does he help me, but he can affect the emotional response of others.

Once this spirit taps into me, we can somehow hear the feelings of others. It makes it easier for me to understand what is going on emotionally. Remember when this spirit comes, it's usually because the person is going through a rough emotional time and needs that type of input. He is all business and does not delve into frivolous things, so if your problem is about childish desires, I doubt he comes in for things like that. It has to be something truly emotionally complicated for him to make his energy known to me and to the person that I'm dealing with at the time.

Black Magic Man

Now I want to speak to you about one of the first spirits I worked with. He has been my constant companion for these many years. My chosen path has set him at my right hand, and on almost every occasion his council is thought after. He is my witch doctor. I like to call him my black arts specialist; from the beginning, he showed me who he was and the place he came from. I must admit the first year I was a bit confused as he manifested both as an African witch doctor and as a Native American mystic. I thought it was two separate entities. This comes with not having experience, and he was attempting to see where he would fit better with me.

Always his job would have been as a mystic, but how he would show himself with me was the question. Remember spirits are but a firefly of energy, and all these shows they do as they represent themselves as man or woman, black or white, or any other attribute, is for our benefit. Since they must work with us, how we can best reason their existence is how they ultimately show themselves. They might take on the form of one of their previous lifetimes here on earth or choose one from our own acceptable and reasoning mind. For example a new medium today might have a spirit that will show as a witch or another popular TV or movie show. Whatever makes it easier for this young medium to relate.

So as far as I know, over all, they as spirits usually show themselves from one of many previous lifetimes. It's not always this way, but by far, it's the popular way for them to work themselves into our lives. This spirit that works with me chooses the African witch doctor's life. He lived many hundreds of years before as I guess he knew that I would be working in this manner as I developed. You must understand this career is not one of my choosing or was it one I was looking into. It chooses me, and I embraced it as I realized I could make a difference in many lives. I still do what I do as a person, and my likes and dislikes have not changed as my wife will attest. I still love movies and television, and yes, we still try and go dancing once a month and dinner with friends as much as time will allow. So on my day-to-day, I'm still just a dad to my daughter and take her to her singing classes and anything else she needs me to do for her.

My work definitely has changed, and now with this second book in the works, I started to work with a local college to set up spiritual development classes based solely on my first book. I have been asked for many years to teach what I know, and in the past, I did do some classes and they were very successful. In a more strict college environment, I believe the people taking the classes will take much more from them. I set up two classes: one will be for beginners and the second for advanced practitioners. I don't care the level; a good ground is always a strong beginning. So even for those who feel they know, they might not know what I know and taking the advanced class might have them at a disadvantage.

Back to the story, this spirit has helped me in almost every cleansing, and he uses a variety of tools. I had one situation where a person had been alone for about fifteen years, and he suggested getting a metal chain. Not plastic or thin, but thick and steel and—on midnight on a moonless night drive to a railroad track and while standing on top of the track—whip himself asking that the entity of loneliness depart and stay where the chains that whipped him were thrown. After several whips, he was to throw the chain into bushes and walk away. Well, after some convincing, he was sold on the idea and went to the hardware store and purchased ten feet of iron chain. I told him it was to be long enough and just thick enough, so he could hit himself hard, but it had to be light enough so he could wield it and then throw it far enough as to hit bushes away from the railroad tracks. This entity of loneliness when it settles on a human, that person will stay alone until it leaves.

On another occasion I had to clean a person with a white dove. This person had lost, believe it or not, thirteen different jobs in a two-year period. So I was to purchase a white dove and make sure it was clean and well cared for. On the day of the ritual I was to place it on my chest and explain that no harm would come to it. As a matter of fact, I told it how it would help this person achieve freedom from this curse, and as it flew away, it would take with it that energy and while in flight it would disperse it harmlessly into the air. Well, just as said to her after I did the ritual and released the animal within twenty-one days, she got a new job. It's now been over five years and she is stable at that job. As a matter of fact, a few months after the third year during a reading, she asked if that dove idea would work for another need of hers.

I asked the spirit, and he said yes. I cleaned her energies again, and unfortunately the dove died in my arms. The spirit explained that often the energies picked up by the animal are so heavy they are unable to withstand them even for the short period. I've done this ritual many times, and this was the first fatality. I believe loss of life should be avoided. After the death of the dove, I inquired if what I had done had failed. The spirit said no, he explained that as it is when bad luck falls upon a home and some animal or animals die this is a similar scenario and death is not given as a failure but a costly success.

Soon after this ritual, the girl met a good man and they are now today living together, and as she has recently told me, he asked her to marry him. She still remembers the dove, and although saddened by its death, she understood the explanation. She assured me had she realized that the outcome was the death of the dove she would have asked for another way to solve her problem. I agreed, and we continued with the reading. She over the years has sent me many clients, and all have been satisfied customers as she told me.

This spirit has great knowledge of the dark arts as he was the chief advisor to the tribe. He showed me how he lived separate from the tribe and any members that had a need of his services would have to leave the tribe and walk to his hut where he would do his consultations and fix the problems of the tribe members. In those days life was much more simplified, and often if a man, the wife was used as payment to the witch doctor. My wife tells him when he channels that mentality will not fly in today's lifestyle, and he can forget her backing that sort of nonsense. I laugh because she talks to him most of all as he is channeled through me. Don't get me wrong she likes him, just not some of the ideas he proposes for me in this life.

He has shown me over the years many ways to clean dark energy out of so many that I've actually learned the process of how energy transfers from one person to another. He's quite the character and in his own way keeps me young. He must have been a ladies' man in those days. As by the time he died, he was in his sixties and had over forty children. Let's just say they were not all his by marriage, but I guess they all worked it out. He not only showed me that life but several others and most was very interesting.

I think over the years that I've worked with him there was only one time he said we could not take the case. I could not believe it; he explained that although we could clean the person, he could not guarantee success on the specific issue as he did not understand the magic. I was confused as I had believed that the cradle of civilization came from Africa. He explained that the magic used was older than he understood. I said older than Africa, he said yes and gave me an explanation. But beside that one time we have taken on many challenging dark spells and have been able to give a solution to the situation.

He does not have to fully possess me to channel his energies through me. He only needs to stay close, and his energies cover me and I'm able to do what needs to be done. More often than not, he takes control to speak clearly to others, and in circumstances where my wife talks to him, he takes over completely. I'm sure there are conversations about me he and her have that they prefer I not hear. Well, bottom line is he is here to help me, so I'm sure it will never be counter to my best interest. I'm a bit nosy, so there have been times where I've tried to stay in control and he asserts himself fully and to sleep my mind goes.

One funny thing about this spirit is that he does not like deep water. He is an earth spirit, and water holds no interest to him at all. I often go to the ocean for cleaning, and he always tells me I'll be here when you return. He expresses to me that if he cannot see the bottom, he wants nothing to do with that water. He is all about nature but not in the water. Who would have thought, but no matter, over the years most ocean spells or cleansings are done by another spirit we will get to in a while. He's a bit of a rebel and does not find a middle ground with the spirit of the mind, that soul professes only using the mind and this spirit is all about spell craft. Both have their point of views, and I'm so glad to have them both as the group as a whole brings me the balance I need to be successful in this arena.

Over the years, he has been my strong right hand in handling magic of the dark kind. He believes to fight fire with fire. Fortunately I have a balance with the other five who believe balance is the way to obtain true enlightenment. So when needed, he steps in and assists in resolving any dark magic that the client might be suffering. Let me tell you that from very simple stuff to elaborate spells, I'm glad to have this spirit on my side. He truly knows his stuff, and so far, except for one time, he has always found the solution to any situation that I'm attempting to solve for my clients.

He lived outside the tribe. The people would have to walk to his place, and he would consult them on the issues they brought to him. He was isolated, but he explains that this was the way of his people, and whenever the opportunity presented, he would have relations with the women of the village, so is why he had over forty children of his bloodline in the village. He explains that those were some of the perks of being the witch doctor. He has on occasion told me that part of having this life as a healer must by definition be a life of distance from others. He explains that the more time in reflection and meditation, the stronger the communication with the spirit world. I believe that to some extent opening to this other plain of existence can overwhelm us and this turbulence comes from all the energies that each of these people around us bring. It's life and the flux of the individual radiates and not always in a positive direction, so being open can mean suffering those indirect currents. Thus what he tells me it's better to be distant in prayer and meditation, so we are always ready for the next client.

He is always with me. I could be driving, and he will tell me move to the right, and a few minutes later an ambulance will fly by my left side. I could be speaking to someone, nothing spiritual, and he will put his two cent's worth like he was part of the conversation. Something strange could be happening, and he will alert me to the situation way before I would have become aware of it. He truly would be the spirit I would categorize as a friend. On many of occasions over the years, he has given advice and not once has he been wrong. A while ago my stepson needed a bit of help on a particular circumstance, and I sent him to be with my stepson, and sure enough not only did he get the help but he realized it was not just him doing the thing.

Oh, that is right, we had not spoken of this as most mediums won't. you once you establish a relationship with one or more of the spirits with you. You can request that spirit go with the person or even help the person more so than just through me but directly. I've had situations where one of my long-term clients have been in a difficult situation and I've given them permission to call upon the spirit and they responded and the assistance was rendered. Cool stuff, of course, the better your spiritual connection the stronger your request.

He is the one spirit that is with me most of the time. We can be driving, and I'll be speaking with my wife and he will put in his two cent's worth. She thinks it's funny how he is just like another person and talks about many topics and has his opinions about things we talk about without even asking him. He's only shy about the water; he definitely does not like the ocean or even the river. If we were supposed to get in, we would have fins he states. So again whenever I go on the boat or any other water activity, he waits for my return. It's not to say that if I need him he does not come, but he definitely prefers to stay away from water.

This spirit amongst the rest of the group I work with has knowledge of things lost through time and ignorance. Lack of record keeping and more, I work with him on many levels; he is my friend and confidant.

I know there is a great power for darkness within him. He and I have spoken of this before, and as he puts it, why is it dark, it's only as applied, and by definition, we live in an energy world and everything can be dark. He said what if I light some dead wood and it burns down the house, the dried wood and fire are dark. But it was I who lit it on fire, so the dark energy was set to motion by me. Furthermore, he said, what if there was a sink hole below, underneath my home, and by burning the house with time, it was shown that it actually saved my entire family.

He said we do not see the big picture of things and must by definition see any cause and effect through to its end. So what is the end of life if not just the beginning of some other form of existence. What if this life we are living is just an aberration of the spirit, like a hiccup to keep things moving? What if by doing nothing, the spirit will get stuck and sedentary; all good questions he had posed to me. I don't have an answer but definitely worth keeping an open mind. If Adolph Hitler was killed as a small boy, the war would have probably not started.

Also because of the war, many new inventions had to be developed; it is said that man's greatest advancements were made in time of war or strife. What does that tell us about the human raise as a whole? We are complacent, and our souls need impute in order to evolve; the best impute so far has been conflict. If he is right then that darkness within each of us has to come out, has to flex its muscle as much as our goodness for the spirit to continue evolving. Scary stuff, especially for a person like me that has worn many hats in his life and has settled on the side of light. That means that both sides are just as important, and I'm just a tool that moves the darkness to continue to push because I try and keep it down.

He like most spirits of his caliber can take completely over a body as I'm an open channel and can feel him. Most of the time, he just inspires in me what I need to do. I have no doubt that if the situation calls for it and his full energy is called for as he has done on multiple occasions, he will take over and help me to resolve the issue. It's funny, he is the one that I work with the most. Besides the card guy does the hands-on stuff that deals with spell magic and all sorts of dark stuff that I come across when cleaning a person. Remember my job is to help people in need, and when you deal in this type of scenarios, what is most often being cleaned is not very nice stuff.

He showed me that in his tribe when the elder witchdoctor dies, he is often beheaded, and the skull is passed on to the next chosen to protect the tribe. He showed me as his elder taught hem and his before all those heads are adorned and kept close to use not only the knowledge bestowed but the life experience of the spirits before. A bit barbaric but something practiced even today in some religions.

My Black Magic Woman

The next spirit that I would speak of is the only female energy within my group; she is like the counterpart of the witch doctor. She, however, unlike him works with water; she is an ocean and freshwater spirit. What I mean that most of the work she does connects me with water of some sort; for example, ocean cleansings are directed by her and all that it entails. When I prepare baths, she is the one who tells me if it's to be well water or river water or rain water, you get the picture. She loves plants, but water is always one of the ingredients. One time she had me look for lake water and well water. She does well water often enough that I had a well done in my backyard. I know where to get it, but I thought in the long run, it would be more efficient to just walk out the back and get it. Besides I built a pond with two cascades on either side, it's a good relaxing place. I had it done in a horseshoe against the wall and a little bridge to walk into the center section. A fire pit in the ground and chairs for people to sit, imagine getting one of my cleansings in there. The energy is great and much easier to disperse whatever negativity might be with the person.

So far several of my spirits like to clean inside this area I built. I also have the tree of life in my backyard. This is a huge tree, and although it's only five years old, it towers over the roof of my two-story home. I planted most of the plants that I use on the side of the home. I like things fresh, and walking to the side and cutting the branches I need is very convenient for me. Not to mention the client gets the freshest possible ingredients. I know a person that runs a business of selling baths and doing readings. He has a freezer where he keeps the plants he uses most often. One time I saw him clean a person and put the plant back in the freezer. I was speechless. Can you imagine clean one person and the next gets cleaned with old used plants. I told him he was crazy. He said no worries the client does not know the difference and the plant is strong enough to go through several cleanings before running out of positive energy.

I say to each their own. I like it fresh from the tree and used once. I like to talk to the plant and explain how it's branches will be of help, how they are doing a good deed for a person in need. I tell them how I feed them and water them and tend to them and in return they give me some of their branches to help the people in need. It's important when working with nature to give the reason or intent for the specific use of nature. When entering the forest let nature know what your intent is and how appreciative you are for nature's bounty. I like to place a toll of sorts when entering a place. If in the ocean, I would eat something and offer a bite to the ocean as I share of what I eat may in return whatever I'm doing have a fruitful solution for the client or me or whomever it is for.

The only thing I don't like about the female spirit as she channels through me I feel all her attributes. She while taking over my body makes me feel her big butt, big breasts, and other parts of her anatomy. It makes me feel a bit uncomfortable; also my walk is like hers, so I'm walking weird. I know this is my own issue as she is just being her, and I have been able to relax enough not to let it bother me and she has tried to back up enough, so I don't feel all these female attributes as strongly. It's a balance and they try to do whatever they can to work with me and not disrupting the work with miscellaneous stuff like the body. When I'm cleaning a person, I've felt everything from broken bones to pain in an ovary. As you can imagine, when I'm cleaning a woman and I tell her that I feel some discomfort in my left ovary, she looks up at me and tells me "yes, me too." As a matter of fact she had set up an appointment for just that issue the week before. Then she realizes that I'm a guy and don't have any ovaries, and well, let's just say it's interesting.

Over the years with cleaning, one of the things they help me with is by reflecting whatever is going on with the body of the person so I can best identify problem areas. One time I had to stop the cleansing and go to the bathroom. I told him and he said that he had been with diarrhea for two days on and off. Soon after my bathroom visit, he felt better and the diarrhea subsided. Along with these physical manifestation are also yearnings; for example, I began to cry while doing a cleaning for a woman, a sense of loss came over me she explained that she had just lost a child and this had been how she had been feeling for a while.

Not only does it help me identify in some circumstances but also, I physically take on some of the maladies and the person feels better. Since it's not mine, they subside from me, and I guess I channel whatever it is and the person feels better. I do this, and to this date still find it amazing how energy transference can occur between people. To a lesser degree it's similar to what can happen to undeveloped mediums. There are many out there and you are not alone. If you feel sick at times when you enter a place or after talking with someone you end up with a headache or spent of energy, you are probably a medium and don't have any idea.

I teach developmental class based on my first book and hope to add this second book to the teachings. If you become a subscriber on my website, I usually send out notices of upcoming events and some words of wisdom as the energy of the planet shifts. So I will advise where I'm teaching. As of the writing of this book, I will be teaching my next class February 5 at Miami Dade College, Kendall campus, the continuing education department. So if you check their curriculum, you will find me there and the spiritual development class!

These classes address not only development but also how to protect you from these unexpected attacks. Most are not targeting the person, just stray energies out there that can affect us all. Remember you can be walking down the street and pass by an area affected by someone with a cold for example and you can pick up the virus or infection. Energy is no different, and if you are susceptible, you could be next. Learning to protect one self and the family can better the human condition. Over the years, I've developed or helped to better the abilities of many mediums and so many that are not mediums learned of this thing called energy.

This woman as she comes to me had a life where she lived and raised her family by a running river; she believes that nature at its best is always in need of water. Most of the magic she works with is water. She can take a plastic container from the supermarket filled with water and radiate healing energy on to it, and as I give it to a client that needs it, by the time the person has drank the gallon, they feel better from the malady.

The Class Act

She loves dancing and making me money. She brings abundance and riches to my life, not only in money but in relationships. She was of the upper class, so she tries to get me with people of affluence. She does not like for me to look bad or not groomed. She always brings good stuff to me; for example, she is the one that always makes sure that I get along with others in business or in any sort of gathering, not a bad spirit to have if you deal with a lot of people. She has a very long name, and there have only been a couple of people that have seen her and that she has given her name to. I guess she is very guarded of my person and does not like the wrong people in my life.

I had one evening that a client wanted to communicate with a specific spirit that I invited to other mediums. As I've stated before, no one person can see all spirits, so I wanted the best chance that if the spirit she wanted to come through came, one of us would be able to pass along whatever messages she had for my client. Well, the night went well, and a grandfather came through along with two others but not the one she expected. This happens, and partially one of the reasons I don't do these types of sessions very often. I did warn her, this could happen, so she was not disappointed and she got a good house and personal energy cleaning along with the visit. I bring this up as it was during this session that one of the mediums I had brought saw the spirit I'm speaking of and gave me her name and a message. I was happy, and it took some doubts I had out of my head. The message for me was directed at the situation I had been worrying about.

The Smokey Spirit

There is a special spirit amongst the group that I work with. I say *special* because he was not of my own commission of spirits. You must understand that most of the mediums work with the spirits that were assigned to work with them from birth. There is another level of spirit that is not quite ready to work with a specific medium. This type works with the ones they find and have an affinity to. There is yet another way to work with spirits for specific reasons, and they may be summoned if one knows how to do it. I will get to that later in this book.

So this one special spirit arrived to work with me while I was working my spiritual temple. One of the other mediums that cleaned people one day told me there is a new spirit around you, and I said good, the more, the better. He smiled and told me to grab a cigar and to get a chair in the middle and pick a person to clean. I have gone in great detail as to the center and what goes on there, so in this book, I will keep it to this spirit and how it arrived.

I did as told; understand that I had never smoked a cigar, so I was less than sure of what would happen. I placed the chair and grabbed the cigar. One of the helpers placed a light in front of me and lit the cigar; soon I began to feel the pull of this spirit. He approached as he was I guess attempting to figure out how to take over my body. He told me his name and that he would like to work with me in cleaning those who needed with tobacco. I acknowledged him, and we began to work together. I looked around and called a person sitting in the audience waiting their turn.

This was an eye-opening experience as I had never channeled this spirit nor smoked cigars, much less use it to clean anyone's energies. So the relationship with this spirit began, he does not take me completely, so I'm there, but his influence is felt by me and the people I'm cleaning. After the first person, the other medium came, and the new spirit introduced him and thanked him and all there for the opportunity to serve at this center. I continued, and that evening I must have cleaned eleven people and used fourteen cigars. Yes, some took more than one cigar to clean their auras, so I started with a new talent. I must say of all the spirits I worked with to date, he was the less chatty. All business no play as they say.

I no longer participate at the center as I closed it a couple of years ago, so less and less he comes to work with me. He is a spirit of work, so he can go on all night long. One cleansings at a time is not his thing, so I think with time, he will retire from my group and find a new person to work with. I'm saddened by this as he has taught me so much about the seriousness of this business I'm in to help all that come. He does not concern himself if guilty or innocent. He feels this is not our job; we do the hard part to clean the energy and give the person another chance to move forward. If they do great, if they don't, again our job is not to judge but to help clear up obstacles in hopes the person is given another opportunity to fix mistakes.

He does not chat very much. Most of the years he and I worked together, he really spoke other than with regards to the cleaning and what he saw and how to best proceed. It's funny, even when during an evening of cleanings, if I get distracted speaking with one or more of the other mediums, he will just nudge me back to work. Very much all business, I've tried to get him to engage me, and the most I get is a yes or no answer. Does not elaborate, truly work, work, work, for this spirit, he feels there are many people in need, and time for socializing should be left for when we are done with our work.

There are many spirits in training, and on occasion, I would see a group of them just observing how we worked in the center with the other mediums and the spirits that each of us worked with. I think it was like a school for them. They in turn when they got what they needed would look for someone like us and like this spirit that cleans with cigar start the relationship of helping the needy. I never actually spoke of this with him but understand the concept and what I have seen leads me to this conclusion. Remember this spirit is all about work and has no time for the nonsense of chatting or mingling. He is all work and no play. He said we are here to evolve through good deeds and how best to do this is in mass how the center works. Many needy people in one place we can break it down and one by one give faith and set what has gone wrong back on track.

I've been told from many years ago that there are two more spirits that I will come to know and work with closely. I've been told that as the need arises, they will come and present themselves. I'm waiting as I've had a very wonderful experience with this spirit. I've come to realize that there are many steps to soul evolution and many souls in need of a medium who truly gives of him or herself in the selfless quest to help others. I gladly invite those two souls to come and begin their journey with me, and so we can together do God's work. I was told that they would be of the same type, not of my own commission. Remember my own commission, as I call them, are spirits that were assigned to work with me since birth. These two will be like this one, souls in an evolutionary path that requires the body of a medium ready and mature to take on their quest in one way or another the betterment of humanity.

The Card Reader

He is not your typical gypsy. He wears suit and tie, and he likes me to be perfect in how I dress; this is why he gets along great with my wife. Not to mention that if you add all the times she gets read by him, it's probably more than all the clients I read put together. She is hooked; talking to the gypsy with the cards is her favorite past time. She gets all the answers to her questions. Imagine how many questions we have on a day to day and that spirit loves it when he is used, so she definitely works him over.

Now that she read the first book and is getting much better at feeling them and identifying who is who, I'm surprised how easy it has become for her to do the exercises and summon her spirits close to her. It's like everything in this world. If you have a natural capability for something, it becomes easier to develop the ability. Otherwise it's doable, but you really have to work for it. Some people can go to class, listen, and get an A; others go to school, listen, do their homework, study, and come up with barely a B.

So back to the gypsy. He comes to me impeccable. His clothing is wrinkle free, and he expects me to be the same. I'm more relaxed; remember I do 99 percent of my readings over the phone, so as I tell him, who cares if I'm in shorts or slacks. He's funny, so he tells me he does, and the energy I put out is more professional. I'm of the belief that I give results by giving each person what they need; as a matter of fact that is my motto: what you need is what you get. Anyway my wife and he hit it off as she is also one that wants me to look good. Hey, I look good; I do events and other activities and never a complaint. I teach the classes at the college, and yes, I wear long sleeve in the winter but short sleeve in the summer. What can I say, I'm not your typical suit-and-tie guy, but I do give results. I have clients from over ten years ago, so I must be doing something right.

If you read my testimonials, it's all good stuff, and in all these years, I have never had a person ask for a refund. As a matter of fact, I had a reversal a few years ago and I called the person. She was very apologetic as my billing does not reflect psychic readings. From the beginning, some clients did not want the significant other to know they were getting a reading, so I had what you get from the credit card very generic. When I called her, she remembered it was me and so immediately put it back. She did not remember what it was, so she disputed it. Bottom line, I give good service, and 80 percent of my clients stay calling with me.

Look, I'm not your smoke-and-mirrors type of medium. I tell it like it is, and my clients appreciate my honesty. I have a life. This is not my life. This is what I do. Some psychics live this, and sooner or later they crash. Imagine constant communications into that realm. We go dancing to the movies, vacation with the kids, and on our own. I do all the handy work around the house and the yard work. That is right, regular guy with this gift having a meltdown is not on my agenda. So as life throws curves as it does all of us field those balls very well and as my life changes I change with it, not alone with my spirits but living this lifetime as I'm supposed to with the additional shore or helping others with the aid of these wonderful souls I've created a relationship with.

Now back to the card reader. He is great; he and I started working together by going through many different decks of cards until we came to the best conclusion. You can see pictures of our deck in an earlier chapter. He and I both feel that more is not better, so a small deck of thirty-six cards with this deck and impute of the spirits, I give a complete reading to the client at the other end of the phone. The cards are like a crutch. They take me where I need to go, but it's always the words of the spirits that give the details. No card will tell you a person's name of infirmity they might have. They are general guides as the situations and the rest is fine-tuning. This is why I tell my clients in my classes that a deck of cards without a spirit working it with you is no reading at all.

The reader and I have developed a good rapport. His cards take me in the general area, and then he gives me the energy I need to see the rest of the message. There are few times when the cards and the reader do not agree. I can tell you an instant where they differ. The cards work with karma, so when they speak of a person that is supposed to be with you, the cards will always follow the line of karma. The reader will tell me more what the reality of the situation for the couple, so by now we know what karma is because he will disagree with the cards. This is not always; as a matter of fact, if karma and he agree, it's 100 percent to happen. If there is a disagreement, he is right, and karma will just cause problems.

I'll give you a scenario. I have a client, been with me for many reasons including her business. She covers her bets and gets readings from three different mediums, I being one of them. The other two mediums like the guy she likes, my cards like him also; however, the reality for her is the person's free will won't let him give in to karma and chooses not to be with her romantically. From the first reading with her give or take eight or nine years ago, I told her that they had a karma connection, but he would not act on it. Over the years, the other medium would give her hope and tell her how he dreams about her and for certain will make his move.

Guess what, she continues to see this, and I continue to tell her that although she is a good medium when it comes to this, I've learned that God is not love but free will. No matter what karma has in mind for any of us, we make the final decision. As free spirits, we choose the life we are to live here on earth, but as we develop this karma, we can choose to veer of and not complete it. Rather live and die without going through with it and come back again to finish it at another point in another life. Remember we choose, and the universe is here to always give us wiggle room; after all, this is growth. But the bottom line is they are not wrong in what they see as my cards are not wrong as they follow the karmic threads. Unfortunately free will always wins out, so as life progresses, we can shift our path by making conscientious decisions to veer from our destined path.

The truth is that life is not as orderly as most believe, but chaos is a factor in all portions of the decision process. So we can embark on our chosen profession, and karma kicks in and woops a change occurs that completely sets a stable and guided future in a new direction. That would be an example where karma superseded free will. If it was strong enough, there would be turbulence, but the chosen path would stick. I hope this gives you an idea of how complex life on this planet can be and the infinite variables that can change our lives.

The topic of the right person is an age-old one that I would like to shed some light on at this time. Yes, there is a right person for each of us; as a matter of fact, there are many. We as free spirits take on human bodies to temporarily act out or live certain things or experiences that would be impossible as souls. So as souls with a temporary body, we live out lessons that teach the soul about relationships and self.

We as romantic emotional beings have to grow and evolve petty jealousies and other unfortunate side effects that emotions bring to the equation. We are given many possible companions, some are reasons, others seasons, and believe it or not many more as possible lifetime partners. With every life we live, there are unresolved issues, so the older the soul, the more unresolved romantic encounters and therefore more to choose from. As the age and maturity of the planet grows, so do the multiple possible life partners for each of us.

As I've stated before, our souls choose the life they are to live, and then we are dropped in time and space to an area in this world where the best chance to accomplish the largest portion of the karma we choose. Unfortunately choice or free will is given to us once we land with certain predetermined likes and desires to guide us to our rightful place. Environment plays another part in this mix of predetermined events and emotions. Back to the concept of the right partners, each have many right partners, so the odds that any of us will stay alone will be diminished to a fraction of a percentage.

This is why in a reading, you might get mixed answers where it concerns the right person as most put it; that is, because they all have the possibility to be the right person. Some might be the right person to bear children with; another might be the right person to be emotionally nurturing to your path of life. Another might be for them, and you are the person that will help them accomplish a task or mission in their life. You might be auxiliary to another in this karma to a large percentage of the folks that would be the right person. It would be narcissistic to believe they are all here for us. True, in some cases, it might be so, but an equal chance exists that we are here to serve their karma.

Difficult concepts? Not really. If you read and read over and over, the concepts will become acceptable; after all, for your lifetime, most of us were told there is that right person to each of us. Back to possibilities, I believe and do my readings to windows of possibilities. What I mean is when I'm shown windows of possibilities and the more possible the possibilities, the bigger the window for that path. As the possibilities are lessened, it still shows to me but at a smaller window. So when I tell the person and they inquire about a lesser window, I give them ideas. I tell them this is only strong because you are headed in that direction. If you want that other window, then you must shift your path and head to that future.

If we are to discuss work and you are headed for a raise and what you really wanted was another position, then you must do things in a way to get the other position. This is if they were both windows of possibilities. So if you are doing a great job and the promotion was imminent, then you want to start dropping hints or asking the boss what you need to do in order to get that position that will open up soon. Otherwise the universe will keep you on track for your promotion and then what follows, so it's still up to you the possibilities exist. It's up to you what window to walk through. The one you are on the path for or shift your energies to get to that secondary window.

Back to the card reader. I will divert if this topic seems important, sorry to those that are one track, but life is not one track and being flexible is part of being successful. In life we must roll with the punches and the song states, don't worry be happy is a good way to live your life. When I do readings and the initial deck is laid out, I read as sentences, so from left to right and up to down and crisscross. There are certain cards that are more important, so the top left is most and the center card is second in overall importance. Oh yeah, my deck is laid out in nine cards. The top left is your path, the middle is optional to alternative paths of importance or subordinate paths that tangent the first. Other cards will clarify the person's path. Remember the cards put you on path, and the spirit gives the verbal information.

The reader often gives impute as to details in the cards or questions. I should ask to interpret what I'm being shown in the cards. When the person has questions, I lay out the deck and tell them to verbally ask the question, not because I want to know but more often than not a person will be asking a question but thinking of something else, so this can make the answer incorrect. So if you ask a question out loud, it grounds the questioner in the question and lessens the chance of thinking of something else. Then I tell them to choose two cards; in order for it to be a yes, both cards have to be positive. This lessens the chance of a false positive; it's all about getting the right information, so you want a yes to be sure.

I've had people not sure of the answer and asked the same questions five or six times, and they will get the same answer. I don't recommend too many times, or the spirit will just give you the answer you want as he feels you do not trust the process. My stepson recently asked some questions after the reading and like most kids was not sure and kept asking similarly the same question four other times and the same answer was given; if he had any doubt, it was set to rest. With time, the answer came to fruition, and he told me that it happened as the cards had predicted.

He comes from Europe but not with any of the attributes you or I would give a typical gypsy. He believes the world moves forward, and either we move with it or become stuck in the past like so many stuffed animals. He is up-to-date with all the slang and other ways of speaking. Sometimes I'm reading a young person, and he gives me the words they understand. I find this amazing as some of these codes they speak in are a foreign language to me. I'm so happy my spirits make this job easier for me. They really do help me in this process and make passing the information so much easier and a pleasure for me.

He does come with another spirit as a second to him. He is the primary and who I deal with, but the other is younger, perhaps learning or assisting. Over the years I'm aware of the presence, but there has been no dialogue between us, so I cannot really as of yet say much about the second spirit that comes with the gypsy. Suffice it to say I was told that often a new spirit to this type of work will apprentice with an older one such as the card reader. I guess to learn the ropes before he or she is assigned to their first charge in this physical existence.

The Indian

I want to briefly cover my main spirit. He is an Indian, an American Indian, and in my coronation, he came forth and became the spirit guide for the rest of the group. As such his responsibilities are to keep any one of the spirits from taking over—that means that if one of the spirits wants to impose his or her way of working beyond the balance set with the group, he steps in and brings balance and harmony, so I work best. He is the one that when I'm in need of extra inspiration, he gives it to me, not for him but to help me receive the guidance of any of the spirits that work with me.

I work with many people and sometimes forget to give myself the same attention I give to my clients. He is the one who reminds me that I have the same need to get cleaned as much as any of my clients and often more because of all the work I do. Remember most people come to me because they have needs that are not currently being met, so my job is to open or close doors so the person gets back on track. When I say close, if there is a negative energy, door opens to them. I'm the one that works my magic to close it and help the person back on track. If they are stuck, no job, no relationship or bad ones—even health-related or emotional issues—I have to find an answer to help them get back on track.

In cases where I'm in trouble, he would be the one to organize my spirits to give that extra push and help bail me out of the difficulty. Although I work with six spirits regularly, there are literary hundreds that I have at my disposal. It's said an army is built from faith, and I have an abundance of that; at one time or another, I've been told there are two more spirits to come and complete my more active spirits on the day to day work. There will be situations where sheer numbers will win the situation. I've yet to experience that scenario and hope never to be there. I was told a very long time ago that there will be in my future a situation where sheer numbers would win the day.

With a single string if pulled, it can be easily broken. As you add more strings, they intertwine and become stronger until almost impossible to break apart. Same with spirits, the more the stronger the body of those they work with, most will be there for support, but each comes with its own wisdom and abilities that can be handy at the right moment. Don't forget what I mentioned earlier, you may always summon the type of spirit that would best help in particular situations. I won't go into great detail, suffice it's important to try it several times, so in time of need, you don't have to scramble and still maybe not get it right. Let's use a brief example: if you are a boxer on an athlete, it's possible to summon a great athlete from the past for inspiration and support. I once ran the pool table with some friends three times straight by summoning a great pool hustler from the past. This is a temporary boost in your talent and don't expect it to stay.

So back to the story of quantity, I was told that there would be a situation that I would be involved in where the opposing side would be very strong, and it will require all my spirits to overcome this obstacle. One of the things they told me, the body must stay strong and pure to channel the needed energies to best my opponent. They did not specify if the opponent would be another person or some sort of energy I had not encountered before. One key thing I will advise, faith in who you are and your abilities are essential to victory; so you must work on your talents and be the best you can be so if the moment ever comes, your energies will flow only in your direction and through the obstacle.

This spirit while in the middle of writing this book made his first appearance as he took over my body for the first time while I was in a trance with my wife. Every once in a while, I sit out back and channel some of the spirits I work with. Although they can speak to me without taking over, the action of temporary possession does give them the advantage of better cleaning me of any negative energy. So I was out back with my wife, and he chooses to pass and talk to her. She loves the cards, so it's not surprising to me he choose that time and with her to make his first manifestation.

She told me how he enjoyed speaking with her. He has a very soft demeanor and loves the cards. He took many months looking with me for the right set, and I included some pictures of the deck we choose in this book. He talked with my wife for a while, and she was so excited. He gave her his name and a little more about himself, where he came from, and such stuff. She told me afterward she can't wait till he does that again. I've been working with him through the cards for many years, and this is the first time, so I don't know if he will come more often, but as I said, it's always good for a medium to have the body cleansed by a spirit while they take over.

A Special Guest

This spirit is not one of mine but of my wife. She does not communicate with him although she can perceive spirits and channels as well. This spirit talks to me as he explains it he wants her to be better with me. I asked him the very first time he came to me who he was. I could see he was a spirit of light but could not identify where he came from or why. So he explained that he was with my wife, girlfriend at the time. He thought I would be good for her and wanted things to go well between us; I asked why, he said I was kind and understanding, and she needed that kind of man.

I told her all this spirit had told me. She was a bit freaked out, but I guess she understood. She did not run. At that time, she was not developed, so she knew what I did but did not understand it completely. As we continued, she found she could feel things and wanted to know more. I helped her develop. With time, I got to know her spirit, and he would give me advice about Vivian and how he wanted her and me to be together.

I remember one time she and I were dating, and she left after an argument; well, the spirit came to talk to me and told me she was at a friend's house and had smoked two cigarettes. That would be fine if she smoked, but she did not, so I called her and inquired. She thought it was funny how her spirit would come to me and tell me these things. When you are in a relationship with another and there is a connection, usually your spirits will stop giving you any information about that important person in your life. So it was with me, however, there was nothing that said one of the other person's spirits could not.

So it has been with my wife and me that particular spirit every once in a while comes and gives her advice in our relationship. By now she has come to accept him as he is. She thinks he is a male chauvinist from the past and still lives there. He was from a time that women were possessions and spoke when spoken to. He has moved on, but he still insists that she and I should be together, so when she does something he thinks is not correct, he lets her know. Funny, I'm easy about most things. He is tougher on her than I ever will be. She understands and we all live happy together even if every once in a while he gives her his opinion on things.

On occasions many souls have come through me and given advice to me or others at the moment. I still hesitate to give any advice unless the person I'm reading can identify the spirit as a family or someone she recognized from her life—someone she respected and knew the information would be for her good. If after describing the spirit to the person, she or he does not know who it is then I will keep that information to myself and not pass it. It has been as with many things in life the person remembers before the end of the reading or cleansing who I was describing I will pass on the information. So far it's much more a hit than a miss as far as my description and their acknowledgment of who the spirit is. You have to appreciate my situation. In this world there are lots of clowns, so there are in the spirit realm and as such can mislead or misguide, sometimes maliciously, often from boredom.

Most of the times that a spirit of light chooses to pass through a medium, they tend to at least temporarily fix some of the physical maladies the body has. I remember while I was working at the spiritual center of a medium that was blind as a bat. I say this because without his glasses, he could not read or drive a vehicle; on multiple occasions after the sessions were over, he would leave his glasses and drive home. I know this because on occasion someone had to drive him back to get his glasses but yet that evening after the session he would be able to get in his car and drive home with twenty-twenty vision and at night. Incredible but true. For me I could be having a cold or a bad cough, and when I would start a cleaning or at the center for hours no cough and I would speak as if I was not sick. Soon after the session ended, I would go home, and the lung congestion would start up again.

In my opinion, most, if not all of us, have spirits that have an agenda, and these spirits are not so concerned with the big picture but with our emotional stability and only this is of importance for this type of spirit. So there is no misunderstanding. We are here for many reasons, and each of the souls assigned to us has a responsibility to fulfill and we must abide and believe that there is a reason for everything they do for us. You know if a spirit makes us hurt ourselves or others, this is not a spirit with sufficient knowledge to guide us. So with some common sense and understanding, we can define a good spirit and one with an anterior reason to be next to us. Keep an open mind and always be on the alert for mischievous souls with an agenda of their own.

This spirit like many my wife works with tries to help as all the souls assigned to work with the living. Unfortunately not all fit well with the personality of the human they are assigned to work with. I guess if it were easy, they would not be here. They need to have as much or more patience with us as we do with them. The fit is not always perfect, and even I don't always agree with the advice of some of my spirits, but we must work together to find neutral ground.

Other Spirits

While I worked at the center and other places, there are other spirits that come and help keep the place or location running smoothly. I call these auxiliary spirits. They are in some cases very wise and not necessarily to work with any one individual but help keep order in the place for the time it's open or spiritual work is being conducted. On more than one occasion, I would see a group of spirits, sometimes more spirits than the people that come for help. You must realize that the centers I've worked with often have more than fifty people in any one session looking for all kinds of help. So I was surprised to see so many souls just sitting looking and observing what was going on in our center.

One of my spirits cleared up this question by explaining how there are souls that will be doing the good work but are not quite ready so they are taken to places like ours to learn and observe how to work in a certain type of way. There are other types of centers that work differently; I've been to some where they are standing up all the time. They pray and sing and channel, the way I work is differently, but who's to say mine is the only way? Keeping an open mind and observing is how we learn, and that night I learned that is how some souls learn as well.

Over the years I've seen many famous souls, Liberace, the piano player, Abraham Lincoln, Joan of Arc, and many more. These souls make visits to locations or make their presence known to someone but are rarely permanent fixtures to any one place or person. I've met death or the reaper as many have come to know it. I do believe some entities are not souls but another sphere or domain they work form opens up for them to do what they must in this realm of the living. Most are not good or bad. Unfortunately we, the living, don't see it that way; after all, who wants to die?

I have certain ideas that I would like to tell you about. This is my own thoughts and are not truth as I have experienced but ideas I've postulated form the years I've spent working this field of spirituality. I've come to believe we are capable of creating our own reality; for example, if many people pray for someone to live even if they are for certain destined to day may find a reprieve. We as spirits with a soul and a mind have no idea of the power that is ours while we possess this temporary body. Imagine if we can focus all our power or thoughts on a single task, there is no way we can fail. We might try and try again, but ultimately we will persevere.

So it is with the mind, if many minds work together, we can manifest reality from thin air. I have yet to master this as the spirits tell me I must become healthier of body and mind before I may take yet the next step in my own evolution. I know this to be true as it has been told to me by monks and others; there is also choice and free will. Do I really want to give my all to this quest for total clarity? In my case I'm not ready and I accept this. I like a balanced life. I like to go dancing, have a couple of drinks. I enjoy my life with family and friends. As I said it's a choice, one that I accept, maybe with time I will decide to give more to this spiritual world. I think we move through life and, with each step, evolve to who we will ultimately become.

If you were to tell me fifteen years ago I would be this person today, I would say you were crazy. I was a network administrator and had no reverence for anything much. I did meditate regularly and had the philosophy of not doing to others what I did not want done to me. Other than that I lived much like the rest of the work, and look at me today. Many changes have occurred, all out of my control. I never searched for this work, and yet it came to me. So I will pose this question, who are we, who were we, and who will we become. A simple answer and one that I followed go with the flow: if your life is not going in the right direction, contemplate. Maybe you are bucking changes that are bigger than you are.

Each step we take will ultimately take us closer to that end of the road or death. Will you leave here having learned all that was given to you, or will you leave wanting for more? All good questions, one simple answer is open the door to life: live it to the fullest and live without regrets. There are man's laws to follow, but life is so immense you may find more than you can handle if you but open your eyes and mind to one of an infinite possibilities for you. The purpose of life is to matter, to be productive, to have it make some difference that you lived at all. Oh yeah, being happy is also a plus of life, one I have chosen not to ignore.

Gratification comes in many ways, so maybe to become a monk is yours, and this lofty goal makes you happy. Me, I like to party, enjoy every aspect within the life I have chosen. If that for me means to go out on the boat and take two vacations a year, so be it. I work hard, so I also like to play till I'm done. Life is different for everyone. At the end of the day, we all take our lives in our hands and what happens at the end. You have no one to blame but yourself if as you look back you find yourself wanting for more. Life is a blank canvas, paint, and keep on painting until you get it right and then paint some more. The river of life has many turns and splits and meanderings along the way, keep moving and you will get to your destination.

The Stinky Spirit

Recently, as I was writing my second book, I started having this very strong odor. I changed my deodorant, sometimes even bathing twice a day. Even my wife brought this odor to my attention. It was not in the armpits, it was just a new odor that sometimes would overwhelm my body. I was at odds to what this was. Another medium friend of mine was the first to describe this new spirit. He told me some of the tendencies, and one was the odor.

I don't have a handle on this one yet. He comes with the abilities over life and death. Cool stuff so I can't wait until we start to work together. From what I've been able to feel and understand, he will be able to heal the sick, at least the ones who were not destined to get sick but by their own hand caused it to be so. He will also be able to help those along the path to death and destruction to end the life on the fast track. Scary stuff! I've been waiting for him for over ten years, and there is still another to come. If I understood some of the messages, the first will be the last, so actually the samurai would be the last one as he comes back in to my group of spirits.

Quick Reminder

One last thought to keep in mind: This simple cleanse should clean, maintain, and—on necessary occasions—clear your home or office from any negative energies. It should be done three times a year. Each time it's executed, it should be done over a six-day period. These ingredients can be purchased from most supermarkets.

On the first three days, get bay leaves and rosemary. Use a deep pot like the picture below.

Place inside at the bottom the bay leaves and rosemary to cover the entire bottom of the pot. In a different container burn at least a dozen carbons like the ones you would buy to do a barbeque, quick light kind to make it easier to burn. Once the carbon is burning red hot but no longer on fire, cover the bay leaves and rosemary with the carbon. I like a deep pot so as to minimize any sparks from burning furniture as you walk throughout the home or office.

Once it starts to smoke, walk the home room by room until the entire house is smoky. Careful, or you may accidently set off your fire alarm. Once the entire house has been smoked, you can then place the pot out the front door if you have a house. If it is an apartment, place it in the balcony until it completely burns the bay leaves and rosemary. Let it burn itself out before disposing of the carbon. This should be done three days in a row. If you have a house and are able to walk around the exterior, grab the handle and walk the exterior to clean the energy of the home from the outside as well.

Once you are done with the first three days, you can do the same procedure again, but this time, at the bottom of the pot, add cinnamon sticks and brown sugar enough so it covers the bottom then you would add the carbon. Same steps walk each room going from corner to corner to cover the four corners until the entire home has been smoked. If you can find it, you may use on both the first three days and the second three days church incense. If not, it's not a necessary ingredient, just add a little more juice to the process.

If you are having some turbulence in the home or office, you may do this monthly until things settle down. If you are being spiritually assaulted, you may do twice a month until things calm down. This is something you should also do before you move in to a new home or office. Remember try and be at peace before you start, perhaps a little meditation or prayers, and always do these things in God's name to give yourself the best chance to have a successful cleanse. These types of cleanse are easy and available to you from most supermarkets. If you feel the need to add another ingredient, you may add star anise as well to both first and second set of cleanses. As you walk the property, ask for your need; for example, if you need things to settle and the family to be at peace, then ask for it. If looking to get more abundance flow into the home or to get a job, ask for it as you do the cleanse. Remember you are getting this smoke yourself, so in a sense, you are cleaning your own energies in the process. Good luck and God bless. Remember nothing is outside your reach as long as you truly believe it is. Thought creates reality, and you are powerful, more so than you can imagine.

Want your struggles to end? Give in to gratitude, turn your life around, be grateful for all you do have—they are the keys to opening blessings in your life. Possessions like toys don't ever fill us for long if at all, so if where you are, with what you have, you are not content, seriously analyze what you want. It might never be enough for a permanent state of happiness and contentment; switch your process and look inside. Reflect to the past, present, and future and realize happiness is a state of mind and not body. Your soul is happy because it is and not for what it temporarily possesses. Free yourself from need and want, and happiness will grow. No matter the situation, be happy and all those other things you want will just flow into your life. Contentment first then gratification arrives! Don't let go of the lifeline that vine. Whatever you choose to call it, hope is its true name, and with it you can swing from tree to tree until you reach your goals!

In life we hardly realize that we receive a great deal more than we give, and that it is only with gratitude that life becomes rich. Start each day with a new zeal for life, and be grateful for life. Past, present, and future—this is called manifest destiny. It's your God-given right! Freedom is the oxygen of the soul; never forget it's a vital ingredient for health and longevity. Life is choice, life is chance. Opportunities abound, so cast your hook no matter the waters; even the least expected can land your desires. That is chance, this is living! When we write about time as if it were an instant, is it not what life becomes. Many moments, many memories—this is the intimacy of time, your time, so reflect and realize the world has moved on. Did you move with it? Rage each moment with a passion that lasts a lifetime!